Modern Somali Dictionary

Somali-English, English-Somali

WILD

kasahorow

Read your language, every day.
Somali
Revised 2018-07-17
www.kasahorow.org

Auntie Dorcas

Contents

Preface

kasahorow loves African languages.

Our mission is to give African languages speakers in the world freedom by modernizing African languages.

The first step to modern usage is to write each language with consistent spelling rules. Consistent spelling may be pronounced in different ways in different places.

In other words, the spelling of a word does not indicate how to pronounce it. In fact, there is no correct pronunciation. Rather, we think your pronunciation is correct when you can be understood by others.

Sign up to receive updates in your favourite African language at `http://kasahorow.org/`.

Sharing License

You may freely photocopy and redistribute this book for private or commercial use. No restrictions. Yes go ahead. Do good by sharing.

Errata

All mistakes are ours. When you find one, please let us know so we can fix it.

Please send corrections to help@kasahorow.org or online at http://kasahorow.org/booktalk.

How To Use This Dictionary

Ma nabad baa! Hello!

This dictionary has two parts.

1. Somali - English
2. English - Somali

Words are in groups. Each group of words starts with one letter.

To find a word, start at the group of the first letter of the word.

English - Somali

The groups of words start with...

aA bB cC dD eE fF gG hH iI jJ kK lL mM nN oO pP qQ rR sS tT uU vV wW xX yY zZ

Somali - English

The groups of words start with...

Each Word

Each word has one type...

- *nom*: A noun is a name.

- *sci*: A noun of science.

- *pro*: A pronoun is a noun to replace a name.

- *adj*: An adjective is a value of a noun.

- *act*: A verb is an action.

- *adv*: An adverb is a value of a verb.

- *det*: A determiner is a word that shows the type of a noun.

- *pos*: A determiner that shows the owner of a noun.

Sound

This sign means "silence".: " "

If the people of a city say a different sound then we write their sound of the word in //.

Thank You

We thank the big community of kasahorow.

Go and read!

Write to us. We will like that.

Thank you!
kasahorow Editors
help@kasahorow.org

Somali - English

A

aabe *(nom)* dad

aad *(adv)* very
you have done very well

aad loo jecelyay *(adj)* very desirable
it is very desirable

aad u badan *(adv)* too much
he insults too much

aad u badan *(adv)* very much
thank you very much

aad u cajiib ah *(adj)* awesome
awesome God

aad u dhuuban *(adj)* tiny
tiny thing

aad u faraxsan *(nom)* exultation
songs of exultation

aalad *(nom)* device
a phone is a device

aale sonkor *(nom)* sugarcane
to chew sugarcane

aaminid *(act)* trust

aaminid *(nom)* trust

aaminsanaan *(nom)* belief

aamusnaan *(nom)* silence
silence, silence!

aan daruuri ahayn *(adj)* unnecessary
unnecessary insults

aan dhamaad lahayn *(adj)* infinite

aan hadli karin/doqon *(adj)* mute

aan hoaray loo aqoon *(adj)* unfamiliar
unfamiliar animal

aan ka badnayn *(adj)* mere
mere fool

aan kibir badnayn *(adj)* humble
humble person

aan lo baahnayn *(adj)* undesirable
it is undesirable

aan mahad celin *(adj)* ungrateful
an ungrateful person

aan shaqeynayn *(nom)* inactive
he is inactive

aan waxtar lahayn *(adj)* useless
useless work

aas *(act)* bury
to bury a corpse

aas *(nom)* funeral
I am going to a funeral
aasaas *(nom)* foundation
foundation of the house
aasaasi ah *(adj)* basic

aasaasid cashuur *(nom)* levy
pay a levy
Aasiya *(nom)* Asia
Asia is a continent
aayad/beyd *(nom)* verse
three verses
abaal marin *(nom)* award
give her an award
Abena - magac *(nom)* Abena
Abena is my daughter
abid *(adv)* forever
she lives forever
abochi - magaca *(nom)* abochi
we are very good friends
aboor *(nom)* termite
many termites
abtirsashada *(nom)* genealogy
the genealogy of Nkruma
abuur *(act)* create
create something new
abuure *(nom)* creator
creator god
abuuritaan *(nom)* creation
all creation
adag *(adj)* difficult
the exam is difficult
adag *(adj)* hard

it is hard
adag *(adj)* tough
tough meat
adag *(adv)* firmly
to stand firmly
adag *(adv)* hard
to work hard
addeecid *(nom)* obedience
obedience and love
addoon *(nom)* slave
my slave
adduun noqosho *(nom)* worldliness
she possesses worldliness
adeec *(act)* obey
obey your parents
adeeg *(nom)* service
thanksgiving service
adeege *(nom)* servant
my servant
adeegenimo *(nom)* servanthood
our servanthood
adeegto *(nom)* maid
she is a maid
adeer/abti *(nom)* uncle
uncle Kofi
adiga *(pro)* you
you eat
adigu *(pos)* your
your house
adkaansho *(nom)* difficulty

adkaansho *(nom)* hardship

great hardship

adkaysi *(nom)* stamina

she has stamina

adke *(adj)* solid

solid water

adoon *(nom)* concubine

Yaa is my concubine

af *(nom)* language

afaf badan *many languages*

af *(nom, c2)* mouth

afkayga *my mouth*

af mugiis *(nom)* mouthful

two morsels

afar *(adj)* four

afar dhaloonyinka *There are four bottles on the wall*

afar iyo toban *(adj)* fourteen

afar iyo toban dhaloonyinka *fourteen bottles*

afar qofood *(plural(adj)* four

afar xaglood/laydi *(nom)* rectangle

a rectangle has four angles

afartan *(adj)* forty

forty bottles

afayn *(act)* sharpen

sharpen a knife

afduubasho *(nom)* kidnapping

kidnapping is evil

Afgaan *(nom)* Afghan

the Afghans

Afgaanistaan *(nom)* Afghanistan

go to Afghanistan

afhayeen *(nom)* spokesperson

the chieftain's spokesperson

Afrika *(nom)* Africa

visit Africa

Afrikaan *(adj)* African

African soccer team

Afrikaan *(nom)* African

I am an African (person)

Afrikaan Dhexe *(nom)* Central African

the Central Africans

ag *(pre)* at

meet me at home

agoon *(nom)* orphan

we are orphans

ah *(exc)* ah

ah yes!

ahaansho *(nom)* being

human being

ahow *(act)* be

You are an important person

ajoya - magac *(nom)* Ajoa

Ajoa is my daughter

Akaan - dad ku nool Gaana *(nom)* Akan

I speak Akan

akadami *(nom)* academy

akhri *(act)* read

to read a book

akhris *(nom)* reading

repeat the reading

akoonada *(nom)* accounts
she made accounts
Akra *(nom)* Accra
I am going to Accra
aktaaniyam *(sci)* actinium
actinium (Ac) has 89 protons
Akubeen - dad ku nool koon-
fur bari Gaana *(nom)* Akuapem
Akuapem is an Akan language
alaab/walax *(nom)* stuff

albaab *(nom)* door
xidh albaabka *close the door*
albaab *(nom)* gate
open the gate
aleelaxay *(nom)* cowry
five cowries
alfabeeto *(nom)* alphabet
I know all the alphabet
Algooriisam - nidaam xisaabiye
oo koombuyuuter *(nom)* algorithm
a new algorithm
Aljeeriya *(nom)* Algeria
go to Algeria
alumuuniyam *(sci)* aluminium
aluminium (Al) has 13 protons
amaah *(nom)* loan
I need a loan
amaahi *(act)* lend
lend me this book
amaahi *(act)* loan
loan me money

amaaho *(act)* borrow
borrow money
Ambaay - Buur ku taala wadan
Beeruu *(nom)* ampay
let's play ampay
Ameerika *(nom)* America
America is a continent
amiir *(nom)* prince
he is a prince
amiirad *(nom)* princess
she is a princess
amiriikiyam *(sci)* americium
americium (Am) has 95 protons
ammaan *(act)* glorify

ammaan *(act)* commend
commend her
ammaan *(act)* praise
to praise God
ammaan *(nom)* glory
glory of humankind
ammaanida *(nom)* praise
she deserves praise
ammar *(act)* command
to command a soldier
ammar *(nom)* authority

ammusan *(nom)* mute
a mute cannot speak
amrid *(nom)* command
give him a command
amuusan *(adj)* silent
be silent

Amxaar *(nom)* Amharic
Amharic and Oromo
Angoola *(nom)* Angola
go to Angola
Angoolaan *(nom)* Angolan
the Angolans
annaga *(pro)* us
show us
annaga *(pro)* we
we eat
anniga *(pro)* me
me and you
anniga *(pro)* I
I eat
Antaraatiga *(nom)* Antartica
Antartica is a continent
aqal *(nom)* bungalow
three bungalows
aqal *(nom)* hut
ten huts
aqbal *(act)* accept
accept her
araanjo *(nom)* orange
araanjo saddex three oranges
araanjo *(nom)* orange
araanjo saddex three oranges
aragti *(nom)* vision
a new vision for Africa
Arbaca *(nom)* Wednesday
Wednesday children
arbushnaan *(adj)* unkempt
an unkempt room
arday *(nom)* pupil

pupil and eyeball
arday *(nom)* student
twenty students
argagaxi *(act)* frighten
frighten evil people
argoon *(sci)* argon
argon (Ar) has 18 protons
Armeeniya *(nom)* Armenia
go to Armenia
Armeeniyaan *(nom)* Armenian
the Armenians
aroos *(nom)* groom
groom's friends
aroos *(nom)* wedding
we are going to a wedding
aroosad *(nom)* bride
bride's husband; groom
arrin *(nom)* affair

arrin *(nom)* issue
new issue
arseenik *(sci)* arsenic
arsenic (As) has 33 protons
arxan-darro *(nom)* apathy
apathy kills good things
aryaa *(exc)* hey

Asarbijaan *(nom)* Azerbaijan
go to Azerbaijan
Asarbijaani *(nom)* Azerbaijani
the Azerbaijanis
ashtako *(nom)* accusation
lay an accusation

asiidh leh *(adj)* acidic
 acidic water
askari *(nom)* soldier
 the soldiers are marching
asluub leh *(adj)* gracious
 a gracious person
astantiin *(sci)* astatine
 astatine (At) has 85 protons
atam *(sci)* atom
 an atom has a nucleus and electrons

awllalada malabka *(nom)* honeycomb
 honey in a honeycomb
awood *(act)* can
 I can read
awood *(nom)* authoritative
 she is authoritative
awood isticmaal *(nom)* access
 give me access
awood leh *(adj)* powerful
 powerful prophet
awood oo dhan leh *(adj)* almighty
 almighty god
awood xirfadeed leh *(adj)* competent

awoodi kara *(adj)* capable
 a capable woman
awoodid *(adj)* able
 an able woman
Awoodo inuu *(act)* be able to
 I am able to climb a tree

awoow *(nom)* grandfather, grandpa
 my grandfather
ax *(exc)* ouch
 Ouch! It hurts
Axad *(nom)* Sunday
 Kwasi and Akosua are Sunday children
axal *(nom)* catarrh
 I have catarrh
axdi *(nom)* covenant
 a new covenant
ayax *(nom)* locust
 locusts and honey
ayeey *(nom)* grandmother, grandma

Ayforiyaan *(nom)* Ivoirian
 the Ivorians
Ayfri Koost *(nom)* Cote d'Ivoire
 go to Cote d'Ivoire
ayodhiin *(sci)* iodine
 iodine (I) has 53 protons
ayron *(sci)* iron
 iron (Fe) has 26 protons

B

baabii *(act)* incinerate
 incinerate all the papers
baabtiis *(act)* baptise
 baptise John
baabuur *(nom)* car
 kaxee baabuur *drive a car*

baabuur *(nom)* lorry
lorry stop
baabuur *(nom)* vehicle
a new vehicle
baadbadiye *(nom)* saviour
my saviour
baadh *(act)* find
find the word
baadhid *(act)* search
search his house
baadiyaha *(nom)* bush
go into the bush
baahi *(act)* need
to need family
baal *(nom)* feather
bird's feathers
baaldi *(nom)* bucket
*baaldigu wuu darrooraa the bucket
leaks*
baaldi *(nom)* pail
pail and soap
baamiye *(nom)* okro, okra

baanadd *(nom)* spanner
a big spanner
baariyam *(sci)* barium
barium (Ba) has 56 protons
baarlaman *(nom)* parliament
elect her to go to parliament
baaruud *(nom)* gunpowder
I smell gunpowder
baaskiil *(nom)* bicycle
baaskiil cusub new bicycle

baaxad *(nom)* depth
the depth of a well
babtiisam *(nom)* baptism
repentance and baptism
bacrin ah *(adj)* fertile
fertile land
bad *(nom)* sea
a river goes into a sea
bad *(nom)* ocean
a large ocean
badal *(act)* change
if time changes, change with the times

badal *(nom)* change
do you have change?
badan *(adj)* many
many vehicles
badan *(adj)* more
more food
badan *(adj)* plenty
plenty of issues
badana *(adv)* always
he is always here
badarka gini *(nom)* guinea grain

badbaadin *(act)* save
save it
badbaado *(nom)* salvation
our salvation
badeeco *(nom)* product
to advertise a product
badhida *(nom)* buttocks
big buttocks

bahriyum *(sci)* bohrium
bohrium (Bh) has 107 protons

bakayle *(nom)* hare
to run like a hare

bakeyle *(nom)* rabbit
a white rabbit

bakhalynimo *(adj)* miserly
he is miserly

bakheyl *(nom)* stinginess
stinginess or generosity

bakhtii *(act)* extinguish
extinguish the flame

Bakistaan *(nom)* Pakistan
go to Pakistan

Bakistaani *(nom)* Pakistani
the Pakistanis

bakoorad *(nom)* cane
bring the cane

balaadhan *(adj)* broad

balaadhan *(adj)* large
a large tiger

balaadhan *(adj)* massive

balaadhiyam *(sci)* palladium
palladium (Pd) has 46 protons

balaari *(act)* expand

balac *(nom)* width
height and width

baladh *(nom)* breadth
breadth and width

balan *(nom)* promise

give me a promise

balanbaalis *(nom)* butterfly
balanbaalistu way qurux badan-
tahay a butterfly is beautiful

balanqaadid *(nom)* pledge
God's pledge has been fulfilled

ballaatiyam *(sci)* platinum
platinum (Pt) has 78 protons

ballan qaad *(act)* promise
promise me

ballaran *(adj)* wide
wide road

banaan *(sci)* area
area (rectangle) = length x width

banaan *(nom)* outdoors
go outdoors

banaan *(nom)* plank
plank and nail

banbo *(nom)* suicide
It is a suicide

bandhagid *(nom)* set

Bangaaladhish *(nom)* Bangladesh
go to Bangladesh

Bangaaladhishi *(nom)* Bangladeshi
the Bangladeshis

bangi *(nom)* bank
my money is at the bank

banku - cunto lagu cuno Gaana
(nom) banku
you eat banku?

baqbaaq *(nom)* parrot
two parrots

baqdin *(nom)* fear
fear has filled her heart
baqid *(act)* scare

baqo *(act)* fear
fear an apparition
baqtii *(act)* shut down
the shop shuts down in the evening

bar-kulan *(nom)* junction, intersection

Baraasfile-Koongaaliis *(nom)*
Brazzaville-Congolese
the Brazzaville-Congolese
baradho macaan *(nom)* cassava
plantain and cassava
baradho macaan *(nom)* sweet potato
I like sweet potato
baradho macaan *(nom)* yam
cook the yam
baradho macaanta biyaha *(nom)* water yam
cook the water yam
baraf *(nom)* snow
there is snow on the mountain
barakaysan *(adj)* holy
holy book
barako *(nom)* blessing
God's blessing
baranbaro *(nom)* cockroach

I see a cockroach
barandaha *(nom)* verandah
let's go to the verandah
barar *(nom)* swallow
a cat and a swallow
bararid *(act)* swell
swollen leg
baras *(nom)* leprosy
leprosy is a disease
barasodimiyam *(sci)* praseodymium
praseodymium (Pr) has 59 protons
barbaarin *(nom)* preschool

barbarad *(nom)* novice
he is a novice
bari *(nom)* orient
go east
barid *(act)* teach
to teach mathematics
Bariga Taymor *(nom)* East Timor
go to East Timor
Bariga Taymoriis *(nom)* East Timorese
the East Timorese
bariis *(nom)* rice
rice and beans
bariis jollof *(nom)* jollof
jollof is food
baro *(act)* learn
they learn a language
baroorasho *(nom)* lamentation
many lamentations
baroorte *(nom)* mourner

18

many mourners

baroosin *(nom)* anchor
anchor of a ship

barte *(nom)* learner
we are learners

barwaaqaysam *(adj)* abundant

barwaaqo *(nom)* prosperity
peace and prosperity

barwaqada *(adj)* plenteous

barwaqaysan *(adj)* fruitful

bas yar *(nom)* van
board a van

basaasnimo *(nom)* espionage
espionage films

basaboor/dal ku gal *(nom)* passport
your passport

basal *(nom)* onion

basali *(adj)* pink
some pigs are pink

basbaas *(nom)* pepper
the pepper burns

baxay *(adv)* out
he is coming out of the house

Baxrayn *(nom)* Bahrain
go to Bahrain

Baxrayni *(nom)* Bahraini
the Bahrainis

baylah ah *(adj)* vulnerable

bayoolaji *(nom)* biology
we are learning biology

baytariyo *(nom)* battery
a new battery

beddelid *(act)* replace
replace me

bedel *(nom)* replacement

beed *(nom)* egg
beedka digaaga *chicken egg*

been *(nom)* lie
lies and discord

been abuur *(nom)* falsification
lies and falsifications

been sheeg *(nom)* perjury
perjury in court

beenaale *(nom)* liar
three liars

beeni *(act)* deny
you cannot deny the truth

beer *(act)* plant
to plant a tree

beer *(nom)* farm
cocoa farm

beer *(nom)* liver
a dog has a liver

beer *(nom)* garden
our garden

Beer xayawaan *(nom)* zoo
zoo tour

beerin *(act)* sow
sow a tree

beerkiliyam *(sci)* berkelium
berkelium (Bk) has 97 protons
beerliyam *(sci)* beryllium
beryllium (Be) has 4 protons
beerwale *(nom)* farmer
she is a farmer
**Bemba - dad ku nool Saam-
biya** *(nom)* Bemba
Bemba language
berri *(adv)* tomorrow
she will arrive tomorrow
biciid *(nom)* antelope
a lion likes antelope meat
bidix *(adj)* left
go left
biibiile *(nom)* balloon
laba biibiile *two balloons*
biibiile *(nom)* pipe
pipe water
biilka *(nom)* bill

biisa *(nom)* pizza
five pizzas
bikaaco *(nom)* lens
lens of a camera
bikro *(nom)* virgin
ten virgins
bil *(nom)* month
one month
bilaa hoy ah *(adj)* homeless
a homeless person
bilaa qadarin *(nom)* impertinence

stop the impertinence
bilaabid *(act)* start
to start early
bilaash *(act)* free
she will free the dog
bilaash *(adj)* free
free food
bilaw *(act)* begin
start eating
bileedh *(nom)* plate
meydh bileedhkaaga
bilic *(nom)* grace
the grace of God
bilow *(nom)* beginning
the beginning
bilyan *(adj)* billion
a billion bottles
Biniin *(nom)* Benin
go to Benin
Biniinoos *(nom)* Beninois
the Beninois
biqlid *(act)* sprout
the maize is sprouting
bir *(nom)* metal
hat of metal
biriij *(nom)* bridge
cross the bridge
birkin *(nom)* pillow
birkin iyo sariir *pillow and bed*
bisad *(nom)* cat, pussy
bisadu waxay leedahay dabo *a cat
has a tail*
bisad duurjoog ah oo weyn

(nom) jaguar
  a jaguar is an animal
bislee *(act)* ripen
  the mango has ripened
bismat *(sci)* bismuth
  bismuth (Bi) has 83 protons
Bisow-Giniyaan *(nom)* Bissau-
  Guinean
  the Bissau-Guineans
bixi *(act)* pay
  I will pay
biyaano *(nom)* piano
  play the piano
biyaha guga *(nom)* springwater
  to drink springwater
biyo *(nom)* water
  waxaad cabtaa biyo *you drink wa-*
ter
biyo ku gubasho *(act)* scald
  hot water scalds
biyomareen *(nom)* gutter
  there is water in the gutter
bog *(nom)* page
  open page twenty-two
bogsasho *(nom)* healing
  he brought healing
bogso *(act)* heal
  heal disease
bohol *(nom)* pit
  dig a pit
boloniyam *(sci)* polonium
  polonium (Po) has 84 protons

bood *(act)* jump
  to jump a wall
boodh calaamadeed *(nom)* signpost
  a tall signpost
bool *(nom)* bolt

boolis *(nom)* police
  five police
boolonboolo *(nom)* duck
  white duck
boonballo *(nom)* puppet
  red puppet
booqasho *(act)* visit
  do come and visit me!
booraan *(nom)* ditch
  there is water in the ditch
boorash *(nom)* porridge
  millet porridge
Boortugaal *(nom)* Portugal

boos *(nom)* position
  a good position
boosto *(nom)* post office
  I am going to the post office
Bootiswaana *(nom)* Botswana
  go to Botswana
boqol *(adj)* hundred
  hundred bottles
boqor *(nom)* king
  he is a king
boqor noqosho *(act)* reign
  God reigns

boqorad *(nom)* queen
she is a queen

boqortooyo *(nom)* kingdom
the kingdom of God

boqortoyada *(nom)* royalty
you are royalty

boqortoyadisi *(nom)* realm
news of the realm

boqoshaa *(nom)* mushroom
mushroom soup

boromiin *(sci)* bromine
bromine (Br) has 35 protons

boromiitiyam *(sci)* promethium
promethium (Pm) has 61 protons

boroon *(sci)* boron
boron (B) has 5 protons

boroorasho *(nom)* wailing
crying and wailing

borotakaniyam *(sci)* protactinium
protactinium (Pa) has 91 protons

borotoroon *(sci)* proton
a proton has a charge of +1

botaashiyam *(sci)* potassium
potassium (K) has 19 protons

bowd *(nom)* fence
behind a fence

bowdada *(nom)* thigh
chicken thigh

bu'da isha *(nom)* eyeball
eye and eyeball

bukaan *(nom)* patient
the patients sleep here

bulsho *(nom)* society

bulsho *(nom)* community
*to integrate a new family into the
community*

buluug *(adj)* blue
blue dress

buluug *(adj)* violet
violet flowers

buluug guduud ah *(adj)* purple
purple flower

buluutooniyam *(sci)* plutonium
plutonium (Pu) has 94 protons

buni *(adj)* brown
brown bird

burburi *(act)* crumble
the house crumbled

burburi *(act)* destroy
destroy everything

burburin *(act)* smash
the plate is smashed

burcad *(nom)* cheese
blue cheese

Burkiina Faaso *(nom)* Burkina Faso
go to Burkina Faso

Burkiinaabe *(nom)* Burkinabe
the Burkinabes

Burunaay *(nom)* Brunei
go to Brunei

Burundi *(nom)* Burundi
go to Burundi

Burundiyaan *(nom)* Burundian
　the Burundians
Buruniyaan *(nom)* Bruneian
　the Bruneians
burush garee *(nom)* brush
　a black brush
bus-buska *(nom)* chickenpox
　chickenpox is a disease
buste *(nom)* blanket
　buste qoyan *wet blanket*
butoon *(nom)* button
　press the button
buug *(nom)* book
　buugan *this book*
buug masiixi ah *(nom)* bible
　the Bible and the Koran
buul *(nom)* lodge
　stay at the lodging for a while
buul shimbireed *(nom)* nest

buun *(nom)* trumpet
　seven trumpets
buur *(nom)* mountain
　mountain peak
buuran *(adj)* fat
　fat cheeks
buuri *(nom)* snuff
　give me some snuff
buuxa *(adj)* full
　full bucket
buuxi *(act)* fill
　fill it
buuxi *(act)* fill up

fill up the barrel

C

caadada *(nom)* menes

caadi ah *(adj)* normal
　normal behaviour
caadi ah *(adj)* usual

caado *(nom)* custom
　love is a good custom
caado *(nom)* habit
　bad habit
caado ama walax la caabudo
　(nom) fetish
　this town has a fetish
caado callool xun wadata *(nom)*
　dysmenorrhoea
　I have dysmenorrhoea
caafimaad *(nom)* health
　food gives health
caag ah *(adj)* plastic
　plastic cup
caajis *(nom)* sluggard
　the sluggard is asleep
caajis ah *(adj)* lazy
　lazy man
caajisnimo *(nom)* laziness
　laziness is not good
caalam *(nom)* planet
　Earth is a planet

caan ah *(adj)* famous
famous person
caanaha naaska *(nom)* breastmilk
drink the breastmilk
caanaqubta *(nom)* porcupine
three porcupines
caano *(nom)* milk
to drink milk
caarada farta *(nom)* fingertip
lick your fingertips
caaro *(nom)* spider
xuubka caarada spider's web
caaro *(nom)* tarantula
a large tarantula
caasimad *(nom)* capital
Accra is the capital of Ghana
caasinimo *(nom)* rebellion
the rebellion has started
caato ah *(adj)* slim
slim person
caawi *(act)* help
you are helping everyone
caawimo *(act)* assist

caawimo *(nom)* help
everyone needs help
caawiye *(nom)* assistant
my assistant
caawiye *(nom)* helper
my helper
cab *(act)* drink
to drink water

cabaadid *(act)* scream

cabasho *(act)* whine
stop whining
cabir *(nom)* measure
three measures of flour
cabsan *(ydy(i(act)* drank

cabsi leh *(adj)* frightening
it is frightening
cad *(adj)* white
white house
cad ceed dhac *(nom)* sunset
from sunrise to sunset
cad ceed soo bax *(nom)* sunrise
from sunrise to sunset
cadaalad *(nom)* justice
freedom and justice
cadar *(nom)* perfume
what perfume is that?
cadar madaxa lamarsado *(nom)*
pomade
fragrant pomade
caday *(nom)* toothbrush
caday iyo dawo caday toothbrush
and toothpaste
cadceed *(nom)* sun
cadceedu way dhalaalaysaa the
sun is shining
caddibaad *(act)* torment

cadeyn *(nom)* proof

show me the proof
cadho *(nom)* bile
green bile
cadow *(nom)* enemy
enemies will tire
cafi *(act)* forgive
forgive me my wrong
cagaar ah *(adj)* greenish
greenish house
cagaaran *(adj)* green
green leaf
cagaha dofaarka *(nom)* pigfeet
pigfeet soup
cagajuglee *(act)* bully
they are bullying him
cago kala baxsan *(adj)* bow-legged
bow-legged man
cajiib ah *(adj)* strange

cajiin *(nom)* dough
he pressed the dough
calaali *(act)* chew
to chew groundnuts
calaali *(act)* masticate
a cow masticates grass
calaamad *(nom)* badge
a white badge
calaamad *(nom)* symbol
symbol of power
calal *(nom)* rag
old rag
calamad dhigid *(act)* stamp

Big Man, please stamp it for me
calan *(nom)* flag
yellow flag
caleen *(nom)* leaf
caleen cagaaran green leaf
caleen *(nom)* foliage
cut the foliage
caleen *(nom)* frond
to cut the fronds
calool *(nom)* stomach, belly

calool xanuun *(nom)* stomach-ache
he has a stomach-ache
caloool xumo *(nom)* grief
grief is killing me
cambaar *(nom)* eczema
eczema is a skin disease
cambe *(nom)* mango
cambuhu wuu bislaaday the mango has ripened
canaanas *(nom)* pineapple
pineapple juice
canab *(nom)* grape
eat the grapes
canab *(nom)* vine
vine leaf
candhuuf *(nom)* spittle
wipe the spittle
canqow *(nom)* ankle
your ankles
caqabad *(nom)* challenge
a good challenge

caqabad *(nom)* obstacle
many obstacles
caqli leh *(adj)* wise
a wise girl
carab *(nom)* tongue
dog's tongue
caraf/udug *(nom)* fragrance
the fragrance of sheabutter
Carafo *(nom)* September
September has 30 days
cararid *(act)* flee
he fled
carfoon *(adj)* fragrant
cinnamon is fragrant
carmal (gabar) *(nom)* widow
she is a widow
carmal (nin) *(nom)* widower
he is a widower
carmalnimo *(nom)* widowhood
a short widowhood
carmaloobay *(adj)* widowed
widowed man
caro leh *(adj)* annoying
it is annoying to you
carqalad *(nom)* hindrance

carruurnimo *(nom)* childhood
my childhood
carsaanyo *(nom)* crab
crab soup
carshi *(nom)* throne
to sit on a throne
caruur *(plural(nom))* child

caruusad *(nom)* doll
caruusadayda *my doll*
cas *(adj)* red
bushimo cas *red lips*
casaan *(adj)* scarlet
a scarlet dress
casayso *(act)* doze
you are dozing
cashar *(nom)* lesson
learn the lesson
cashuur *(nom)* tax
to pay tax
cawaaqib *(nom)* consequence
its consequences
caws *(nom)* grass
a cow chews grass
cay *(act)* insult
stop insulting her
cay *(nom)* diss
it is not a diss
cay *(nom)* insult
many insults
cayayaan *(nom)* insect
a cockroach is an insect
cayayaan duula *(nom)* blowfly
blowflies are annoying
caytinta *(nom)* insults
unnecessary insults
ceeb *(act)* shame
shame him
ceeb *(nom)* shame
shame and disgrace

ceebayn *(act)* disgrace
 you are disgracing yourself
ceel *(nom)* borehole
 dig a borehole
ceeryaamo *(nom)* mist
 morning mist
ceeryaan *(nom)* fog
 dark fog
cida diiga *(act)* crow
 a cockerel is crowing
ciddi *(nom)* snail
 I eat snails
ciddiyaha aroosada *(nom)* pawpaw, papaya

cidhib *(nom)* heel
 toe and heel
cidhiidhi *(nom)* anguish

cidi *(nom)* nail
 plank and nail
cidida farta *(nom)* fingernail

cidida suulka *(nom)* thumbnail
 click on the thumbnail
cidiyaha faraha lugaha *(nom)*
 toenail

Ciid *(nom)* Eid
 Eid is a holiday
ciid *(nom)* sand
 beach sand

Ciida masiixiga *(nom)* Christmas
 Christmas is coming
Ciise *(nom)* Jesus
 Jesus Christ!
cilin *(nom)* dwarf
 seven dwarves
cillad *(nom)* defect
 the building has many defects
cillad lahaan *(nom)* imperfection

cilmi nafsi *(nom)* psychology
 to learn pyschology
cimilo *(nom)* weather
 we have good weather
cimlaaq *(adj)* giant
 he is a giant man
cimlaaq *(nom)* giant
 four giants
ciqaab *(act)* punish
 punish him
Ciraaq *(nom)* Iraq
 go to Iraq
Ciraaqi *(nom)* Iraqi
 the Iraqis
cirka *(nom)* sky
 to fly into the sky
ciwaan *(nom)* address
 your address
ciyaar *(act)* play
 we are playing
ciyaar *(nom)* game

play a game
ciyaar *(nom)* play
watch a play
Ciyaaraha Olombikada *(nom)*
Olympics
Olympics competition
ciyaaro *(nom)* sport
she likes sports
cod *(nom)* voice
soften your voice
cod dheer *(adj)* loud
loud siren
cod leh *(nom)* sound
loud sound
codayn *(act)* vote
vote for me
codeyn *(nom)* voting
the voting is going well
codsadaha *(nom)* requester
who is the requester?
codsi *(nom)* petition

codsi *(nom)* application
job application
codsi *(nom)* request
my request
codso *(act)* request
to request food
colnimo *(nom)* enmity
great enmity
coloosha *(nom)* abdomen
abdomen of a dog
cudbi *(nom)* cotton

cloth of cotton
cudud *(nom)* arm
lift up your arm
cudur *(nom)* disorder

cudur *(nom)* disease
heal disease
cudur *(nom)* plague
no plagues there
cudurka duumada *(nom)* malaria
malaria is a disease
cudurka ebola *(nom)* ebola
ebola is a disease
cudurka yaawis *(nom)* yaws
yaws is a disease
cuf *(sci)* mass
you can change mass into energy
culayska maskaxda/cadaasi
(nom) stress

culeys *(nom)* burden
very heavy burden
culus *(adj)* heavy
it is heavy
Cumaan *(nom)* Oman
go to Oman
Cumaani *(nom)* Omani
the Omanis
cun *(act)* eat
*si aad wax kasta u cunto to eat
everything*
cun casho *(act)* dine

Cunaha *(nom)* throat
clear your throat
cuncun *(nom)* herpes
herpes is a disease
cuncun *(nom)* irritation

cunto *(nom)* food
cun cunto *eat food*
cunto cajiin ka sameysan *(nom)*
dumpling
we are eating Chinese dumplings
cunto carruureed *(nom)* pap
eat the pap
cunto jarjarid *(nom)* cube
a cube of sugar
curyaamin *(act)* sabotage
sabotage her
curyaamin *(nom)* sabotage
this is sabotage
curyaan *(nom)* cripple
he is a cripple
curyanimo *(nom)* paraliesis
paraliesis is a disease
cusbitaal *(nom)* hospital, clinic

cusbo *(nom, c1)* salt

cusko *(act)* grab
grab his hand
cusub *(adj)* fresh
fresh leaves
cusub *(adj)* new
new family

cusub /casri *(adj)* modern
modern language
cutub *(nom)* chapter
chapter 12
cutub *(nom)* unit
five units
cuyaanimo *(nom)* lameness
her lameness is improving

D

da' ah *(adj)* old
old pan
da' yar *(nom)* teenager
she is a teenager
da'aha isku dhow *(nom)* age
group
your age group
da'da *(nom)* age
your age
daa'in *(nom)* eternity
from now to eternity
daa'uus *(nom)* peacock
three peacocks
daabac *(act)* print
they print books
daabace *(nom)* printer
book printer
daac *(act)* belch
eat then belch
daacad ah *(adj)* loyal
my loyal friend

daacadnimo *(nom)* loyalty
loyalty and love

daacadnimo ah *(adv)* frankly
say it frankly

daad *(nom)* flood
Accra flood

daaf *(nom)* conjunctivitis
conjunctivitis is a disease

daah *(nom)* curtain
the window needs a curtain

daal *(nom)* fatigue
tiredness and fatigue

daal *(nom)* tiredness
tiredness and fatigue

daalid *(act)* tire
enemies will tire

daan *(nom)* jaw
my jaw

daanyeer *(nom)* chimpanzee
I saw a chimpanzee

daanyeer *(nom)* monkey
daanyeerku wuxuu jecelyay muuska
a monkey likes bananas

daanyeer *(nom)* ape
an ape and a monkey

daanyeer *(nom)* baboon
three baboons

daaqad *(nom)* window
fur daaqadaha open the windows

daarada danbe *(nom)* back-yard
the backyard is overgrown

daawasho *(act)* watch
to watch football

daawasho *(nom)* watch
a small watch

daawo *(nom)* medicine
bitter medicine

dab *(nom)* fire
light the fire

daba-qalooc *(nom)* lobster
I eat lobster

dabaalasho *(act)* swim
to swim well

dabaaldeg *(nom)* festival
a yearly festival

dabacsan *(adj)* flexible
a flexible stick

dabagaale *(nom)* squirrel
a squirrel likes palm nuts

dabaly leh *(adj)* windy
a windy day

dabaqa hoose *(adv)* downstairs
he is downstairs

dabaqa sare *(adv)* upstairs
he is upstairs

dabayl *(nom)* wind
the wind is blowing

dabey qalalan *(nom)* harmattan
harmattan winds

dabo *(act)* tail
to tail someone

dabo *(nom)* tail
a cat has a tail

dabool *(act)* cover
  cover it up
dabool *(nom)* lid
  lid of a cup
dacas *(nom)* slippers
  waxaad xidhan tahay dacas *you are wearing slippers*
dacawo *(nom)* fox
  three foxes
daciifnimo *(nom)* weakness
  in her weakness
dacwayn *(act)* sue
  to sue someone
dacwee *(act)* litigate
  we are litigating
dacwo maxkameed *(nom)* litigation
  he likes litigation
dad *(nom)* people
  some people
dadaal *(nom)* effort
  a good effort
Dadka Galbeedka Saxaaraha *(nom)* Western Saharan
  the Western Saharans
dadweynaha *(nom)* public
  you don't say 'vagina' in public
dafo *(act)* hawk
  hawk things
dafo *(nom)* hawk
  a hawk and a chicken
dag *(act)* descend
  descend to the ground

dagaal *(nom)* battle
  we are going to battle
dagaal *(nom)* war
  we are going to war
dagaal gar daro ah *(nom)* aggression
  too much aggression
dagaal sokeeye *(nom)* civil war
  stop the civil war
dagaalan *(act)* battle
  we are going to battle them
dagaalan *(act)* fight
  Ali and Frazier fought
dagaalyahan *(nom)* warrior
  warrior of antiquity
dagaalyahano *(nom)* warriors
  the warriors are coming
daganaan u seexasho *(exc)* so there
  I say, "So there!"
dahab *(nom)* gold
  fragrance and gold
dahab *(nom)* jewelry
  pretty jewelry
dahab *(sci)* gold
  gold (Au) has 79 protons
dahab xaddi yar oon qiimo badan lahayn *(nom)* trinket
  she has many trinkets
daloolin *(act)* pierce
  pierce your ear
damaaci *(adj)* greedy
  greedy fool

damac *(nom)* greed
 gred and envy
dambas *(nom)* ash
 charcoal and ashes
dameer *(nom)* arse

dameer *(nom)* donkey
 ten donkeys
dameer farow *(nom)* zebra
 seven zebras
damiir *(nom)* conscience
 your conscience
damin *(act)* turn off
 to turn off the light
dan *(nom)* interest
 loan interest
danbas *(nom)* soot
 black soot
danbe *(nom)* behind
 the end has neared
daneystenimo *(nom)* selfishness
 selfishness is not good
daqiiq/bur *(nom)* flour
 corn flour
daqiiqad *(nom)* minute
 five minutes
darajo *(nom)* appellation
 proclaim her appellations
darajo *(nom)* title
 "Mighty One" is a title
darawal *(nom)* driver
 the driver has braked

darbi-jiif *(nom)* bum
 large bum
dardaaran *(nom)* testament
 new testament
dareemaya *(adj)* feeling
 your mind and your feelings
dareemayaasha *(nom)* nerve
 brain and nerves
dareemid *(act)* sense
 I sense we will score a goal
dareen *(act)* feel
 I am feeling good
dareen *(nom)* sense

dareere *(adj)* liquid
 liquid water
dareeri *(act)* drain
 use the collander to drain the rice
darmastiyam *(sci)* darmstadtium
 darmstadtium (Ds) has 110 protons

daruur *(nom)* cloud
 daruur cad *a white cloud*
daruur *(act)* cloud
 the sky has clouded
daruuro leh *(adj)* cloudy
 a cloudy day
daryeel *(act)* care

dawlad *(nom)* government
 Nkrumah's government
dawo caday *(nom)* toothpaste
 caday iyo dawo caday *toothbrush*

and toothpaste
dayax *(nom)* moon
  dayax iyo xiddigo moon and stars

dayr *(nom)* Autumn
 I spend Autumn in France
deeq bixiye *(nom)* philanthropist
 she is a philanthropist
deeq waxbarasho *(nom)* scholarship
 I have a scholarship
deeqsinimo *(nom)* generosity
 your generosity
deeqsiya *(adj)* bountiful

deero *(nom)* deer
 a lion likes deer meat
degaanka *(nom)* habitat
 habitat of animals
degid *(act)* reside
 I reside in Osu
degid *(act)* settle
 settle there
dekad *(nom)* port
 Takoradi has a port
deked *(nom)* harbour
 Takoradi has a harbour
dembi *(nom)* sin
 sin and forgiveness
deris *(nom)* neighbor

deris *(nom)* neighbour
 my neighbour

derisnimo *(nom)* neighborhood, area

derisnimo *(nom)* neighbourhood
 we live in the same neighbourhood

deyn *(nom)* debt
 he has many debts
deyr *(nom)* yard
 big yard
dhaaf *(act)* pass
 if you are passing, call me
dhaar *(nom)* oath
 great oath
dhaarasho *(act)* swear
 swear that you and me will die (together)
dhaasheer *(adj)* gaudy
 gaudy necklace
dhaawac *(act)* injure
 I am injured
dhab ah *(adj)* serious
 a serious work
dhab ah *(adv)* truly
 truly God is good
dhaban *(nom)* cheek
 fat cheeks
dhabar *(nom)* spine
 ear, nose and spine
dhabar jab *(nom)* blow
 give him a blow
dhabta ah *(adj)* actual

dhac *(act)* fall
 a rope fell from the roof of the house

dhacay *(adj)* outdated
 outdated lorry
dhacdo *(nom)* event
 the event has started
dhadhan *(act)* taste
 taste the food
dhado *(nom)* dew
 morning dew
dhag *(nom)* ear
 ear and nose
dhag la gashto *(nom)* earpiece
 new earpiece
dhagax *(act)* rock
 I shall never be rocked
dhagax *(nom)* rock
 a big rock
dhagax *(nom)* stone
 stones and cement
dhagax madow *(nom)* flint
 use the flint to light the fire
dhageyso *(act)* listen
 to listen to music
dhageyste *(nom)* listener
 hello listeners
dhago la gashto - sida da-habka *(nom)* earring
 he wears earrings
dhakho leh *(adv)* soon
 she is coming soon

dhakhtar *(nom)* doctor
 she is a doctor
dhakhtar *(act)* doctor
 they have doctored the thing
dhakso ah *(adj)* quick

dhal *(act)* birth
 to birth twins
dhalaalaya *(adj)* bright
 bright room
dhalaalaya *(adj)* glossy
 a glossy magazine
dhalashada ilmo *(nom)* child-birth
 a childbirth brings joy
dhalasho *(nom)* advent

dhalasho *(nom)* birth
 place of birth
dhaleecayn *(act)* diss
 diss someone
dhalin yaro ah *(adj)* young
 young person
dhalinyaro *(nom)* youth
 in my youth, I was strong
dhalo *(nom)* bottle
 shan dhalooyinka *five bottles*
dhalo *(nom)* jar
 seven jars
dhamaad *(nom)* end
 the end has come
dhamaan *(det)* all
 all things

34

dhamaan *(pro)* all
 all came
dhamee *(act)* accomplish

dhamee *(act)* end
 you will end the war
dhamee *(act)* finish
 they will finish the food
dhan *(adj)* whole

dhankay wax isu badaleen
 (nom) trend
 a good trend
dhaqaale *(nom)* economy
 the economy of Africa
dhaqaaq yar *(act)* flicker
 the light is flickering
dhaqan *(nom)* behaviour
 normal behaviour
dhaqan *(nom)* culture
 the culture of my school
dhaqan *(nom)* tradition

dhaqan wanaagsan *(nom)* virtue
 vice and virtue
dhaqdhaqaad degdeg ah *(act)*
 wriggle
 stop wriggling
dhar *(nom)* clothes
 Iibso dhar buy clothes
dhar *(nom)* cloth
 wear cloth
dhar *(nom)* dress

 blue dress
dhar *(nom)* fabric
 buy fabric for me
dhar *(nom)* garment
 wear a garment
dharka dumarka ee qaarka
 sare marka laga reebo gacmaha
 (nom) bodice
 she wears a bodice
dhas *(nom)* dust
 red dust
dhawr *(act)* preserve
 to preserve the food
dhawray *(ydy(i(act)* kept

dhaxaltoyo *(nom)* inheritance
 claim your inheritance
dhayal *(act)* be trivial
 working is not trivial
dhedig *(adj)* female
 a female child
dhedig *(nom)* female
 female's womb
dheeman *(nom)* diamond
 a white diamond
dheer *(adj)* long
 long beard
dheer *(adj)* tall
 a tall tree
dheerow *(act)* be lengthy
 your story is lengthy
dhego yare *(nom)* clove
 add some cloves to the food

dheh macaasalaama *(act)* say
goodbye
we take ten minutes to say goodbye

dherer *(nom)* height
height and width
dherer *(nom)* length
height, width and length
dheri *(nom)* pot
metal pot
dhexda *(nom)* middle

dhexda *(nom)* waist
your waist
dhexe *(nom)* centre
be in the centre
dhib *(act)* bother
you are bothering me
dhib *(nom)* trouble
trouble and pain
dhibaatee *(act)* hassle
hassle him so that he pays
dhibaateysan *(adj)* distressed
a distressed mind
dhibaato *(nom)* problem
many problems
dhibcaha *(act)* score
to score a goal
dhibic *(nom)* drop
drop by drop a chicken drinks water
dhibic *(nom)* point
1 point 5 (1.5) is one and a half.

dhibic dhado ah *(nom)* dewdrop
many dewdrops
dhibicda oohinta *(nom)* teardrop
a few teardrops
dhibid *(nom)* bother
too much bother
dhicid *(act)* happen
let it happen
dhicid *(ydy(i(act)* fell

dhig *(act)* put

dhigasho *(act)* study

dhihid *(act)* say
I say yes
dhiig *(nom)* blood
water and blood
dhiig bax *(act)* bleed
he is bleeding
dhiigbax *(nom)* bleeding
stop the bleeding
dhiiri geli *(act)* encourage
encourage her
dhiirigelin *(nom)* courage
she has courage
dhiirigelin *(nom)* encouragement
encouragement and joy
dhiirigelin badan *(adj)* courageous

dhilo *(nom)* slut
 a male prostitute
dhilqaha *(nom)* bedbug
 to kill bedbugs
dhim *(act)* reduce
 reduce it by five
dhimasho *(nom)* death
 place of death
dhimo *(act)* die
 to die young in the play
dhinac *(nom)* angle
 two angles
dhinac *(nom)* side
 love is on our side
dhinac aayar u dhaqaaqid
(nom) wobble

dhinaca *(nom)* corner
 the table is in the corner
dhinaca kale *(adv)* other side
 let us go to the other side
dhinacyada *(nom)* corners
 all corners of the world
dhintay *(adj)* dead
 a dead tree
dhir *(nom)* herb

dhir *(nom)* plant
 red plant
dhir yar *(nom)* grove
 grove of spirits
dhirbaax *(act)* blow
 blow air

dhirbaaxid *(act)* slap
 slap him
dhirbaaxid - gaar ahaan dabada
(act) spank
 I will spank you
dhis *(act)* construct
 he has constructed a new machine
dhisid *(act)* build
 build a house
dhismaha dabaq *(nom)* storey
 building
 I am building a storey building
dhisoboriyam *(sci)* dysprosium
 dysprosium (Dy) has 66 protons
dhokumenti *(nom)* document

dhoobo *(nom)* clay
 clay vase
dhoobo *(nom)* mud
 wash the mud
dhoola caddayn *(act)* smile
 to smile a bit
dhow *(adv)* near
 pull near to me
dhowr *(adj)* several
 several people came
dhudhun *(nom)* cubit
 three cubits
dhufeys *(nom)* shield
 He is my shield
dhul *(act)* land
 the aeroplane has landed
dhul *(nom)* land

buy land
dhul gariir *(nom)* quake
big earthquake
dhul xad leh *(nom)* territory

dhulalka bariga *(nom)* orient
go east
dhulka *(nom)* soil
people of the earth
dhulka *(nom)* ground

dhunko *(act)* kiss
kiss my lips
dhuuban *(adj)* thin
thin stick
dhuus *(act)* fart
someone has farted
dhuusid *(act)* flatulate
he flatulated
dhuuso *(nom)* fart
her fart smells badly
dhuxul *(nom)* charcoal
sack of charcoal
dib *(nom)* back
the back of the door
dib u cusbonaysii *(act)* regenerate

dib u dhig *(act)* delay
you have delayed
dib u dhigis *(nom)* procrastination
procrastination is not good

dib u dhisitaan *(adj)* pitch black
pitch black darkness
dib u kulan *(nom)* Reunion
go to Reunion
dib u soo nolee *(act)* revive
revive yourself
diba-qalooc *(nom)* scorpion
a black scorpion
dibada *(adv)* outside
stroll outside
dibada *(nom)* abroad
she goes abroad
dibi *(nom)* ox
I see an ox
dibi-dibaded *(nom)* buffalo
one buffalo
dibin *(nom)* lip
red lips
diciifsan *(adj)* weak
I am weak
digaagad *(nom)* chicken
hilib digaag *chicken meat*
digir *(nom)* bean
bariis iyo digir *rice and beans*
digniin *(nom)* warning
listen to the warning
digniin siin *(act)* warn
warn someone
digniin u diyaari *(act)* alert
alert them
digo *(nom)* dung
cow dung
digsi *(nom)* saucepan

cook in the saucepan
digtoon *(adj)* discreet

diid *(act)* reject
I will reject fear
diidmo ah *(adj)* negative
negative one
diig yar *(nom)* cockerel
a cockerel is crowing
diin/amuur *(nom)* tortoise
a tortoise walks slowly
diir *(act)* peel
to peel plantain
diirad saarid *(nom)* focus
my focus
diirka ka qaad *(act)* peel off
peel off the plaster
dil *(act)* kill
to kill a goat
dilaa *(nom)* murder
goessip and murder
**dile - qofka dila dadka dil
tooagsho lagu xukumo** *(nom)*
executioner
the king's executioner
dille *(nom)* killer

dimuqraadiyad *(nom)* democracy
peace and democracy
**Dinka - dadka ku nool Suu-
daan** *(nom)* Dinka
cmd(tu(act:write)) nom:Dinka

dirid *(act)* send
send me
dirindir *(nom)* caterpillar
a caterpillar becomes a butterfly
dirxi *(nom)* maggot
many maggots
dirxi *(nom)* worm
worm, where are you going?
dirxi lugo badan leh *(nom)*
centipede
look at the centipede
diyaar ah *(adv)* ready
I am ready
diyaarad *(nom)* aeroplane
laba diyaaradood two aeroplanes

diyaarad *(nom)* plane
board a plane
diyaarin *(nom)* preparation
make preparation
diyaarinta *(nom)* preparations
make preparations
dood *(nom)* argument
many arguments
dood *(nom)* debate
the debate is starting
doofaar yar *(nom)* piglet
piglets
doofaarka *(nom, c1)* pig
some pigs are pink
doofaarka *(nom)* pork
pork and beef
doolar *(nom)* dollar

ten dollars
doolshe *(nom)* pie
three pies
doon *(nom)* boat
  doon cas *red boat*
doon doonid *(act)* seek
to seek meaning
doonid *(nom)* aspiration
good aspirations
doorasho *(act)* select
to select a book
doorasho *(nom)* choice

doorasho *(nom)* option
five options
dooro *(act)* choose

dooxo/tog *(nom)* valley
hills and valleys
doqon *(nom)* rascal
she is a rascal
dub *(act)* bake
bake bread
dub *(act)* roast
roast a little corn
dubbe *(nom)* anvil
hammer and anvil
dube *(nom)* hammer
hammer and nail
dubniyam *(sci)* dubnium
dubnium (Db) has 105 protons
ducee *(act)* bless
bless me

dufan *(nom)* grease
grease in a pan
dugsi/iskul *(nom)* school
I learn to read at school
duhur *(nom)* noon
noon has arrived
duhur wanagsan *(exc)* good
afternoon
good afternoon Esi
dukaamaysi *(nom)* shopping
my shopping
dukaan *(nom)* shop

dukshi *(nom)* housefly
a housefly can carry disease
duleed *(nom)* outskirt
I live in the outskirts
dulmi *(act)* oppress
you are oppressing me
dulmi *(nom)* oppression
such oppression!
dulsaara *(pre)* on
sleep on the table
dunida *(nom)* world
children of the world
duq *(adj)* elder
my elder sibling
duqsiyo *(nom, c1)* beetle

durbaan *(nom)* drum
I hear the drums
durbaan tume *(nom)* drummer

she is a drummer

durbaanka la cadaadiyo *(nom)*
squeeze drum
play the squeeze drum

**Durbaano dhawaaqyo kala
duwan leh** *(nom)* talking drum
four talking drums

durdur *(nom)* stream
cross the stream

duri *(act)* inject
inject me

duris *(nom)* injection
an injection is painful

duufaan *(nom)* storm
storm with thunder

duul *(act)* fly
to fly into the sky

duulid *(nom)* fly
a fly flies

duur joog *(adj)* wild
wild animal

E

edbin *(act)* discipline
discipline your child

Eebbe *(nom)* god
dependable god

eed saar *(act)* blame

eedayn *(nom)* indictment
nine indictments

eedee *(act)* accuse
they accused him

eedo/habaryad *(nom)* aunt
Aunt Ama

eedo/habaryad *(nom)* auntie

eedo/habaryad *(nom)* aunty

eerbiyasm *(sci)* erbium
erbium (Er) has 68 protons

eex *(nom)* favor

eex *(nom)* favour
favour and kindness

eexasho *(nom)* bias

eexsasho *(nom)* favoritism

eexsasho *(nom)* favouritism
stop the favouritism

eey *(nom, c1)* dog
a dog barks

Ereteriya *(nom)* Eritrea
go to Eritrea

Ereteriyaan *(nom)* Eritrean
the Eritreans

erey *(nom)* word
I know 100 words

ereyga sirta ah *(nom)* password
change password

eri/ceyri *(act)* fire
fire him; sack him

eryasho *(act)* chase
 no one is chasing him
eryo *(act)* pursue
 pursue him

F

faa'iido *(nom)* advantage
 they have an advantage
faas *(nom)* axe
 four axes
faash *(nom)* billhook
 three billhooks
fadhi *(nom)* couch
 the red couch
fadhi *(nom)* sofa
 five sofas
fadhi-sare kac *(act)* squat
 hold your waist and squat
fadlan *(adv)* please
 to say 'please'
fahamsan *(act)* understand
 to understand something very well

fakhri ah *(adj)* poor
 a poor country
fakuu *(sci)* vacuum
 space is a vacuum
fal *(nom)* act
 Act 1 of the play
fal-kaabe *(nom)* adverb
 ten adverbs

falaar *(nom)* arrow
 bow and arrow
Falastiin *(nom)* Palestine
 go to Palestine
Falastiiniyaan *(nom)* Palestinean
 the Palestineans
falsafad *(nom)* philosophy
 I am learning philosophy
fanaadiyam *(sci)* vanadium
 vanadium (V) has 23 protons
faqiir *(nom)* indigent
 an indigent has nothing
far *(nom)* finger
 how do you me sr finger
farageeto *(nom)* fork
 farageeto iyo midi *fork and knife*
faragelin *(nom)* influence

faraha lugaha *(nom)* toe
 toe and heel
Faransiis *(nom)* French
 she speaks French
Faransiiska *(nom)* France
 go to France
faras *(nom)* horse
 faras cad *white horse*
farax *(act)* exult
 exult her
faraxsan *(adj)* happy
 today is a happy day
fargal *(nom)* ring
 put on the ring
fariin *(nom)* message

when the message arrived

farkaniyam *(sci)* francium
francium (Fr) has 87 protons

farmasiile *(nom)* pharmacist

faro badan *(adj)* plentiful
a plentiful harvest

faro xumeyn *(nom)* pedophile
he is a pedophile

farqi/dallool *(nom)* gap
she has a beautiful gap between her teeth

farsamo leh *(adj)* technical
technical work

farshaxan *(nom)* art
food and art

farxad *(nom)* joy

farxad *(nom)* happiness
happiness has arrived

farxad geli *(act)* rejoice
rejoice, I say, rejoice

farxad leh *(adj)* amusing

fasal *(nom)* class
he is in class 2

fasax *(nom)* holiday
today is a holiday

fasax *(nom)* vacation
a long vacation

fasir *(nom)* discord
lies and discord

fastaleeti *(nom)* handkerchief

do you have a handkerchief?

fayada *(nom)* ringworm
he has ringworm

faylasoof *(nom)* philosopher
she is a philosopher

feedh *(act)* comb
use a comb to comb your hair

feedh *(nom)* boxing
boxing is a sport

fees- weel ubaxa lagu rido
(nom) vase
clay vase

fekirid *(nom)* thinking

Fenesiweela *(nom)* Venezuela
go to Venezuela

Fenesiweeliyaan *(nom)* Venezuelan
the Venezuelans

ferminam *(sci)* fermium
fermium (Fm) has 100 protons

feyl *(nom)* file
computer file

fican *(adj)* nice
make it nice

fican *(adv)* well
do it well

ficil *(nom)* verb
nine verbs

fidid *(act)* spread
spread it

fiican *(adj)* fine
grind it finely

fiican *(adj)* well

fiican *(nom)* well
well water
fiid *(nom)* evening
evening meal; dinner
fiid wanagsan *(exc)* good evening
good evening Kofi
fiidmeer *(nom)* bat
three bats
fiirasho *(act)* see
to see ghosts
fiiri dhinac kale *(act)* look away
I look away
fiirin *(act)* look
look at the boy
fiisigis *(nom)* physics
we are learning physics
Fiitnaam *(nom)* Vietnam
go to Vietnam
Fiitnaamiis *(nom)* Vietnamese
the Vietnamese
fikir *(act)* think
I think that ...
fikrad *(nom)* idea
I have an idea
filaromiyam *(sci)* flerovium
flerovium (Fl) has 114 protons
Filibiinees *(nom)* Philippines
go to Philippines
Filibiino *(nom)* Filipino
the Filipinos
filim *(nom)* film

cast of a film
fin *(nom)* pimple
I have a pimple
firfircoon *(adj)* active
an active lifestyle
firfircoon *(adj)* energetic
an energetic dog
firimbi *(nom)* siren
loud siren
fodka- nooc alkoolada kamid ah *(nom)* vodka
rum or vodka?
foloriin *(sci)* fluorine
fluorine (F) has 9 protons
fooda madaxa *(nom)* forehead
look at her forehead
fool maroodi *(nom)* ivory
ivory necklace
fool xun *(adj)* ugly
it is ugly
foorjeyn *(act)* tease
tease him
foorno *(nom)* oven
the bread is in the oven
foosto *(nom)* barrel
fill up the barrel
fosfooras *(sci)* phosphorus
phosphorus (P) has 15 protons
fudud *(adj)* easy
the exam is easy
fudud *(adj)* lightweight
the book is lightweight
fudud *(adj)* simple

fur *(act)* open
  I open the door
furaash *(nom)* mattress
  a new mattress
fure *(nom)* key
  door and key
fursad kasta *(adv)* by any chance
  have you seen her by any chance?
fuud *(nom)* stew
  make stew
fuufuu - cunto laga isticmaalo galbeedka afrika *(nom)* fufu
  eat fufu
Fuutaan *(nom)* Bhutan
  go to Bhutan
Fuutaani *(nom)* Bhutann
  the Bhutanns

G

gaaban *(adj)* short
  short man
gaadh *(act)* achieve
  to achieve something
gaadh *(nom)* rearguard
  they are the rearguard
gaagaab *(act)* germinate
  the corn is germinating
gaajo *(nom)* hunger
  hunger and thirst
Gaambiya *(nom)* Gambia
  go to Gambia

Gaambiyaan *(nom)* Gambian
  the Gambians
Gaana *(nom)* Ghana
  people from Ghana are called Ghanaians
Gaaniyaan *(nom)* Ghanaian
  the Ghanaians
gaar ah *(adj)* specific
  show me the specific thing
gaar dhacdadii uu dambeysay *(act)* reach a final milestone
  if the time comes
gaari xamuul ah *(nom)* truck
  a red truck
gaas/hawo *(nom)* gas
  gas stove
gaaseysan *(adj)* gaseous
  gaseous water
gaasta la shito *(nom)* kerosene
  bottle of kerosene
gaasta rinjiga lagu daro *(nom)* turpentine
  turpentine and kerosene
gabadh *(nom)* woman
  gabadh qurux badan a pretty woman

gabadh *(nom)* daughter
  my daughter
gabadh *(nom)* lady
  Lady Danso
gabadh aan guursan *(nom)* damsel
  this damsel is pretty
gabadh weyn *(nom)* old lady

my old lady
gabadh weyn oo aan guursan *(nom)* maiden
beautiful maiden
gabadha gudmooyaha ah *(nom)* chairwoman

gabagabee *(act)* conclude

gabar *(nom)* girl
gabar dheer tall girl
gabar adoon ah *(nom)* slavegirl
six slavegirls
gabi ahaanba *(adv)* utterly
utterly finished
gabigaba *(adv)* totally
it is totally burnt
Gaboon *(nom)* Gabon
go to Gabon
Gabooniis *(nom)* Gabonese
the Gabonese
gacaliso *(nom)* sweetheart
he is my sweetheart
gacaliye/gacaliso *(nom)* dear
don't worry dear
gacan *(nom)* hand
lift up your hand
gacan haadin *(nom)* wave
the waves are breaking
gacankudhiigle *(nom)* murderer
he is a murderer

gadaal *(act)* rear
rear animals
gadaal *(nom)* rear
Gadagme - luqad lagaga hadlo meelo kamida Afrika *(nom)*
GaDangme
I speak GaDangme
gadh *(nom)* beard
long beard
gado *(act)* purchase
purchase a few things
gadoloniyam *(sci)* gadolinium
gadolinium (Gd) has 64 protons
gajoonaya *(adj)* hungry

gal *(act)* enter
enter into the room
galab *(nom)* afternoon
I will come in the afternoon
galab *(nom)* nightfall
daybreak and nightfall
galadiyam *(sci)* gallium
gallium (Ga) has 31 protons
galayr *(nom)* falcon

Galbeed *(nom)* west
go west
Galbeedka Saxaaraha *(nom)*
Western Sahara
go to Western Sahara
gallaan *(nom)* gallon
a gallon of water

gallayda *(nom)* maize, maize
corn and groundnuts
galley *(nom)* maize, maize
corn and groundnuts
ganacsade *(nom)* trader
I am a trader
ganacsanaya *(nom)* trading
trading profit
ganacsasho *(act)* trade
to trade quickly
ganacsi *(nom)* business
business and politics
ganacsi *(nom)* commerce

ganacsi *(nom)* trade
a good trade
gar *(nom)* chin
hold your chin
garaac *(act)* beat
beat someone
garaam *(nom)* gram

garaam *(nom)* gramme
ten grammes
garab *(nom)* shoulder
stand on my shoulders
garan *(nom)* t-shirt
white t-shirt
garanka dumarka *(nom)* camisol
garfeedh *(nom)* comb
use a comb to comb your hair
gargaaar *(nom)* assistance

gargaar *(nom)* aid

gargaarid *(nom)* consolation
love and consolation
**gari - cunto laga cuno meelo
kamida Galbeedka Afrika** *(nom)*
gari
beans and gari
gariirid *(act)* tremble
his lips are trembling
gariirid *(act)* vibrate
the tree is vibrating
gariirid *(nom)* trembling
fear and trembling
garo *(act)* guess

garoon *(nom)* playing field
they are on the field
garoon diyaradeed *(nom)* airport
I'm going to the airport
garsoore *(nom)* judge
seven judges
gebi ahaanba *(adj)* entire
the entire house
geed *(nom)* tree
beer geed *plant a tree*
geed shukulaato ah *(nom)* cocoa
cocoa tree
geed suuf xariir ah *(nom)* silk
cotton tree

cut the silk cotton tree

geedo la karkariyay *(nom)* boiled herbs

drink the boiled herbs

geel *(nom)* camel

six camels

geerash *(nom)* garage

car garage

geesi *(adj)* bold

a bold man

geesi *(adj)* brave

brave man

geesi *(nom)* hero

she is a hero

geesi *(nom)* horn

horn music

geesi ah *(adj)* valiant

valiant woman

gelitaan *(nom)* entry

a new entry in the book

geri *(nom)* giraffe

gerigu waa xayawaan *a giraffe is an animal*

gidaar *(nom)* wall

sit on the wall

giiji *(act)* fasten

giitaar yar *(nom)* ukelele

play the ukelele

Gikuuyu - luqad lagaga hadlo Kiiniya *(nom)* Gikuyu

I can read Gikuyu

gilgil *(act)* sway

the tree is swaying

Gini *(nom)* Guinea

go to Guinea

Gini-Bisow *(nom)* Guinea-Bissau

go to Guinea-Bissau

Giniyaan *(nom)* Guinean

the Guineans

Ginseen - geed ka baxa Aasiya *(nom)* ginseng

ginseng is a plant

girgire *(nom)* hearth

there is fire in the hearth

go'aan *(nom)* decision

a good decision

go'aansasho *(nom)* determination

we will do it with determination

gobol *(nom)* region

three regions

gobol *(nom)* state

look at our pitiful state

god *(nom)* hole

small hole

gogoldhig *(nom)* preface

book preface

goo *(act)* carve

carve the wood

goob *(nom)* location

from here to a new location

goobo *(nom)* circle

three circles

gool *(nom)* goal

score a goal

goon-goon - waa wax biyaha ku jira oo ay caabudaan Jeyni- isku *(nom)* gong gong
play the gong gong

goor danbe ah *(adv)* late
to come late

goorma *(cjn)* when
he came when you went

goortii *(cjn)* while
he danced while the old man was singing

gorgor *(nom)* eagle
two eagles

gorgor *(nom)* vulture
a vulture is a bird

gorgortan *(act)* bargain
bargain over price

goroyo *(nom)* ostrich
an ostrich is a bird

gub *(act)* burn
burn papers

gudaha *(adv)* inside
go inside

gudoomiye *(nom)* chairman

guga *(nom)* spring
I spend Spring in England

guji *(act)* click
click here

guji *(act)* poke
poke me on Facebook

gujis *(nom)* submarine
a new submarine

gumaar *(nom)* groin
groin of a man

gunti *(nom)* knot
tie the knot

gurguuro *(act)* crawl
the child is crawling

guri *(nom, c2)* house
guriga *the house*

guri danbays *(nom)* lastborn
your lastborn

guri quraanjo *(nom)* anthill
a tall anthill

guriga *(nom)* home
your home

gus *(nom)* dick

gus *(nom)* penis
you don't say 'penis' in public

guul *(nom)* achievement
your achievement is appreciated

guul *(nom)* milestone
an important milestone

guul *(nom)* success
success and happiness

guulaysasho *(act)* triumph
you triumphed

guuleyso *(act)* win
to win a competition

guuleyste *(nom)* conqueror
she is a conqueror

guuleyste *(nom)* victory
victory and defeat

guuleyste *(nom)* winner, victor

guumeys *(nom)* owl
guumeystu waa shimbir an owl is
a bird
guur *(act)* move

guur *(nom)* marriage
good marriage
guursasho *(act)* wed
I will wed you
guurso *(act)* marry
marry me
guuxid *(act)* sigh
he sighed

H

haa *(pro)* ye
me and ye
haadka-gini *(nom)* guinea-fowl
three guinea-fowls
haaf - dharka hablaha *(nom)*
skirt
short skirt
haafniyam *(sci)* hafnium
hafnium (Hf) has 72 protons
haajire *(nom)* immigrant
we are immigrants
haashtaag *(nom)* hashtag
Twitter hashtag
hab sii *(act)* embrace
embrace me

hab wax u dhacaan *(nom)* manner
his manner is amusing
habaar *(nom)* curse
a prayer and a curse
habee *(act)* arrange
arrange the chairs
habee/dalbo *(act)* order
to order food
habeen madoobaad *(nom)* night
8 o'clock in the night
hadal *(act)* speak
to speak the truth
hadal *(act)* talk
to talk too much
hadda *(adv)* now
go now
haddi aanay/aanuu *(cjn)* unless
she will come unless it rains
haddi ay dhacdo taasi *(adv)*
in that case
in that case come
haddii *(cjn)* whether

haddii *(cjn)* if
if someone loves you
haddii... ka dibna *(cjn)* if ...
then
if A then B
hadh *(nom)* shade
I am sitting under the shade
hadhow *(adv)* later

they will eat later

hadiyada *(nom)* present
　hadiyad wanaagsan a good gift

hag *(act)* guide
　to guide people

hagaaji *(act)* adjust
　to adjust the door

hagaajiye *(nom)* fixer
　she is a fixer

hagid *(nom)* guide
　she is our guide

hakad *(nom)* comma
　comma and fullstop

hal *(adj)* one
　hal dhalo There is one bottle standing on top of the house

hal *(pro)* one
　one does not believe fables

hal abuurnimo leh *(adj)* creative
　a creative person

hal qof *(nom)* one person
　one person is coming

hal qof *(nom)* singleton
　combine the singletons

hal xiraale *(nom)* riddle
　puzzles and riddles

halbeeg - lacageed oo laga isticmaalo Gaana *(nom)* cedi
　hundred pesewas make one cedi

halbeeg lacageed oo laga isticmaalo Gaana *(nom)* pesewa
　one cedi makes a hundred pesewas

halbeega dhererka *(nom)* meter
　ten meters

halbeega dhererka *(nom)* metre
　ten metres

halbowle dhiig *(nom)* artery
　a large artery

halkaas *(nom)* there
　here and there

halkan *(adv)* here
　click here

halkee *(adv)* where
　where do you live?

halleluuya - erey ay idhaahdaan kiristanku *(exc)* hallelujah
　sing hallelujah

hamaansasho *(act)* yawn
　stop yawning

hammi *(nom)* ambition

hanaanka gelinta hawo ama dareere malawadka *(nom)* enema
　I need an enema

hanaqaad *(nom)* adult
　he is an adult

hanjabaad *(nom)* threat
　stop the threats

hanti *(nom)* asset
　a good asset

51

hanti *(nom)* property
my property
hanti *(nom)* wealth
we have great wealth
haraad *(nom)* thirst
I feel thirst (I am thirsty)
haraga lo'da *(nom)* cowhide
waache and cowhide
haramcad *(nom)* cheetah
a cheetah is an animal
haramcad *(nom)* leopard
a leopard has a tail
harame *(act)* weed
wed grass
hareerayay *(act)* surround
to surround the house
haro *(nom)* lake
the lake has overflowed
haro bada *(nom)* lagoon
Elmina lagoon
hasa yeeshee *(cjn)* however

hasiyam *(sci)* hassium
hassium (Hs) has 108 protons
Hausa - luqad *(nom)* Hausa
Hausa language
hawada sare *(sci)* space
space is a vacuum
hawlgal *(nom)* mission

hawo *(nom)* air
the air is blowing
hay *(act)* keep

keep the change
haydarojiin *(nom)* hydrogen
hydrogen car
haydorojiin *(sci)* hydrogen
hydrogen (H) has 1 proton
haye *(exc)* yes
I say yes
haye *(exc)* okay
okay let's go
heeniyam *(sci)* rhenium
rhenium (Re) has 75 protons
heer sare *(adj)* advance
give me an advance warning
hees *(nom)* music
play music
hees *(nom, c1)* song
play a song
hees jama *(act)* sing jama
let us sing jama
heesid *(act)* sing
to sing a sweet song
heesid *(nom)* singing
I like her singing
heh *(exc)* heh
sorry, heh
hel *(act)* gain
if I have life, I have gained every-thing
hel *(act)* get
get the book
helay *(act)* found
let us found a group
helay *(ydy(i(act)* gotten

52

helikobtar *(nom)* helicopter
two helicopters
heysasho *(act)* take hold of
take hold of me
heyso *(act)* have
she has money
heystaa *(tdy(i(act)* has

hilaac *(nom)* lightning
lightning and thunder
hilaac *(nom)* thunderbolt
a loud thunderbolt
hilib *(nom)* meat
hilibka riyaha *goat meat*
hilib *(nom)* flesh
flesh and blood
hilib qale *(nom)* butcher
she is a butcher
hilyam *(sci)* helium
helium (He) has 2 protons
hinaas *(act)* be jealous
be jealous over her husband
hinaase *(nom)* jealousy

hindhisid *(act)* sneeze
to sneeze loudly
Hindi *(nom)* Indian
the Indians
hindise *(nom)* proposal
a good proposal
Hindiya *(nom)* India
go to India

hingo *(nom)* hiccups
he has got the hiccups
hogaami *(act)* lead
lead us
hogaamiye *(nom)* chief
she is a chief
hogaamiye *(nom)* leader
this is our leader
holmiyam *(sci)* holmium
holmium (Ho) has 67 protons
hoobiye *(nom)* mortar
pestle and mortar
hoodiyam *(sci)* rhodium
rhodium (Rh) has 45 protons
hoonka ka digista dagaal *(nom)*
warhorn
blow the warhorn
hoos *(adv)* down
go down
hoos u dhac *(act)* fall down
the egg has fallen down
hooseysiin *(nom)* humility
you show humility
hooyo *(nom, c1)* mother
my mother's child is my sibling
hooyo *(nom)* mom

hore *(adj)* early
early morning
hore *(adv)* early
come early
hore u wad *(act)* proceed
he proceeded to see

horteeda *(pre)* in front
go in front
horumar *(nom)* development
good development
horumar *(nom)* progress, improvement

horyaal *(adj)* ideal
an ideal woman
horyaal *(nom)* pioneer
they are pioneers
hub *(nom)* weapon
we sell weapons
hubi *(nom)* check

hubin *(nom)* cheque
write a cheque
hudheel la seexdo *(nom)* hotel
she sleeps at a hotel
hunguri *(nom)* covetuousness
covetuousness is not good
hunqaacid *(nom)* vomit
dog's vomit
hurdo *(nom)* sleepiness
food causes sleepiness
hurdo heyso *(nom)* drowsiness

hurid *(nom)* sacrifice
offer a sacrifice
huudhi *(nom)* canoe
canoe and paddle

I

idingu *(pos)* your
your house
idinka *(pro)* you
you eat
iftiimin *(act)* shine
sun is shining
iftiin *(nom)* light
light of the sky
iga rali ahaw *(exc)* excuse me
Sorry. Excuse me.
Igo - luqad *(nom)* Igbo
Igbo language
iibin *(act)* sell
to sell houses
iibiye *(nom)* seller
buyers and sellers
iibsade *(nom)* buyer
buyers and sellers
iibso *(act)* buy
to buy something
iidheh *(nom)* advertisement

iimaan *(nom)* faith
faith and peace
iimayl *(nom)* email
print the email
iinseetiniyam *(sci)* einsteinium
einsteinium (Es) has 99 protons
il *(nom)* eye
il iyo sunayaal eye and eyebrow
il biriqsi *(nom)* second
ten seconds

il jabi *(act)* grind
 to grind corn
ilaa *(pre)* till

ilaa iyo *(pre)* until
 until we meet again
ilaali *(act)* guard
 guard the house
ilaali *(act)* protect
 protect us
ilaalin *(nom)* preservation
 the preservation of food
ilaalin *(nom)* protection
 give me protection
ilaalinta *(nom)* preservative
 it has no preservatives in it
ilbaxay *(adj)* civilized
 a civilized world
ilig *(nom)* tooth
 white tooth
ilko xanuun *(nom)* toothache
 I have toothache
ilmo *(nom)* baby
 waxaan leeyahay ilmo *I have a baby*

ilmo *(nom)* child
 my mother's child is my sibling
ilmo galeen *(nom)* womb
 female's womb
ilmo iska so ridid *(nom)* abortion
 the doctor performs abortion
ilmo uu/ay dhalay/dhashay

sayigu/xaasku *(nom)* step-child
 my step-child
ilow *(act)* forget
 I have forgotten
ilowshiiyo *(nom)* forgetfulness
 her forgetfulness
imanaya *(nom)* coming
 the second coming
immika *(adj)* just
 it is just folly
immika *(cjn)* now
 so what now?
immisa *(adj)* how much
 how much is it?
imtixaan *(nom)* exam
 the exam is easy
in ka badan *(pre)* more than
 she eats more than me
in kastoo *(cjn)* though
 I see though it is dark
in la dareemo eed *(act)* be guilty of
 we are guilty
in la dhameeyo *(act)* be finished
 the oil is finished
in la jabiyo *(act)* be defeated
 you were defeated
in la kariyo *(act)* be cooked
 food is cooked
in la sakhraamo *(act)* be high
 you are big and you are high
In la wanaagsanaado *(act)* be

good
prayer is good
ina keen *(exc)* let's go

inakeen *(exc)* let's go
let's go home
inanta aad abti/adeer u tahay
(nom) niece
my nieces
inbadan *(nom)* lot
a lot of hard work
indheyn *(nom)* scout

indhiyam *(sci)* indium
indium (In) has 49 protons
indhoolnimo *(nom)* blindness
blindness is a disease
Indooniisiya *(nom)* Indonesia
go to Indonesia
Indooniisiyaan *(nom)* Indonesian
the Indonesians
Ingiriis *(nom)* English
I speak English
Ingiriisi *(nom)* Inglish
I can read Inglish
Ingiriiska *(nom)* England
I spend spring in England
iniin *(nom)* saw
three orange saws
injiil *(nom)* goespel
the goespel of Jesus
injiin *(nom)* engine

a new engine
injineer *(nom)* engineer
an engineer makes tools
injir *(nom)* louse
chicken lice
inkaar *(act)* curse
do not curse me
inkastoo *(pro)* thou

insaan *(nom, c1)* human
we are humans
insi *(nom)* humankind
we are humankind
inta badan *(adv)* often
she often comes here
inta u dhaxeysa laba wakhti
(nom) lapse
too many lapses
inta ugu badan *(adj)* maximum
maximum amount
inta ugu yar *(adj)* minimum
minimum quantity
interneet *(nom)* internet
internet link
inuu haboonaado *(act)* be fitting
it is fitting that
inyar inyar *(adv)* little by little
*little by little a chicken drinks wa-
ter*
Iqwaatooriyaal Gini *(nom)* Equa-

torial Guinea
go to Equatorial Guinea
Iraan *(nom)* Iran
go to Iran
Iraani *(nom)* Iranian
the Iranians
irbad *(nom)* needle
string and needle
iridhiyam *(sci)* iridium
iridium (Ir) has 77 protons
is cadee *(act)* bleach
some women bleach their skins to become fairer
is dabci *(act)* loosen
to loosen the belt
is daji *(act)* calm
calm your anger
is diiwaangeli *(act)* book
book a ticket
is goys *(nom)* junction, intersection

is mudhxin *(act)* strip off
strip off your shoes
isaga *(pro)* him
show him
isagoo haysta *(pro)* having
tea with sugar (literally, tea having sugar)
Isbaanish *(nom)* Spanish
I speak Spanish
isbahaysi *(nom)* union
African Union

Isbayn *(nom)* Spain
we will go to Spain
isbiinaaj *(nom)* spinach
spinach stew
isbuunyo *(nom)* sponge
my sponge
isfuris (laba isqaba) *(nom)* divorce
marriage and divorce
isjeclaansho laba qof *(nom)* courtship
courtship and marriage
iska dhig *(act)* pretend
you are pretending
iska hadal - maalaayacni *(nom)* balderdash

iska tuur *(act)* throw away
throw away the water
iskaandiyam *(sci)* scandium
scandium (Sc) has 21 protons
iskibriya/cawaandi *(adj)* arrogant
arrogant man
Iskootlaan *(nom)* Scotland
visit Scotland
isku dar *(act)* combine

isku dar *(act)* integrate
to integrate a new person into the family
isku dar *(act)* mix
to mix tomatoes and pepper

isku dhufasho *(nom)* multiplication

2 x 1 = 2; this is multiplication

isku gayn *(nom)* addition

1 + 1 = 2; this is addition

isku mid ah *(adj)* same

we are the same

isku simid *(act)* smoothen

to smoothen the plank

isku xayeysii *(nom)* sponsor

many sponsors

iskufil *(nom)* peer

your peers

isla markiiba *(adv)* immediately

cut off immediately

Islaam *(nom)* Islam

Christianity and Islam

Islaami ah *(adj)* Islamic

Islamic holiday

Isniin *(nom)* Monday

Monday children

Israa'iili *(nom)* Israel

go to Israel

istaagid *(act)* stand

to stand slowly

istaroontiyam *(sci)* strontium

strontium (Sr) has 38 protons

isticmaal *(act)* use

you will use it like that

isticmaal hub/qalab *(act)* wield

she is wielding the pan

isticmaale *(nom)* user

how many users?

isticmalid *(nom)* surf

look at the surf

isu ekaan *(nom)* likeness

Iswaasi *(nom)* Swazi

the Swazis

Iswaasilaan *(nom)* Swaziland

go to Swaziland

Iswaati *(nom)* Swati

Swati language

isxoqid *(nom)* friction

friction came between us

Itaaliiya *(nom)* Italy

to visit Italy

Itoobiya *(nom)* Ethiopia

go to Ethiopia

Itoobiyaan *(nom)* Ethiopian

the Ethiopians

ixtiram *(nom)* respect

show respect

iyada *(pro)* it

it falls

iyada *(pro)* she

she eats

iyada *(pos)* its

its house

iyaga *(pro)* them

show them

iyaga *(pro)* they

they eat

iyo *(cjn)* and

Kofi iyo Ama Kofi and Ama

J

Jaadiyaan *(nom)* Chadian
the Chadians

jaajuusid *(act)* spy
to spy on a country

jaalle/huruud *(adj)* yellow
yellow flag

jaamacad *(nom)* university
Legon University

jaamomayl - geed yuribiyaan
ah oo ubax soo saara *(nom)*
chamomile
chamomile tea

jaariyot *(nom)* chariot
chariot of iron

jaas *(act)* dance
to dance with joy

jaas *(nom)* dancing
singing and dancing

jaas - laga ciyaaro Gaana *(nom)*
azonto
I know how to dance azonto

Jabaan *(nom)* Japan
go to Japan

Jabaaniis *(nom)* Japanese
the Japanese

jabad *(nom)* twig
how many twigs?

jaban *(adj)* cheap
be cheap

jabi *(act)* break
break the stick

jabin *(nom)* defeat
victory and defeat

jabsi *(nom)* burglary
burglary is increasing

jabso *(act)* burgle
they burgled me

Jabuuti *(nom)* Djibouti
go to Djibouti

Jabuutiyaan *(nom)* Djiboutian
the Djiboutians

jadeeco *(nom)* measles
measles is a disease

Jadwal taariikheed/kaalandar
(nom) calendar
a new calendar

jajab *(nom)* fraction
three fractions

jalas/ dawan *(nom)* bell
school bell

jaldi *(nom)* cover

jalxad *(nom)* earthenware

jama *(nom)* jama
sing jama

James - magac *(nom)* James
my name is James

Jamhuuriyada Afrikada Dhexe
(nom) Central African Republic
go to Central African Republic

jaqaf *(nom)* dustpan
broom and dustpan

jar *(act)* cut

to cut the cake in two
jar jarid *(act)* slice
slice the bread up
jaranjaro *(nom)* stair
climb the stairs
Jarmalka *(nom)* Germany
I spend the winter in Germany
jasiirad *(nom)* island
Seychelles island
jawaab *(nom)* answer
give me an answer
jawaab *(nom)* response
song's response (i.e. chorus)
jawaab celin *(act)* reply

**jayfis - geed yar oo ka baxa
  Yuuroraashiya** *(nom)* chives
chives and onions
Jayna *(nom)* China
go to China
jeclah *(act)* love
I love you
jecle *(nom)* lover
my lover has tricked me
jeeb *(nom)* pocket
nothing inside my pocket
jeedalayn *(nom)* whip
horse whip
jeel *(nom)* jail
go to jail
jeer *(nom)* hippopotamus
jeertu waxay leeday calool weyn
a hippopotamus has a big stomach

jeer *(nom)* hippo

jeermaniyam *(sci)* germanium
germanium (Ge) has 32 protons
jees *(nom)* oware
can you play oware?
**Jeewa - luqad lagaga hadlo
  wadano badna oo Afrikaan
  ah** *(nom)* Chewa
Chewa language
jeexid *(act)* tear
tear some of the paper
jeexid *(nom)* tear
my eyes filled with tears
jellaato *(nom)* ice-cream
One evening, he told them a story
jidh *(nom)* body
a person is body, soul and spirit
jiil *(nom)* generation
five generations
jiilaal *(nom)* winter
I spend winter in Germany
jiir *(nom)* mouse
jiir weyn a big mouse
jiir *(nom)* rat
a big rat
jiir *(sci)* mouse
computer mouse
jilcin *(act)* soften
soften your voice
jilib *(nom)* knee
my knees

jilicsan *(adj)* gentle
a gentle tongue
jilicsan *(adj)* soft
soft bread
jillaab kalluun *(nom)* fish-hook
two fish-hooks
Jimca *(nom)* Friday
Friday children
jinis *(nom)* jeans
blue jeans
jinsi *(nom)* sex
what is sex?
jinsi ahaan soo jiidasho leh
(adj) sexy
a sexy man
jiraya/waaraya *(adj)* everlasting

jirdil *(nom)* torture
torture is evil
jiriirico *(nom)* goosebumps
I have got goosebumps
jiriqaa *(nom)* grasshopper
ant and grasshopper
jirro *(nom)* sickness
what sickness have you?
jismiga hadalka *(nom)* figure
of speech
every language has figures of speech

John - magac *(nom)* John
to baptise John
Jokolaynt *(nom)* chocolate

the chocolate has become cheap
joogid *(act)* remain

joogsi *(nom)* full stop
add a full stop after the word
joogto ah *(adj)* permanent
a permanent job
jooji *(act)* block
to block the way
jooji *(act)* brake
the driver has braked
jooji *(act)* cancel
cancel the meeting
joojin *(act)* stop
stop making noise
joojin *(nom)* brake
brake of a car
joojin *(nom)* stop
bus stop
Joorjiya *(nom)* Georgia
go to Georgia
Joorjiyaan *(nom)* Georgian
the Georgians

K

ka badan *(cjn)* than
he is taller than me
ka bax *(act)* exit
pass here to exit
ka baxsan *(nom)* outside
go outside

ka cabasho *(nom)* suffering
fear with suffering
ka danbeeya *(pre)* behind
go behind
ka degid *(act)* touch down

ka dhaafid *(act)* weave
weave a basket
ka dhalin/keenid *(nom)* delivery
the delivery has arrived
ka dhex gal *(act)* interrupt
interrupt him
ka dhiman/hadhaa *(nom)* remainder
the remainder of the food
ka dhufasho *(act)* snatch
snatched the phone
ka dib *(cjn)* then

ka dibna *(adv)* then
then he slept
ka duwan *(adj)* different
different things
ka fiijin *(act)* startle
I was startled
ka gudbid *(act)* pass by

ka gudbid *(nom)* cross
the cross of Christ
ka gudub *(act)* cross
cross the stream
ka hadh *(act)* cut ties

he and I have cut ties
ka hel *(act)* like
a frog likes water
ka helid *(adv)* like
it feels like fufu
ka hor *(adv)* in advance
eat in advance
ka hor *(pre)* before
eat before (you) sleep
ka hor *(pre)* by
written by a teacher
ka hor imaansho *(act)* bump
into
the car has bumped into something

ka jar *(act)* deduct
deduct one from two
ka jawaabid *(act)* answer
answer me
ka jawaabid *(act)* respond
he responded
ka koobnaw *(act)* consist
*water consists of hydrogen and oxy-
gen*
ka mid ah *(pre)* among
among people
ka nixitaan *(adj)* pitiable
pitiable child
ka rali ka noqo luqadayda
(cjn) excuse my language
*excuse my language, shit smells but
someone collects it*
ka reebid *(act)* discard

discard the ball
ka saarid *(act)* remove
to remove the shoes from here
ka sameysan *(act)* made up

ka sare marid *(act)* surpass
God surpasses man
ka sareeya *(pre)* above
above the house
ka shaki *(act)* doubt

ka tag *(dtv)* depart
depart from here
ka wanaagsan *(adj)* better

ka xanaaji *(act)* annoy
you are annoying me
ka yar *(adj)* smaller
smaller house
kaa *(pro)* that
that bird
kaabash *(nom)* cabbage
cabbage stew
kaabsid - galka booratiinka ee fayraska *(nom)* capsid
capsids eat cocoa trees
kaadh *(nom)* card
a white card
kaadi *(nom)* urine
the urine smells
kaadin *(act)* urinate
to urinate there
kaaki *(nom)* khakhi

khakhi shorts
kaalay *(act)* come
to come here
kaalay *(cmd(tu(act)* come

kaalay/imaw *(act)* arrive
when you arrive, call me
Kaalifoorniya *(nom)* California

Kaamboodhiya *(nom)* Cambodia
go to Cambodia
Kaamboodhiyaan *(nom)* Cambodian
the Cambodians
kaamil ah *(adj)* perfect
a perfect ending
kaarbon *(sci)* carbon
carbon (C) has 6 protons
Kaaribiyaan *(nom)* Caribbean
go to the Caribbean
kaarood *(nom)* carrot
four carrots
kabaab *(nom)* khebab
khebabs and beer
kabo *(nom)* shoe
xidho kabohaaga *wear your shoes*

kabtan *(nom)* captain
she is a captain
kacsan *(nom)* tense
past tense

kaftan *(nom)* joke
tell me a joke
kaftan hadal *(act)* jest
who is the one jesting?
kala badal *(act)* exchange

kala bixid *(act)* withdraw
she will withdraw money
kala duduwan *(adj)* diverse
a diverse group
kala duwan *(adj)* various

kala duwanaan *(nom)* diversity
diversity gives a group strength
kala fidid *(act)* spread out
spread out a mat
kala firdhid *(act)* scatter
to scatter everywhere
kala garasho *(adj)* distinguished
a distinguished frog
kala goyn *(nom)* subtraction
2-1 = 1; this is subtraction
kala goys *(nom)* joint
stretch your joints
kala jabin *(act)* split
split in two
kala jarid *(act)* subtract
subtract one from two
kala jeedsasho diyaaradeed
(nom) Yaw
Yaw is my son
kala saaray *(nom)* distinguished

a distinguished frog
kala wareeg *(act)* overturn
the pan has overturned
kalabaash - geed ka baxa maraykanka
(nom) calabash
drink from the calabash
kalgacayl *(nom)* benevolence

kali ah *(adv)* alone
he will go alone
kalida *(nom)* kidney
a cat has a kidney
kaliforniyam *(sci)* californium
californium (Cf) has 98 protons
kaligiis nocaas ah *(adj)* unique
an unique thing
kaliya *(adj)* only
only you
kaliya *(adj)* sole
my sole child
kaliya *(adv)* just
just see!
kaliya *(nom)* sole
how do you me sr soles
kaliya *(pre)* just
just as he got there
kalkaaliso *(nom)* nurse
she is a nurse
kalkulas *(nom)* calculus
I am learning calculus
kalluumayso *(act)* fish
let's go and fish
kalluumeyste *(nom)* fisherman

he is a fisherman
kalluun *(nom)* fish
  kalluun la shiilay *fried fish*
kalluun *(nom)* eel
  seven eels
kalluun la shiilay *(nom)* fried-
fish
  I am eating fried-fish
kalluun milix leh *(nom)* salted
fish
  salted fish makes food tasty
**kalluunka - sanduuqa biyaha
  lagu rido** *(act)* barb
  barb hair; cut hair
kalluunka dhoobada hoos gala
(nom) mudfish
  catch the mudfish
kalluunka la cuno *(nom)* herring
  a herring is a fish
kalshiyam *(sci)* calcium
  calcium (Ca) has 20 protons
kalsooni *(nom)* confidence
  I have confidence
kamarad *(nom)* camera
  lens of a camera
Kamaruun *(nom)* Cameroon
  go to Cameroon
kamuun *(nom)* cumin
  cumin grows in Asia
kan *(pro)* this
  is this your book?
kan *(det)* this

lend me this book
Kanada *(nom)* Canada
  I spend the summer in Canada
kandhiyam *(sci)* cadmium
  cadmium (Cd) has 48 protons
kaneeco *(nom)* mosquito
  a mosquito has bitten me
kansar *(nom)* cancer
  the cancer has disappeared
karaahiyo *(nom)* abomination
  it is an abomination
karaahiyo ah *(adj)* disgusting
  the place is disgusting
karaybton *(sci)* krypton
  krypton (Kr) has 36 protons
karbaash *(nom)* stripe
  many strips
kari *(act)* boil
  the soup is boiling
kari *(act)* cook
  cook a little rice
kariyaha *(nom)* stove
  gas stove
karkarin *(nom)* boil
  a boil is painful
kartoon *(nom)* cartoon
  new cartoons
kasaafada *(nom)* yuca
  plantain and yuca
Kasakhasitan *(nom)* Kazakhstan
  go to Kazakhstan
Kasakhasitani *(nom)* Kazakhstani
  the Kazakhstanis

kashifaad *(nom)* revelation
 he had a revelation
kasiyam *(sci)* caesium
 caesium (Cs) has 55 protons
kasta *(adj)* every

kaxee *(act)* drive
 drive a car
kayd *(nom)* bench
 to sit on the bench
kayga *(pos, c2)* my
 gurigayga *my house*
kayn *(nom)* forest
 animals in the forest
kee *(det)* which
 which child?
kee/ayo/tee *(pro)* who
 who is he?
keeg *(nom)* cake
 we will eat the cake
keen *(act)* bring
 wuu buug keeni doonaa *he will bring*
 a book
keen *(act)* deliver
 deliver money to me
keyd/bakhaar *(nom)* store
 I will buy food from the store
khaa'in *(act)* replace
 replace me
khaa'in *(nom)* traitor
 two traitors
khaa'in wadan *(nom)* treason
 treason is evil

khaanado *(nom)* drawers
 are you wearing drawers?
khaas ah *(adj)* special
 special day
khad *(nom)* ink
 ink in a pen
khalad *(nom)* mistake
 everyone makes mistakes
khaldanaw *(act)* be wrong
 am I wrong?
Khamiis *(nom)* Thursday
 Thursday children
khamri *(nom)* beer
 we are drinking beer
kharibid *(act)* spoil

khariirad *(nom)* map
 read the map
khasaar *(act)* lose
 He lost his way home
khasaariyay *(adj)* wasted
 wasted food
khasnad maaliyadeed *(nom)*
 treasure
 great treasure
khatar *(nom)* danger
 I see danger
khatar ah *(adj)* dangerous
 a dangerous game
khayraad *(nom)* resource
 a good resource
khibrad *(nom)* experience
 she has experience

khilaaf *(act)* oppose
 we will oppose evil
khilaaf *(act)* dispute
 dispute him
khilaaf *(nom)* controversy

khiyaame *(nom)* cheater
 they are cheaters
khiyaamee *(act)* betray
 do not betray me
khiyaamee *(act)* cheat
 don't cheat me
khiyaameyn *(act)* deceive

khiyaamid *(nom)* deception
 deception and discord
khiyaamo *(nom)* trick
 stop the tricks
khudaar *(nom)* apricot
 two apricots
khudaar laamo leh *(nom)* celery
 eat the celery
khusee *(act)* be relevant to
 it is not about me
khuurin *(act)* snore
 I snore
khuurin *(nom)* snoring
 loud snoring
kibir *(nom)* pride
 his pride
kicin *(act)* stimulate
 to stimulate the wind

kiiloogaraam *(nom)* kilogram
 ten kilograms
kiiloogaraam *(nom)* kilogramme
 ten kilogrammes
kiiloomitir *(nom)* kilometer
 ten kilometers
kiiloomitir *(nom)* kilometre
 ten kilometres
Kiiniya *(nom)* Kenya
 go to Kenya
kiisa *(pos)* his
 his house
kiish *(nom)* sack
 sack of charcoal
kijin/madbakh *(nom)* kitchen
 I am in the kitchen
kilkilo *(nom)* armpit
 smelly armpit
kimsir *(nom)* parsley
 parsley is a plant
kiniisad *(nom)* church
 go to church
kinkee - cunto cajiin ah oo lagu cuno Waqooyiga Africa *(nom)* kenkey
 kenkey and stew
kinte - walxdo midabo leh oo lagu sameeyo Gaana *(nom)* kente
 kente cloth
Kirigistaan *(nom)* Kyrgyzstan
 go to Kyrgyzstan
Kirigistaani *(nom)* Kyrgyzstani

the Kyrgyzstanis
kirishboy *(nom)* steward
a good steward
kirishboyga baska *(nom)* bus
conductor
he's a bus conductor
kitaab *(nom)* scripture
to read the scriptures
Kiwame - magac *(nom)* Kwame
Kwame is my son
Kiweku - magac *(nom)* Kweku
My son is Kweku
Kiwesi - magac *(nom)* Kwesi
my son is called Kwesi
kiyaawo *(nom)* wrench

kobalt *(sci)* cobalt
cobalt (Co) has 27 protons
kobarnishiyam *(sci)* copernicium
copernicium (Cn) has 112 protons
kobcid *(act)* thrive
the ants are thriving
Kobiina - magac *(nom)* Kobina
Kobina is my son
koboca *(nom)* vitality
water gives vitality
koloraydh *(sci)* chloride
sodium chloride
koloriin *(sci)* chlorine
chlorine (Cl) has 17 protons
Komoroos - jasiirad *(nom)* Komoros

go to Komoros
kondhom *(nom)* condom
wear a condom
Kongo - dadka ku nool wadanka
Koongo *(nom)* Kongo
Kongo language
konton *(adj)* fifty
fifty bottles
koob *(nom)* cup
koobka shaaha *tea cup*
koob *(act)* cup
her hand is cupped over her mouth

koob aan dhag la qabto la-
hayn *(nom)* tumbler
one tumbler of water
koob iyo tobnaad *(adj)* eleventh
eleventh house
kooban *(adj)* brief
let your story be brief
koobitaan *(nom)* summary
*the summary of it is that you have
done well*
kood *(nom)* code
to write code
koodh *(nom)* coat
she is putting on a coat
Koofi - magac *(nom)* Kofi
Kofi is my son
koofiyad *(nom)* hat
he is wearing a hat
Koojo - magac *(nom)* Kojo
Kojo is my son

koollo *(act)* paste
  to paste it on the wall
koonfur *(nom)* south
  go south
Koonfur Afrikaan *(nom)* South
  African
  the South Africans
Koonfur Kuuriya *(nom)* South
  Korea
  go to South Korea
Koonfur Kuuriyaan *(nom)* South
  Korean
  the South Koreans
Koonfur suudaan *(nom)* South
  Sudan
  go to South Sudan
Koonfurta Afrika *(nom)* South
  Africa
  go to South Africa
Koonfurta Sudaaniinta *(nom)*
  South Sudanese
  the South Sudanese
Koongo *(nom)* Congo
  go to Congo
Koongo-Baraasifiile *(nom)* Congo-
  Brazzaville
  go to Congo-Brazzaville
Koongo-Kinshaasa *(nom)* Congo-
  Kinshasa
  go to Congo-Kinshasa
koox *(nom)* group
  let us found a group
koox *(nom)* team

  my team
kopar *(sci)* copper
  copper (Cu) has 29 protons
kor *(adv)* up
  look up
kor u qaad *(act)* rise
  to rise at six in the morning
kor u qaadid *(act)* lift up
  lift yourself up!
kordhi *(act)* extend
  extend your palms
kordhi *(act)* increase
  burglary is increasing
kordhin *(nom)* extension
  house extension
kori *(act)* grow
  the child has grown
korkiisa/korkeeda *(pre)* upon
kormeer *(nom)* monitor
  heart monitor
koromiyam *(sci)* chromium
  chromium (Cr) has 24 protons
koronto *(sci)* electricity
  *electricity is when charges go from
  one place to a new place*
koronto *(sci)* electron
  an electron has a charge of -1
koronto *(adj)* electric
  electric light
korso *(act)* adopt
  to adopt a child
Koryaander *(nom)* cilantro

cilantro is a plant
Koryaander *(nom)* coriander
you can eat coriander
kow iyo toban *(adj)* eleven
  kow iyo toban dhaloonyinka *eleven bottles*
ku *(pro)* you
I love you
ku biir *(act)* join
words join together to make sentences

ku celin *(act)* repeat
repeat the reading
ku dadaalid *(act)* strive
she strives
ku dar *(act)* add
add sugar
ku dhac *(act)* fall into
fall into a pit
ku dhawaaq *(act)* announce
announce that
ku dhawow *(act)* approach
to approach quickly
ku dhufo *(act)* hit
do not hit me
ku filan *(adj)* adequate

ku haboonow *(act)* befit
it befits you
ku jira *(pre)* amongst

ku lifaaq *(act)* attach
attach to wall

ku saabsan *(pre)* about
I think about you
ku socda *(nom)* heading
book headings
ku socota *(pre)* to
  xagan ka timi ku socota halkaa *from here to there*
ku tabaruc *(act)* donate
let us donate to them
ku tiiri *(act)* prop
prop the door
ku tiirso *(act)* lean on
lean on me
ku wareejin *(nom)* disposition
a person's disposition
ku xigeen *(nom)* vice
vice and virtue
ku yeelo *(act)* owe
I owe you
kub *(nom)* calf
every leg has a calf
kubad *(nom)* ball
play ball
kubad *(nom)* football
football competition
kubada cagta *(nom)* soccer
football competition
kubra *(nom)* cobra
black cobra
kulan *(act)* tie
tie it
kulan *(nom)* meeting
cancel the meeting

kulayl *(adj)* hot
  hot water
kulliyad *(nom)* college
  where is the college?
kumanaan *(adj)* thousands
  thousands of ants
kun *(adj)* thousand
  thousand bottles
kuraniyam *(sci)* curium
  curium (Cm) has 96 protons
kursi *(nom)* chair
  habbee Kuraasta *arrange the chairs*

kursi *(nom)* seat
  to sit on the seat
kurtin *(nom)* stump
  stump of a tree
kutiri-kuteenka suuqa dhex-maraysa *(nom)* grapevine

kuug *(nom)* chef
  a good chef
kuul *(nom)* bead
  good beads
kuumbuyuuter *(nom)* computer
  kiiboodhka kuumbuyuuterka *computer keyboard*
kuus yar *(nom)* nub
  nub of a pen
kuus/buro *(nom)* lump
  a lump of gold
kuwaa *(pro)* these
  these people came

kuwan *(det)* these
  these books
Kuwayt *(nom)* Kuwait
  go to Kuwait
Kuwayti *(nom)* Kuwaiti
  the Kuwaitis
kuweeda *(pro)* hers
  this thing is hers

L

la dubay *(adj)* parched
  parched skin
la haasow *(act)* date
  will you date me?
la isku aamini karo *(adj)* dependable
  dependable god
la jecelyahey *(nom)* beloved

la kulan *(act)* meet
  meet me at home
la qabsasho *(nom)* adoption
  give her up for adoption
la qooyay *(adj)* soaked
  soaked cloth
la rabi karo *(adj)* desirable
  it is desirable
la saaxiib *(act)* befriend
  befriend me
la sharfay *(adj)* solemn
  a solemn promise

la wadaag sarriirta sayiga *(act)*
share bed with husband
Yaa will share a bed with her husband this night

la xisaabtan *(nom)* accountability
responsibility and accountability

la yaabid *(nom)* wonder
wonder and love

la yaqaan *(adj)* familiar
a familiar animal

la'o - luqada wadanka La'oos *(nom)* Lao
the Laos

La'oos - wadan ku yaala aasiya *(nom)* Laos
go to Laos

laab *(nom)* lab

laab-qarrar *(nom)* heartburn
I have heartburn

laakiin *(cjn)* nevertheless
I like it, but

laalaab *(act)* fold
to fold mother's cloth

laaluush *(nom)* bribe
he wants a bribe

laaluushid *(nom)* bribery
bribery and corruption

laan *(act)* branch
branch here

laan *(nom)* branch
family branch

laastiig *(adj)* elastic
elastic string

lab *(adj)* male

lab *(nom)* male
Mandela is male

laba *(adj)* two
laba dhaloonyinka *There are two bottles on the wall*

laba iyo toban *(adj)* twelve
laba iyo toban dhaloonyinka *twelve bottles*

laba qofood *(nom)* two persons
two persons are coming

labaatan *(adj)* twenty
labaatan dhaloonyinka *twenty bottles*

labadaba *(adj)* both
both sides

labis *(nom)* attire
your attire is beautiful

lacag *(nom)* money
money helps

lacag *(nom)* currency

lacag *(nom)* fees
school fees

lacag bixin *(sci)* charge
electricity has positive charge and negative charge

lacag kaash ah *(nom)* cash
I have cash

ladnaansho *(act)* recover
a sick person recovers
laf *(nom)* bone
my hand has bones
lafta madaxa *(nom)* skull
my skull
laga yabee *(adv)* maybe
maybe he will come
laguu kalsonaan karo *(adj)*
reliable

lahow *(act)* possess

lallabo *(nom)* nausea
she has nausea
lama degaan *(nom)* desert
water is scarce in the desert
lama filaan *(nom)* surprise
great surprise
lamaane *(nom)* partner
she is my partner
lamid ah *(adj)* equal

lantaanum *(sci)* lanthanum
lanthanum (La) has 57 protons
lawrensiyam *(sci)* lawrencium
lawrencium (Lr) has 103 protons
laws *(nom)* nut
they eat nuts
lax dhedig ah *(nom)* Ewe
Ewe language
laxle *(nom)* wasp
many wasps

layaab leh *(adj)* wonderful
amazing story
Laybeeriya *(nom)* Liberia
go to Liberia
Laybeeriyaan *(nom)* Liberian
the Liberians
layn/xariiq *(nom)* line
the ball has crossed the line
leben *(nom)* brick
red bricks
leben *(nom)* tile
bathroom tiles
ledh *(sci)* lead
lead (Pb) has 82 protons
leef *(act)* lick
to lick the spoon
leexo *(nom)* hammock
sleep in the hammock
libaax *(nom, c1)* lion
a lion eats flesh
libaax *(nom)* loin
my loins
lifermooriyam *(sci)* livermorium
livermorium (Lv) has 116 protons
Liibiya *(nom)* Libya
go to Libya
Liibiyaan *(nom)* Libyan
the Libyans
liimi *(adj)* orange
wear the orange cap
liin *(nom, c1)* lemon
three lemons

liinki/xidhiidh *(nom)* link
  Internet link
Lili - magac *(nom)* lily
  a lily is a flower
Lingaala - luqad lagaga hadlo meelo kamida Afrika *(nom)*
  Lingala
  I speak Lingala
liq *(act)* swallow
  swallow medicine
Lisooto *(nom)* Lesotho
  go to Lesotho
lityam *(sci)* lithium
  lithium (Li) has 3 protons
lix *(adj)* six
  lix dhaloonyinka six bottles
lix iyo toban *(adj)* sixteen
  lix iyo toban dhaloonyinka sixteen bottles
lix qofood *(nom)* six persons
  six persons are coming
lix xagal leh *(nom)* hexagon
  a hexagon has six angles
lixdan *(adj)* sixty
  sixty bottles
lo' *(nom)* cow
  hilibka lo'da cow meat; beef
lo' *(nom)* beef
  eat beef
lohod *(nom)* oyster
  I eat oysters
Londhon *(nom)* London
  I am going to London

loogu talogaly *(pre)* for
  for ourselves
Lubnaan *(nom)* Lebanon
  go to Lebanon
Lubnaani *(nom)* Lebanese
  the Lebanese
lug *(nom)* leg
  swollen leg
Lugandha - luqad lagaga hadlo Yugaandha *(nom)* Luganda
  Luganda language
lugeyn *(act)* walk about
  she walks about
lugeyn *(nom)* pedestrian
  nine pedestrians
Lugsembeeg *(nom)* Luxembourg
  go to Luxembourg
Lugsembeeger *(nom)* Luxembourger
  the Luxembourgers
lulid *(nom)* swing
  play on a swing
lumay *(ydy(i(act)* losaw

luteetiyam *(sci)* lutetium
  lutetium (Lu) has 71 protons
Luwo - dad ku nool waqooyiga Suudaan *(nom)* Luwo
  I can read Luwo

M

ma haysto *(act)* not have

I don't have money but I have property

ma nabad baa *(exc)* hello
hello sir

maad leh *(adj)* funny
funny story

maahmaah *(nom)* proverb
quote a proverb

maahmaayo *(nom)* Proverbs
read Proverbs 27:17

maal leh *(adj)* rich
a rich country

maalgashi *(nom)* investment
I need an investment

Maali *(nom)* Mali
go to Mali

maalin *(nom)* day
the day has arrived

maalinta dhalashada *(nom)*
birthday
today is my birthday

maalintii kale *(adv)* the other
day
I saw a lion the other day

Maaliyaan *(nom)* Malian
the Malians

maamul *(act)* manage
to manage someone

maamul *(nom)* administration
her administration brought progress

maamule *(nom)* boss
my boss

maamule *(nom)* governor
she is the governor

maamule *(nom)* manager
a good manager

maamulid *(nom)* governance
good governance

maanganiis *(sci)* manganese
manganese (Mn) has 25 protons

maansalugaleyda *(nom)* chameleon
I see the chameleon

maantay *(adv)* today
she arrives today

Maaritiyaan *(nom)* Mauritian
the Mauritians

Maaritiyuus *(nom)* Mauritius
go to Mauritius

macaan ah *(adj)* sweet
the tea is sweet

macalin *(nom, c2)* teacher
I am a teacher

macbudyo *(nom)* sacrilege
what sacrilege is this?

macmiil *(nom)* customer
a good customer

madadaali *(act)* amuse

madadaalo *(adj)* fun
today is a fun day

madadaalo leh *(adj)* entertaining
it is entertaining

Madagaskar *(nom)* Madagascar

go to Madagascar

madax *(nom)* head

your big head

madax banaani *(nom)* freedom

freedom and justice

madax banaani *(nom)* independence

independence day

madax foorarin *(nom)* bow

bow and arrow

madax furasho *(nom)* ransom

pay a ransom

madax xanuun *(nom)* headache

headache medicine

madaxweyne *(nom)* president

the president has arrived

madaxweyne ku xigeen *(nom)* vice-president

the vice-president has arrived

madfac *(nom)* cannon

shoot the cannon

madhalays *(adj)* barren

barren woman

madhan *(adj)* empty

empty bucket

madiibad *(nom)* bowl

a red bowl

madow *(adj)* black

black cloth

madow *(adj)* dark

dark night

madow *(nom)* darkness

night brings darkness

maeekrowevu *(nom)* microwave

pro:my$_n$om : mothertdy(f(act : want))det : a$_n$om : microwave

mafiiq *(nom)* broom

mafiiq iyo jaqaf broom and dustpan

magaalo *(nom)* town

go into town

magac *(nom)* noun

four nouns

magac *(nom)* name

magacayga my name

magac hableed - laga isticmaalo Gaana *(nom)* Efua

Efua is my daughter

magac hableed - laga isticmaalo Gaana *(nom)* Ekua

Ekua is my daughter

magac u yaal *(nom)* pronoun

two pronouns

magacow *(act)* nominate

name a time

magalada hooyo *(nom)* hometown

I'm going to my hometown

magdhow *(nom)* compensation

have you received your compensation?

magniisiyam *(sci)* magnesium

magnesium (Mg) has 12 protons

mahad celin *(act)* thank

to thank your Father

mahadnaq la'aan *(nom)* un-appreciativeness

how do you do not sr unapprecia-tiveness

mahadnaqida - ciida gaal-ada *(nom)* thanksgiving

thanksgiving service

mahadsanid *(exc)* thanks

Thanks Mandela!

mahadsanid *(nom)* thanks

thanks be to God

majalad *(nom)* magazine

a new magazine

majarafad *(nom)* shovel

majarafad *(nom)* spade

eight spades

makhaayad/hudheel laga cun-teeyo *(nom)* restaurant

a new restaurant

maktabad *(nom)* library

we will go to the library

Malaawiyaan *(nom)* Malawian

the Malawians

malab *(nom)* honey

honey is sweet

Malagasi - luqada wadanka Madagaskar *(nom)* Malagasy

Malagasy language

Malawi *(nom)* Malawi

go to Malawi

Malayshiya *(nom)* Malaysia

go to Malaysia

Malayshiyaan *(nom)* Malaysian

the Malaysians

Maldhafiyaan *(nom)* Maldivian

the Maldivians

Maldhifees *(nom)* Maldives

go to Maldives

malin kasta *(adv)* daily

he comes here daily

malqaacad *(nom)* spoon

lix iyo toban malqaacadood six-teen spoons

malqaacad *(act)* ladle

ladle some for her

malqaacad shaandho ah *(nom)* spatula

three spatulas

malqaacad weyn *(nom)* ladle

soup ladle

mamnuuc *(act)* forbid

forbid her

mamul *(act)* have a hold on

hunger has a hold on me (I am hun-gry)

maqaal *(nom)* article

maqaar *(nom)* skin

dry skin

maqal *(act)* hear

she heard the whistle

maqas *(nom)* scissors

give me the scissors

maqlid *(ydy(i(act)* heard

mar labaad *(adv)* again
see her again
marag *(nom)* testimony
what is your testimony?
maraq *(nom)* soup
palm nut soup
mararka *(nom)* times
ten times
mareeg/barta interneetka *(nom)*
website
make a website for me
Mareykan *(nom)* American
she is an American
Mareykanka *(nom)* United States
of America
he was born in the United States of
America
Mark - magac *(nom)* mark
my name is Mark
marka laga reebo *(cjn)* except
except God
marka laga reebo taas *(cjn)*
except that
except that I want salt
markab *(nom)* ship
a big ship
markhaati *(nom)* witness
three witnesses
maroodi *(nom)* elephant
maroodigu aadbuu u weyn yahay
an elephant is very big

maroojin *(act)* twist
twist it a little
maroojin *(act)* wring
wring the cloth
Marooko *(nom)* Morocco
go to Morocco
marti *(nom)* guest
I am a guest
maruwaana - maandooriye
(nom) marijuana
she smokes marijuana
marwo *(nom)* madam
madam Mary
marwo *(nom)* mistress
master and mistress
mas *(nom)* snake
masku malaha cago a snake has
no legs
mas weyn/luqada koombuyu-
uter ee bayton *(nom)* python
a python is a snake
mas'uuliyad *(nom)* responsibility
it is your responsibility
masaal *(nom)* parable
the parables of Jesus
Masaari *(nom)* Egyptian
the Egyptians
masaf *(nom)* beaker
there is water in the beaker
masago *(nom)* millet
millet porridge
Masar *(nom)* Egypt

go to Egypt
masax *(act)* wipe
to wipe the seat
mashquul *(adj)* busy

mashruuc *(nom)* project
ten projects
Masiix *(nom)* Christ
Jesus Christ!
masiixa *(nom)* messiah
are you the messiah?
Masiixi *(nom)* Christian
a Christian and a Muslim
Masiixinimo *(nom)* Christian-ity
Christianity and Islam
maskax *(nom)* brain
my brain
maskax *(nom)* mind
her mind
masuul *(adj)* responsible
he is a responsible man
mataan *(nom)* twin
she is a twin
mataano *(nom)* twins
we are twins
matag *(act)* vomit
you have vomitted
matal *(act)* act
to act now
Mathew - magac *(nom)* Matthew
read Matthew 19:14
maweeli *(act)* entertain

entertain yourself
Mawliid *(nom)* June
June has 30 days
maxaa yeelay *(cjn)* because
because I like you
maxay *(pro)* what
what is that?
maxkamad *(nom)* court
I am going to court
maxkamada hindiyaan ah *(nom)*
durbar
we will go to the durbar
maya *(exc)* no
I say no
maya *(adv)* not
it is not a snake
mayl *(nom)* mile
ten miles
Maynaama *(nom)* Myanma
the Myanmas
Maynamaar *(nom)* Myanmar
go to Myanmar
meel *(nom)* place
which place?
meel *(pro)* somewhere
we are going somewhere
meel kasta *(pro)* everywhere
everywhere is hot
meel-tobnaadka *(nom)* tithe
pay your tithe
meerkuri *(sci)* mercury
mercury (Hg) has 80 protons
meesha ay shimbruhu u hoy-

daa *(act)* roost
if a bird does not fly, it roosts
meetreeniyam *(sci)* meitnerium
meitnerium (Mt) has 109 protons
mendaliiniyam *(sci)* mendelevium
mendelevium (Md) has 101 protons

meyd *(nom)* corpse
the corpse is rotting
meydhid *(act)* wash
to wash the bottles
micno *(nom)* meaning
seek meaning
mid kasta *(adj)* each
each thing
mid kasta iyo qofkasta *(pro)*
each and everyone
each and everyone came
mid mid *(adv)* one by one
they came one by one
midab *(nom)* color

midab *(nom)* colour
seven colours
midabee *(act)* colour
colour and learn
midabeyn *(nom)* dye
black dye
midabyo *(sci)* antimony
antimony (Sb) has 51 protons
midig *(adj)* right

go right
midnimo *(nom)* trinity
holy trinity
midnimo *(nom)* unity
unity and peace
midoobay *(act)* unite
Africa will unite
Midowga Africa *(nom)* African
Union
African Union troops
miis *(nom)* table
kursi iyo miis *chair and table*
miisaamid *(act)* weigh
weigh your child
miisaan *(nom)* weight
a heavy weight
miisaniyad *(nom)* budget
this year's budget
mijiin *(nom)* machine
new machine
mil *(act)* melt
the sheabutter is melting
milicsi *(nom)* reflection
his reflection
milyan *(adj)* million
a million bottles
mindi *(nom, c1)* knife
afee midi *sharpen a knife*
miro *(nom)* fruit
pluck fruit
miro goosasho *(nom)* harvest
a plentiful harvest
miro soo saar *(act)* bear fruit

the tree has borne fruit
miro ukun u eeg oo la cuno
(nom) eggplant
eggplant stew
mise *(cjn)* or
Kofi mise Ama *Kofi or Ama*
mishaar *(nom)* saw
the carpenter's saw
misig *(nom)* hip
my hips
miyir *(nom)* prudence
prudence and love
molibednum *(sci)* molybdenum
molybdenum (Mo) has 42 protons
Moongooliya *(nom)* Mongolia
go to Mongolia
Moongooliyaan *(nom)* Mongolian
the Mongolians
Morookaan *(nom)* Moroccan
the Moroccans
Mosoto *(nom)* Mosotho
the Basotho
Motiswaana *(nom)* Motswana
the Batswana
mucaarad *(nom)* rebel
the rebels won
mudalab *(nom)* waiter
he is a waiter
mudane *(nom)* gentleman
senior gentleman
mudane *(nom)* mister
Mister Annan

mudane *(nom)* sir
I thank you sir
muddo *(nom)* period
my period came early
mudnaan *(nom)* priority
what is your priority?
mug *(nom)* volume
turn up the volume
muhiim ah *(adj)* essential

muhiim ah *(adj)* important
you are an important person
mulac *(nom)* lizard
a lizard eats grass
mulkiile *(nom)* owner
the owner of the car
mulkiile *(nom)* proprietor
she is a proprietor
munaafaqnimo *(nom)* hypocrisy
hypocrisy and lies
munaarad/taallo *(nom)* tower
Tower of London
muraayad *(nom)* mirror
muraayad weyn *big mirror*
muraayadaha indhaha *(nom)*
spectacles
she wears spectacles
muran *(act)* argue
argue with him
muran *(nom)* quarrel
a big quarrel
muran *(nom)* squabbles
squabbles and insults

murti *(nom)* wisdom
strength and wisdom
murugo *(act)* grieve
my soul grieves
murugsan *(adj)* sad
a sad face
Murutaaniya *(nom)* Mauritania
go to Mauritania
Murutaaniyaan *(nom)* Mauritanian
the Mauritanians
Musaabiqiyaan *(nom)* Mozambican
the Mozambicans
Musaambiqiyuu *(nom)* Mozambique
go to Mozambique
musabiir iyo cirbado *(nom)*
pins and needles
pins and needles is not a disease
mushaax *(act)* roam
roam everywhere
muslim *(nom)* muslim
a Christian and a Muslim
musqul *(act)* go to the toilet
to go to the toilet weekly
musqul *(nom)* bathroom, shower
go to the bathroom
musqul *(nom)* latrine
where is the latrine?
musqul *(nom)* toilet
go to the toilet

musqusha *(nom)* lavatory
mustaqbalka *(nom)* future
I see luxury in your future
musuq-maasuq *(nom)* corruption
bribery and corruption
muuji *(act)* reveal
reveal the truth
muuji ...u nixid *(act)* show ...
pity
show her pity
muujin *(act)* show
muuqaal *(nom)* apparition
fear an apparition
muus *(nom)* banana
daanyeerku wuxuu jecelyay muuska
a monkey likes bananas
muusikiiste *(nom)* musician
the musicians
muuska balaantayn *(nom)* plantain
plantain and cassava
muwaadin *(nom)* citizen
I am a citizen

N

Naamiibiyaan *(nom)* Namibian
the Namibians

naas *(nom)* breast
breast milk
nabad *(nom)* peace
I want peace
nabad galiyo *(exc)* goodbye
say goodbye
nabada ilaalin *(nom)* security
good security
nabadeey *(exc)* hi

nabadeyn *(act)* pacify
pacify the fight
nabadgalyeyn *(nom)* bye

nabar *(act)* bruise
*you swat the fly in anger and you
bruise your wound*
nac *(act)* hate
to hate laziness
nac-naclayn *(nom)* bumblebee
a fat bumblebee
nacas *(nom)* idiot, imbecile

nacas *(nom)* fool
Fool! Dimwit!
nacasnimo *(adj)* foolish
a foolish story
nacasnimo *(nom)* folly
it is just folly
nacasnimo *(nom)* foolishness

naceyb *(nom)* hatred
hatred has no cure

naceyb *(nom)* prejudice
fear and prejudice
nacnac *(nom)* candy

nadiifi *(act)* clean
clean your teeth
nadiifin *(act)* scrape
to scrape the fish scales
naf *(nom)* self
myself, yourself
naf *(nom)* soul
my soul exults
nafihina *(pro)* yourselves
look after yourselves well
nafisiin *(act)* unburden
unburden me
naftaada *(pro)* yourself
look after yourself well
naftayada *(pro)* ourselves
for ourselves
naftayda *(pro)* myself
I love myself
nafteeda *(pro)* herself
she respects herself
naftiisa *(pro)* himself
he respects himself
naftooda *(pro)* themselves
they look after themselves well
naqaska kasii daa *(act)* deflate
your tyre is deflating
nasiib *(nom)* luck
luck and success

nasiib badan *(adj)* lucky
lucky girl
nasiib daro *(nom)* misfortune
many misfortunes
naso *(act)* rest

naxariis *(nom)* compassion
she has compassion
naxariis *(nom)* kindness
favour and kindness
naxariis *(nom)* mercy
goodness and mercy
naxariis leh *(nom)* kind
he and his kind
naxariisasho *(nom)* leniency
show him leniency
naxdin leh *(adj)* pitiful
pitiful child
Nayjar *(nom)* Niger
go to Niger
Nayjeeriya *(nom)* Nigeria
go to Nigeria
Nayjeeriyaan *(nom)* Nigerian
the Nigerians
Nayjeriyeen *(nom)* Nigerien
the Nigeriens
Nayroobi *(nom)* Nairobi
go to Nairobi
naytarojin *(sci)* nitrogen
nitrogen (N) has 7 protons
nebi *(nom)* messenger
the messengers arrived
nebi *(nom)* prophet

powerful prophet
nebiyo *(nom)* messengers
the messengers have come
neefsasho *(nom)* breath
collect your breath; rest
neefso *(act)* breathe
breathe a little; take a breather
neofhmiyam *(sci)* neodymium
neodymium (Nd) has 60 protons
nibiri *(nom)* whale
a large whale
nibtiiniyam *(sci)* neptunium
neptunium (Np) has 93 protons
nidaam daran *(adj)* chaotic
the place is chaotic
nidaamin *(act)* tidy
tidy up the room
nidar ku gelid *(nom)* vow

nigis *(nom)* underwear
he is not wearing underwear
Niibaal *(nom)* Nepal
go to Nepal
Niibaali *(nom)* Nepali
the Nepalis
niibiyam *(sci)* niobium
niobium (Nb) has 41 protons
niikal *(sci)* nickel
nickel (Ni) has 28 protons
nijaarnimo *(nom)* carpentry
she knows carpentry
nijaasee *(act)* defile
do not defile yourself

nin *(nom)* man
  nin dheer *a tall man*
nin asal ah *(nom)* aborigine
  we are the aborigines
nin mararka sameeya xiri-irada jinsiga ee aan joogtada ahayn *(nom)* philanderer
  you have made yourself a philan-derer
nin weyn *(nom)* old man
  he is an old man
nin yar *(nom)* young man
  a young man like you
niyad jab *(act)* disappoint
  my lover has disappointed me
niyadjab *(nom)* disappointment
  love has disappointment
niyoon *(sci)* neon
  neon (Ne) has 10 protons
niyutoron *(sci)* neutron
  a neutron has a charge of 0
njiaar *(nom)* carpenter
  he is a carpenter
nolol *(nom)* life
  live your life well
nolol dheeraansho *(nom)* longevity
  wealth and longevity
nolol heer sare ah *(adj)* afflu-ent
noloosho *(adj)* living
  living god
noobeeliyam *(sci)* nobelium

nobelium (No) has 102 protons
nooc *(act)* type
  I type fast
nooc *(nom)* type
nooc *(nom)* version
  which version?
nooc basbaaska kamida *(nom)* alligator pepper
  add some alligator pepper to the food
nooc dhagaxa kamid ah *(nom)* slate
  wipe the slate
nooc khamriga kamid ah *(nom)* liquor
  pour a little liquor
nooc khamriga kamid ah *(nom)* palmwine
  drink palmwine
nooc lawska ka mid ah *(nom)* walnut
  ten walnuts
nooc masaska kamida *(nom)* puff-adder
  the puff-adder is dead
noole *(nom)* organism
noole yar *(nom)* microorgan-ism
noolow *(act)* live
  we live here

Noorway *(nom)* Norway
go to Norway
noqdo mid qurux badan *(act)*
be beautiful
a butterfly is beautiful
noqo caan *(act)* become famous
Nkrumah has become famous
noqo mid weyn *(act)* be big
you are big and you are high
noqoshada mid dareen adag
(act) be emotionally charged
today will be emotionally charged
noqoshada shaydaan *(act)* be
evil
abusing drugs is evil
nukliyas *(sci)* nucleus
*a nucleus contains protons and neu-
trons*
nuugid *(act)* suckle
suckle the breast
nuurad *(nom)* lime
lime juice
Nuux *(nom)* Noah
Noah is a man

O

ogeysiis muhiim ah *(nom)* proclamation
proclamation of the rights of humankind

ogolaansho *(nom)* acceptance
love, acceptance and forgiveness

ogolaansho *(nom)* permission

ogolaansho sii *(act)* consent

ogolow *(act)* agree
do you agree?
ogolow *(act)* allow
allow them
ogow *(act)* know
I know her
Ogsajiin *(nom)* oxygen
oxygen is in air
ogsijin *(sci)* oxygen
oxygen (O) has 8 protons
oh *(exc)* oh
oh my sister!
ololaysa *(adj)* blazing
blazing fire
onkod *(nom)* thunder
storm with thunder
oomman *(adj)* thirsty

oosmiyam *(sci)* osmium
osmium (Os) has 76 protons
Ootiisam *(nom)* autism
autism is a disease
ooy *(act)* cry
to cry each time
orday *(ydy(f(act)* ran

ordid *(act)* run
to run like a hare
orodyahan *(nom)* athlete

she is an athlete
Oromo *(nom)* Oromo
Oromo language

Q

qaab *(nom)* shape, structure
the shape of the house
qaab nololeed *(nom)* lifestyle
an active lifestyle
qaad *(act)* lift
to lift higher
qaad *(act)* pick up
pick up the stones
qaad *(nom)* pick
to break rocks with a pick
qaadada *(act)* scoop
scoop up sand
qaadid *(act)* carry
carry the book
qaadir *(nom)* Almighty
The Almighty
qaado *(act)* take
to take medicine
qaadsii *(act)* infect
the disease has infected me
qaali ah *(adj)* expensive
it is expensive
qaamuus *(nom)* dictionary
picture dictionary
qaanso-robaad *(nom)* rainbow
I see a rainbow

qaar ka mid ah *(det)* some
some food
qaarad *(nom)* continent
African continent
qabo *(act)* catch
catch the ball
qabooji *(act)* cool
the food has cooled
qaboojin *(adj)* freezing
night is freezing
qabow *(adj)* cold
cold water
qabow *(adj)* cool
a cool beer
qabri/xabaal *(nom)* grave
four graves
qabso *(act)* grasp
grasp my hand
qabso *(act)* hold
to hold something firmly
qadar *(nom)* destiny
a good destiny
Qadar *(nom)* Qatar
go to Qatar
Qadari *(nom)* Qatari
the Qataris
qadhaah *(adj)* bitter
bitter medicine
qadiimi ah *(adj)* ancient
ancient house
qalab *(nom)* tool

qalab muusik *(nom)* xylophone

play a xylophone
qalab wax lagu jaro *(nom)* chisl
hammer and chisl
**qalab yar oo la wareejiyo si
la isugu maaweeliyo** *(nom)*
spin-top
five spin-tops
**qalab yar oo la wareejiyo si
la isugu maaweeliyo** *(nom)*
spinning top
Kofi plays with a spinning top
qalal *(act)* dry
to dry clothes
qalalan *(adj)* dry
dry land
qalcad *(nom)* castle
the white castle
qalcad *(nom)* fortress
God is my fortress
qaldan *(act)* err
I have erred
qalin *(nom)* pencil
　qalin iyo qalin *pencil and pen*
qalin *(nom)* pen
ink in a pen
qalinjabiye *(nom)* graduate
she is a graduate
qallin *(nom)* silver
silver and gold
qalooci *(act)* bend
bend it a bit
qamadi *(nom)* wheat
to eat wheat

qanacsanoow *(act)* be satisfied
I am satisfied
qandho *(nom)* fever
she has a fever
qanid *(nom)* cast
cast of a film
qaniin *(act)* bite
the dog can bite
qaniinyo shimbireed *(act)* peck
the chicken is pecking corn
qaraabo *(nom)* relative
he is a relative
qaran *(adj)* national
a national bank
qaran *(nom)* nation
your nation
qarax *(nom)* bomb
the bomb exploded
qare *(nom)* melon
green melon
qare/xab-xab *(nom)* watermelon
eat the watermelon
qareen *(nom)* lawyer
four lawyers
qari *(nom)* hide
animal hide
qariib *(nom)* stranger
three strangers
qarni *(nom)* century
this century
qarqan *(act)* drown
to drown quickly

qarsho dabiici ah *(nom)* criestal
  a beautiful criestal
qarsoon *(act)* fade
  the cloth has faded
qarxi *(act)* explode
  the bomb exploded
Qasa *(nom)* Gaza
  go to Gaza
qasaacad *(nom)* tin
  five tins
Qasaan *(nom)* Gazan
  the Gazans
qasab *(act)* force
  you are forcing me
qasan *(adj)* turbulent
  a turbulent world
qashin *(nom)* junk
  there is junk in the room
qashin *(nom)* rubbish
  throw away the rubbish
qashin *(nom)* waste
  the work has been a waste
qashin qub *(nom)* dump
  rubbish dump
qasri/madaxtooyo *(nom)* palace
  new palace
qaxooti *(nom)* refuge
  our refuge
qaxwe *(nom)* coffee
  she drinks coffee
qayb *(nom)* part
  the book has three parts
qaylin *(act)* shout

  to shout for help
qaylo eey *(nom)* bark
  bark of a tree
qaynuun *(nom)* ordinance

qeexitaan *(nom)* definition
  a good definition
qeyb *(nom)* category
  five categories
qeyb *(nom)* division
  2/1 = 2; this is division
qeybi *(act)* divide
  divide the bread
qeylin *(act)* yell
  we will yell
qiimaha *(nom)* price
  how much is the price?
qiime *(nom)* cost
  price = cost + profit
qiimey *(nom)* value
  great value
qiimo leh *(nom)* worth

qiiq *(nom)* smoke
  belch smoke
qir *(act)* admit

qiyaas *(act)* estimate
  estimate your height
qiyaas *(act)* measure
  measure two spoonfuls
qiyaas *(nom)* scale
  to measure with the scale

qod (*act*) dig
to dig a hole
qodax (*nom*) thorn
remove the thorn
qof (*nom*) person
important person
qof (*pro*) someone
someone is coming
qof aad wada shaqeysaan (*nom*)
colleague
your colleagues
qof aan nadiif ahayn (*adj*) dishevelled
dishevelled self
qof baras leh (*nom*) leper
ten lepers
qof cir weyn (*nom*) glutton
he is a glutton
qof dadka ka qosliya (*nom*)
clown

qof madow (*nom*) ebony
black ebony
qof masiix raacay nolishiisa
(*nom*) disciple

qof nacas ah (*adj*) dimwit
Fool! Dimwit!
qof u shaqeeya din faafin (*nom*)
missionary
they are missionaries
qof wacan (*adj*) congenial
a congenial place

**qof wado baabuur oo cusub
sameeya** (*nom*) trailblazer
Gandhi is a trailblazer
qof wax bartay (*nom*) savant
they are savants
qof weyn (*nom*) elder
the elders
qof/dabeecad (*nom*) character
her character
qof/koox horyaal ah (*nom*)
champion
she is a champion
qofka dhirta yaqaana (*nom*)
herbalist
she is a herbalist
qofka gudoomiyaha ah (*nom*)
chairperson
she is the chairperson
**qofka hogaamiyaha dad ama
qabiil** (*nom*) chieftain

qofka kaydiya hantida ee isticmaala inyar (*nom*) miser
he is a miser
qofka ku lugelh dacwad maxkamadeed (*nom*) litigant
she is a litigant
qofka wada doon/markab (*nom*)
helmsman
helmsman of a boat
qofkaa (*pro*) that person
that person said it

qofma *(pro)* whose
whose house is this?
qol *(nom)* room
she is sleeping in the room
qol weyn *(nom)* hall
we are sitting in the hall
qolka fadhiga *(nom)* living-room

qolka hurdada *(nom)* bedroom
the house has two bedrooms
qolka martida *(nom)* guest room
sleep in the guest room
qolof *(nom)* shell
shell of a crab
qoolley *(nom)* dove
white dove
qoolley *(nom)* pigeon
a pigeon is a bird
qoomamee *(act)* regret
I regret I said that
qoomameyn *(nom)* regret
pain and regret
qoomamo *(nom)* remorse
he showed no remorse
qoor *(nom)* neck
the tie hangs on his neck
qoraa *(nom)* writer
I am a writer
qoraal qabyo ah *(nom)* draughts
play draughts
qorfe *(nom)* cinnamon
cinnamon is fragrant

qori *(nom)* gun
a soldier has a gun
qorid *(act)* write
to write a letter
qorid/bolog gareyn *(nom)* blog
food blog
qoriga *(nom)* powder-keg
three powder-kegs
qorrax leh *(adj)* sunny
a sunny day
qorshe *(nom)* plan
a pot and a plan
qorshee *(act)* plan
one head does not plan
qosol *(act)* giggle

qosol *(act)* laugh
he is laughing
qoto dheer *(adj)* deep
a deep hole
qoy *(act)* get wet
the place has gotten wet
qoyan *(adj)* wet
wet blanket
qoys *(nom)* family
new family
qubayso *(act)* bathe
to bath each morning
qubo *(nom)* turtle
a turtle swims
Qubrus *(nom)* Cyprus
go to Cyprus
qudhaanjo *(nom)* ant

thousands of ants
qudhaanjooyin *(nom)* ants
the ants are thriving
qufac *(act)* cough
to cough profusely
qufac *(nom)* cough
he has a cough
quful *(nom)* padlock
padlock and key
quful/xidh *(nom)* lock
five locks
quman *(adj)* upright
upright person
qumbe *(nom)* coconut
two coconuts
quraac *(nom)* breakfast
he will eat breakfast
Quraanka *(nom)* koran
the Bible and the Koran
Quran *(nom)* quran

qurmid *(act)* rot
the mango is rotting
qurmuun *(act)* stink
something is stinking
quruurad *(nom)* bottle
shan dhalooyinka *five bottles*
quruurad/muraayad *(nom)* glass
a glass of water
qurux *(nom)* beauty
beauty and love
qurxoon *(adj)* beautiful, handsome

it is beautiful
qurxoon *(adj)* pretty
a pretty woman
quudhsi *(nom)* scorn
stop the scorn
quus *(nom)* desperation

quusi *(act)* immerse
immerse him in the water
quusid *(act)* sink
the boat is sinking
quusid *(nom)* sink
drain the sink

R

raac *(act)* follow
follow me
raadhiyam *(sci)* radium
radium (Ra) has 88 protons
raadiyow *(nom)* radio
switch on the radio
raadon *(sci)* radon
radon (Rn) has 86 protons
raaga *(adj)* chronic
raam *(nom)* rum
rum or vodka?
Raashiyaan *(nom)* Russian
the Russians
raaxeysi *(nom)* pleasure
how do you sr pleasure

raaxo *(nom)* comfort
give me comfort

raaxo *(nom)* luxury
I see luxury in your future

raaxo leh *(adj)* pleasant
a pleasant person

rab *(act)* desire
I desire a banana

Rabaani ah *(adj)* divine
divine power

rabitaan *(act)* want
I want four books

rabitaan *(nom)* desire
your heart's desire

rabitaan *(nom)* will
God's will

rah *(nom)* frog
rahu wuxuu jecel yahay biyaha
a frog likes water

Rajalood kow *(nom)* October
October has 31 days

Rajalood labaad *(nom)* November
November has 30 days

Rajalood sedex *(nom)* December
December has 31 days

rajee *(act)* wish

rajo *(nom)* hope
I have hope

raq *(nom)* carcass
the carcass is rotting

rasaas *(nom)* bullet
two bullets

rash *(nom)* firewood
pickup firewood

rayrayn leh *(adj)* delightful
delightful work

reer boqoreed ah *(adj)* royal
royal family

reer-aakhiraad *(nom)* ghost
I see a ghost

reexaan *(nom)* mint, thyme
mint and water

ri' *(nom)* goat
ri' iyo ido *a goat and a sheep*

rif *(act)* pluck
pluck fruit

riix *(act)* press
to press it seven times

riix *(act)* push
to push the lorry

rinji *(nom)* paint
white paint

rioonjiinayam *(sci)* roentgenium
roentgenium (Rg) has 111 protons

riwaayad *(nom)* drama
I like drama films

riyo *(nom)* dream
many dreams

riyood *(act)* dream
to dream a lot

roog *(nom)* carpet
new carpet

roomaaniyiinta *(nom)* Romans
read Romans 5:1
rooti *(nom, c1)* groundnut
corn and groundnuts
rooti *(nom)* bread
rooti jilicsan soft bread
rubiidhiyam *(sci)* rubidium
rubidium (Rb) has 37 protons
rubuc *(nom)* quarter
two quarters make half
rumeyso *(act)* believe
believe Kofi
run *(nom)* truth
she spoke the truth
run ah *(adj)* true
it is true
ruteeniyam *(sci)* ruthenium
ruthenium (Ru) has 44 protons
Ruumatiisamka *(nom)* rheumatism
rheumatism is a disease
Ruush *(nom)* Russia
go to Russia
ruuteriindhiyam *(sci)* rutherfordium
rutherfordium (Rf) has 104 protons

ruux *(nom)* spirit
he has a strong spirit
Ruwaandha *(nom)* Rwanda
go to Rwanda
Ruwaandhaan *(nom)* Rwandan

the Rwandans
ruxruxid *(act)* quake

S

saabuun *(nom)* soap
baag iyo saabuun pail and soap
saacad *(nom)* clock
tell me the time on the clock
saacad *(nom)* hour
ten hours
saacado yar *(nom)* wee hours
1am
saadaali *(act)* foresee
I foresee victory
saadaali *(act)* predict

saafi ah *(adj)* pure
pure gold
saamaxaad *(nom)* forgiveness
love, acceptance and forgiveness
saamayn *(nom)* effect

Saambiya *(nom)* Zambia
go to Zambia
Saambiyaan *(nom)* Zambian
Tendayi is a Zambian
saameyn *(nom)* impact
learning has great impact
Saantoomiyaan *(nom)* Santomean
the Santomeans

saaxiib *(nom)* friend
my friend

saaxiibad *(nom)* girlfriend

saaxiibtinimo *(nom)* friend-ship
friendship is good

saaxir *(nom)* wizard
he is a wizard

saaxirad *(nom)* witch
she is a witch

sabab *(nom)* reason
everything has a reason

sababid cuncun *(act)* cause itch-iness
the medicine causes itchiness

sabiib *(nom)* raisin
eat the raisins

saboolnimo *(nom)* poverty
poverty or wealth

Sabti *(nom)* Saturday
Saturday children

Sabuux *(nom)* February
February has 28 or 29 days

sacab *(nom)* palm
open out your palms

sacabi *(act)* clap
to clap for Yaa

sacfaraan *(nom)* toffee
muudso sacfaraan lick a toffee

Sadataal *(nom)* January
January has 31 days

saddex *(adj)* three

saddex dhaloonyinka three bottles

saddex gees *(nom)* triangle
a triangle has three angles

saddex ilmood oo mar wada dhasha *(nom)* triplets
they are triplets

saddex iyo toban *(adj)* thir-teen
saddex iyo toban dhaloonyinka thir-teen bottles

saddex qofood *(nom)* three per-sons
three persons are coming

saf *(nom)* row
three rows of chairs

Safar *(nom)* August
August has 31 days

safiiir *(nom)* ambassador
ambassador of Kenya

safka/ taxid *(act)* row
row your boat

sagaal *(adj)* nine
sagaal dhaloonyinka Nine bottles

sagaal iyo toban *(adj)* nine-teen
sagaal iyo toban dhaloonyinka nine-teen bottles

sagaal qofood *(nom)* nine per-sons
nine persons are coming

sagaal xagale *(nom)* nonagon

a nonagon has nine angles
sagaashan *(adj)* ninety
  ninety bottles
sagxad dhul/dabaq *(nom)* floor
  on the floor
sahan *(nom)* reconnaisance

sahay *(nom)* supply
  demand and supply
sakhraan *(act)* be drunk
  you are drunk
sakhraan *(nom)* drunkard
  he is a drunkard
sakhraanimo *(nom)* drunkenness
  drunkenness and pain
Sako *(nom)* May
  May has 31 days
salaad *(nom)* prayer
  prayer is good
salaan *(act)* greet
  greet Ama
salaan *(nom)* greeting
  a new greeting
salaan *(nom)* salutation

Salaasa *(nom)* Tuesday
  Tuesday children
salaaxid *(act)* caress
  her hand caresses it
salaaxid *(nom)* plaster
  remove the plaster
saldhig/xarun *(nom)* station

train station
saliid *(nom)* oil
  the oil
saliid isku shub *(act)* anoint
  she anointed my head with oil
saliida khudaarta *(nom)* vegetable oil
  use vegetable oil to fry fish
sallaan *(nom)* ladder
  long ladder
sallad *(nom)* basket
  carry a basket
salli *(nom)* mat
  spread out a mat
samaariyam *(sci)* samarium
  samarium (Sm) has 62 protons
samayn *(ydy(i(act)* did

samee *(act)* do
  she is doing something
samee *(act)* make
  make food
samir *(nom)* patience
  love and patience
san *(nom)* nose
  ear and nose
sanam/qof lagu daydo *(nom)* idol

sanduuq *(nom)* box
  sanduuqa A ayaa ka weyn sanduuqa B *box A is bigger than box B*

96

sannad *(nom)* year
  a new year has come
sannad kasta *(adj)* yearly
  a yearly festival
sannadka oo dhan *(nom)* whole
  year
  two whole years
sannadle ah *(adj)* annual

Sao Toome iyo Birinsayb *(nom)*
  Sao Tome and Principe
  go to Sao Tome and Principe
saqaf *(act)* roof
  roof the house
saqaf *(nom)* roof
  the house with the red roof
saqee *(act)* work
  to work hard
sarbeeb *(nom)* metaphor
  a good metaphor
sare u qaad *(act)* raise
  raise your hand
sariir *(nom, c3)* bed
  Ku *seexo* sariirta *sleep on the bed*

sawaxan *(nom)* noise
  stop making noise
sawaxan leh *(adv)* raucously
  to laugh raucously
sawir *(nom)* picture
  sawir *qurux badan* *beautiful picture*
sawir *(act)* draw

draw a bird
sawir *(act)* figure
  you figure it is hard?
sawir *(nom)* drawing
  my new drawing
sawir *(nom)* image

sawir *(nom)* photograph
  take a photograph
sax *(nom)* tick
  three ticks
saxafi *(nom)* journalist
  we are journalists
saxan ballaaran *(nom)* tray
  put the food on the tray
saxan muusik *(nom)* cymbal
  play the cymbals
saxariir *(nom)* distress
  shame and distress
saxaro *(nom)* faeces

saxaro *(nom)* feces

saxaro *(nom)* poop

saxaro *(nom)* stool
  sit on the stool
saxarood *(act)* defecate
  the chicken has defecated everywhere

saxaroon *(act)* shit
  the child is shitting
saxgad taag ah *(nom)* rump

look at his rump
saxiib *(nom)* pal

saxiibtinimo *(adj)* friendly
a friendly child
saxiix *(nom)* sign
a sign of hope
say'i *(nom)* husband
I love my husband
Saybiiriyot *(nom)* Cypriot
the Cypriots
sayid *(nom)* master
Master Kofi
saynis *(nom)* science
we are learning science
saytuun *(nom)* guava
the guava is sweet
seeriyam *(sci)* cerium
cerium (Ce) has 58 protons
seex yar *(nom)* cutlass
give me the cutlass
seexasho *(act)* sleep
si aad u seexato habeenkii to sleep
at night
Sekondi *(nom)* Sekondi
Sekondi and Takoradi
seleeniyam *(sci)* selenium
selenium (Se) has 34 protons
Seseelwa *(nom)* Seselwa
the Seselwas
Seyjeelees *(nom)* Seychelles
go to Seychelles
shaag *(nom)* tyre

roll a tyre
shaag *(nom)* wheel
my car has four wheels
shaah *(nom)* tea
the tea is sweet
shaandho miir *(nom)* collander
der
use the collander to drain the rice
shaandho miir *(nom)* strainer

shaati/shaadh *(nom)* shirt
she is wearing a shirt
shabaga kalluumeysiga *(nom)*
fishing-net
a new fishing-net
shabakad *(nom)* network
the network light is on
shabaq *(nom)* net
a fisherman's net
shabeel *(nom)* tiger
a large tiger
shaf/xabad *(nom)* chest
chest hair
shahaado *(nom)* certificate
when you complete school you get a
certificate
shaki *(nom)* doubt
she has doubts
shalay *(adv)* yesterday
she arrived yesterday
shamac *(nom)* candle

shan *(adj)* five

shan dhaloonyinka *Five bottles*

shan geesle *(nom)* pentagon
a pentagon has five angles

shan iyo toban *(adj)* fifteen
shan iyo toban dhaloonyinka *fifteen bottles*

shan qofood *(nom)* five persons
five persons are coming

shandad *(nom)* bag
look at the bag

shandad dhar *(nom)* suitcase
a black suitcase

shaneemo *(nom)* cinema
I am going to a cinema

shaqaale *(nom)* staff
wooden staff

shaqada *(adj)* occupational

shaqeynaya *(nom)* working
working is not trivial

shaqo *(nom)* job
I need a job

shaqo wanagsan *(exc)* good job

shar leh *(adj)* wicked
you are very wicked

sharabaad *(nom)* sock
you are wearing socks

sharaf *(nom)* honor

sharaf *(act)* honour

honour the Lord

sharaf *(nom)* honour
honour and love

sharaf dhac *(nom)* disgrace, humiliation
shame and disgrace

sharaf rid *(act)* dishonor

sharaf rid *(act)* dishonour
you have dishonoured me

sharax *(act)* explain
to explain to me

sharaxaad *(nom)* explanation
the explanation is clear

sharci *(nom)* rule
she follows the rules

sharci *(nom)* law
the law says

shaxda sariirta *(nom)* bedstead
to buy a bedstead

shaydaan *(nom)* devil
don't fear devils

shaydaan *(nom)* evil
which evil is this?

sheef *(nom)* razor
sharpen the razor

sheegid *(act)* state
he stated that

sheegid *(act)* tell
he is telling the story

sheego *(act)* claim

sheekee *(act)* converse

I will converse with someone
sheeko *(nom)* fable
one does not believe fables
sheybaadh *(nom)* laboratory
hospital laboratory
Sheyniis *(nom)* Chinese
the Chinese
shid *(act)* kindle
kindle a fire
shid *(act)* switch on
switch on the radio
shiil *(act)* fry
use vegetable oil to fry fish
shil *(nom)* accident
car accident
shilin *(nom)* coin
afar shilin *four coins*
shimbir *(nom)* bird
shimbirtu way duushaa *a bird flies*

shimbir biyeed *(nom)* Comoran
the Comorans
shimbirta wiifar *(nom)* weaverbird
eight weaverbirds
shinni *(nom)* bee
shinni badan *many bees*
shir *(nom)* conference
we are going to the conference
shiraac *(nom)* canvas
a large canvas
shirkad *(nom)* company
a small company

shirweyne *(nom)* summit
mountain summit
shisheeye *(nom)* foreigner
the foreigners have arrived
Shoona *(nom)* Shona
I speak Shona
shub *(act)* pour
pour water
shuban *(nom)* diarrhoea
I have diarrhoea
shucaac *(sci)* radiation
the radiation of the sun
shucuur *(nom)* emotion

shucuur aan caadi ahayn *(nom)*
paraesthesia

shucuur aan caadi ahayn *(nom)*
paresthesia

shugux shugux *(nom)* castanet
play the castanets
shukumaan *(nom)* towel
shukumaan qoyan *wet towel*
si adag *(adv)* to-and-fro
the swing goes to-and-fro
si cad *(adv)* clearly
you see it clearly
si dag dag ah *(adv)* quickly

si dagan u seexasho *(exc)* sleep
tight

si dagdag ah *(adv)* quickly

si dahsoon u hadal *(act)* insinuate
they insinuate that

si degdeg ah u cun *(act)* devour

si dhakhso ah *(adj)* fast
a fast horse

si jilicsan *(adv)* gently
to shake gently

si kadis ah *(adv)* suddenly
it came suddenly

si miyir leh *(adj)* prudent
a prudent person

si qaniinyo ah *(adv)* pungently
smell pungently

si sax ah u adeegid *(exc)* serves you right
serves you right! come again tomorrow

si tartiib ah *(adv)* slowly
a tortoise walks slowly

si taxadir leh *(adv)* carefully
to walk carefully

si xoog leh *(adv)* strongly
I warned them strongly

Si'eera Liyoon *(nom)* Sierra Leone
go to Sierra Leone

Si'eera Liyooniyaan *(nom)* Sierra Leonean
the Sierra Leoneans

Si'eera Liyooniyaan *(nom)* Sierra Leonean
the Sierra Leoneans

sibidh *(nom)* cement
stones and cement

sida *(adv)* as
as it is

sida *(pre)* like
to think like a human

sida cad *(adv)* obviously

sida kan oo kale *(exc)* such as this
a person such as this!

sidaa darteed *(cjn)* so
why so?

siddeed iyo toban *(adj)* eighteen
siddeed iyo toban dhaloonyinka eighteen bottles

sidee *(adv)* how
how to eat

sidee tahay *(exc)* how do you are
how do you are ?

sideed *(adj)* eight
sideed dhaloonyinka Eight bottles

sideed maalmood *(nom)* eight days
wait eight days

sideed qofood *(nom)* eight per-

sons
eight persons are coming
sideed xagale *(nom)* octagon
an octagon has eight angles
sideetan *(adj)* eighty
80 bottles
sidoo kale *(adv)* also
he will also come
sidoo kale *(adv)* too
you are walking too slowly
sifeeye *(nom)* adjective
three adjectives
sifooyinka *(adj)* characteristic

sigaar *(nom)* cigarette
smoke a cigarette
sii *(act)* give
give the water to him
sii *(act)* provide

sii dayn *(act)* leak
the bucket leaks
sii wad *(act)* continue
continue the work
siib *(nom)* zip
to fasten a zip
siibasho *(act)* slip
she slipped and fell
siiboorgiyam *(sci)* seaborgium
seaborgium (Sg) has 106 protons
siidh *(nom)* melon saw
melon sed stew
siidhi *(nom)* pito

drink pito
siil *(nom)* vagina
you don't say 'vagina' in public
siin baar *(nom)* flute
play the flute
Siira Laanka *(nom)* Sri Lanka
go to Sri Lanka
Siira Laankaan *(nom)* Sri Lankan
the Sri Lankans
Siiriya *(nom)* Syria
go to Syria
Siiriyaan *(nom)* Syrian
the Syrians
siiyay *(ydy(f(act)* giveed

silfer *(sci)* silver
silver (Ag) has 47 protons
Silinge *(nom)* syringe
a nurse's syringe
silisoon *(sci)* silicon
silicon (Si) has 14 protons
silsilad *(nom)* chain
she has broken my chains
silsilad *(nom)* necklace
ivory necklace
siman *(adj)* flat
flat table
Simbaabwi *(nom)* Zimbabwe
People from Zimbabwe are called Zimbabweans
Simbaabwiyaan *(nom)* Zimbabwean
the Zimbabweans

Singabuur *(nom)* Singapore
  go to Singapore
Singabuuri *(nom)* Singaporean
  the Singaporeans
Sinigaal *(nom)* Senegal
  go to Senegal
Sinigaaliis *(nom)* Senegalese
  the Senegalese
Sinik *(sci)* zinc
  zinc (Zn) has 30 protons
sinjibiil *(nom)* ginger
  ginger soup
sino *(nom)* adultery
  adultery and divorce
sir *(nom)* secret
  I have a secret
siraad *(nom)* lantern
  turn on the lantern
sirdoon *(nom)* spy
  he is a spy
Sirkooniyam *(sci)* zirconium
  zirconium (Zr) has 40 protons
sixir *(act)* bewitch
  your love has bewitched me
sixir *(nom)* sorcery
  practise sorcery
sixroolanimo *(nom)* witchcraft
  practise witchcraft
siyaasad *(nom)* politics
  you like politics
siyaasi *(nom)* politician
  Mahama is a politician
so dhawaw *(exc)* welcome

welcome welcome!
socdaal *(nom)* journey
  a long journey
socdaal *(nom)* trip
  trip to India
socdaal marin *(act)* travel
  we are travelling to Africa
socdaale *(nom)* traveller
  four travellers
socod *(nom)* procession
  join the procession
socod baabuur *(nom)* traffic
  traffic light
socod barad *(nom)* toddler
  toddler, where are you going?
socod tamashle *(nom)* stroll
  take a stroll
soddon *(adj)* thirty
  thirty bottles
sonkor *(nom, c1)* sugar

soo bandhigaya *(nom)* offering
  we will receive an offering
soo celi *(act)* return
  to return home
soo gebogabayn *(nom)* conclusion

soo jiid *(act)* pull
  to pull the rope
soo jiidasho leh *(adj)* cunning
  a cunning woman

103

soo jiidasho leh *(adj)* ostentatious
an ostentatious dress
soo nooleyn *(nom)* revival
revival has come to town
soo noqnoqosho *(adj)* recurring
recurring disease
soo saarid *(nom)* resurrection
the resurrection of Christ
soobax *(cmd(tu(act)* come out

soodiyam *(sci)* sodium
sodium (Na) has 11 protons
Soomaali *(nom)* Somali
af Soomaali *Somali language*
Soomaaliya *(nom)* Somalia
go to Somalia
Soomaaliyaan *(nom)* Somalian
the Somalians
soomid *(nom)* fasting
prayer and fasting
soon *(act)* fast
fast and pray
Soon *(nom)* March
March has 31 days
Soonfur *(nom)* April
April has 30 days
soosali *(adj)* indigo
indigo cloth
su'aal *(nom)* question
I have a question
subag *(nom)* butter

bread and butter
subaga shiya *(nom)* sheabutter
the fragrance of sheabutter
subax *(nom)* morning
early morning
subax wanagsan *(exc)* good morning
good morning Kofi
Sucuudi Carabiya *(nom)* Saudi Arabia
go to Saudi Arabia
Sucuudi Carabiyaan *(nom)* Saudi Arabian
the Saudi Arabians
Sudaaniis *(nom)* Sudanese
the Sudanese
sugid *(act)* wait
to wait a bit
suldaan *(nom)* Lord
my soul bless The LORD
Sulu *(nom)* Zulu
Zulu language
summad *(nom)* logo
church logo
sun ah *(adj)* poisonous
a poisonous man like you
suniyaasha isha *(nom)* eyebrow
eye and eyebrow
sunta xayawaanka - sida maska *(nom)* venom
venom of a snake

sur *(act)* hang
 hang it there
surwaal *(nom)* trouser
 she wears trousers
surwaal gaaban *(nom)* shorts
 khakhi shorts
Suudaan *(nom)* Sudan
 go to Sudan
suudh *(nom)* suit
 she wears a suit
suugan *(nom)* literature

suugo *(nom)* sauce

suul *(nom)* thumb
 use your thumb to vote
suun *(nom)* belt
 black belt
suuq *(nom)* market
 go to market
suxul *(nom)* elbow
 elbows and knees
suxul *(nom)* wrist
 hold her wrist

T

taabasho *(act)* touch
 to touch her hair
taag *(nom)* hill
 hill top
taageere *(nom)* spectator
 the spectators

taageere *(nom)* supporter
 hundred supporters
taageere/maraxawad *(nom)*
fan
 electric fan
taageerid *(act)* support
 I support him
taahid *(nom)* sighing
 many sighings
taaj *(nom)* crown

Taajiik *(nom)* Tajik
 the Tajiks
Taajikistaan *(nom)* Tajikstan
 go to Tajikstan
Taakaroodi *(nom)* Takoradi
 Sekondi and Takoradi
taaliyam *(sci)* thallium
 thallium (Tl) has 81 protons
taallo *(nom)* heap
 a heap of books
Taano *(nom)* Tano
 Tano River
taantalum *(sci)* tantalum
 tantalum (Ta) has 73 protons
taariikh *(nom)* date
 which date is today?
taariikh *(nom)* history
 learn history
taariikh hore *(nom)* antiquity
 they have been here from antiquity

taas/kaas *(cjn)* that

I say that
Taay *(nom)* Thai
 the Thais
tacliiq *(act)* remark

tafaariq *(act)* retail

tafiir *(nom)* ancestor
 my ancestors
tag *(act)* get lost
 to get lost in town
tag *(act)* go
 to go to school
tag *(act)* leave
 leave it behind
tagsi *(nom)* taxi
 call me a taxi
talaabo *(nom)* action
 show me the action
tallaabo cageed *(nom)* foot-step
 follow in your mother's footsteps
tallaagad *(nom)* refrigerator
 open the fridge
tallaalid *(act)* vaccinate
 to vaccinate the child
tallabayn *(act)* step
 step on it
tallo *(nom)* advice
 a priest has advice
tallo bixi *(act)* advise
 Samia advises Olu
tamaashiir *(nom)* chalk

white chalk
tamar *(sci)* energy
 you can change mass into energy
tamashle/booqasho *(nom)* tour
 zoo tour
tamashleyn *(act)* stroll
 stroll outside
tangestin *(sci)* tungsten
 tungsten (W) has 74 protons
Tansaaniya *(nom)* Tanzania
 go to Tanzania
Tansaaniyaan *(nom)* Tanzanian
 the Tanzanians
tantooyo *(nom)* fist
 your fist
tarabuun *(nom)* crowd
 noisy crowd
tareen *(nom)* train
 ***tareen cusub** new train*
tartame *(nom)* rival
 she is my rival
tartan *(nom)* competition
 football competition
tartan *(nom)* race
 run a race
tartan *(nom)* rivalry
 stop the rivalry
tartiib *(adj)* slow
 slow tortoise
tawbad keenid *(act)* repent
 they repented
taxadir leh *(adj)* careful

a careful person
taxadirnimo *(nom)* carefulness
too much carefulness
tay *(nom)* tie
the tie hangs on his neck
Taylaan *(nom)* Thailand
go to Thailand
Taywaan *(nom)* Taiwan
go to Taiwan
Taywaaniis *(nom)* Taiwanese
the Taiwanese
teerbiyam *(sci)* terbium
terbium (Tb) has 65 protons
teerbiyam *(sci)* ytterbium
ytterbium (Yb) has 70 protons
tejnatiyam *(sci)* technetium
technetium (Tc) has 43 protons
telefishan *(nom)* television
shid telefishanka *switch on the tele-*
vision
telefoon *(nom)* phone
telefoonkeeda *her phone*
telefoon *(act)* phone
you phone me
telefoon *(nom)* telephone
house telephone
teluuriyam *(sci)* tellurium
tellurium (Te) has 52 protons
testis - unuga soo saara manida
raga *(nom)* testis
testes of a dog
tie-and-dye - waa midabaynta
garamada *(nom)* tie-and-dye

she is wearing a tie-and-dye dress
tigidh *(nom)* ticket
look at my ticket
Tigriinya *(nom)* Tigrinya
Tigrinya language
tiibey *(nom)* tuberculosis
tuberculosis is a disease
tiir *(nom)* ledge
sleep on the ledge
tiir *(nom)* pillar
build the pillars
tiitaaniyam *(sci)* titanium
titanium (Ti) has 22 protons
tijaabin *(act)* test
I was testing you
tijaabin *(act)* try
try again
tijaabo *(nom)* test
the test is difficult
tiknoolaji *(nom)* technology
new technology
tilmaame *(nom)* pointer
use the pointer
tilmaamid *(act)* signify

tima-jarasho *(nom)* haircut
I need a haircut
timo *(nom)* hair
chest hair
tin *(sci)* tin
tin (Sn) has 50 protons
tirada *(nom)* quantity
quantity of the food

tirakoob *(nom)* census

tiri *(act)* count
count money
tiro *(nom)* number
number 5
tirtir *(act)* annul
annul a marriage
tirtiran *(act)* disappear
she has disappeared
tituus *(nom)* Titus
Titus 1:1
Tiwiyaan *(nom)* Twi
Twi is an Akan language
tobabarasho *(act)* train
he will train me
tobabare *(nom)* coach
a football team coach
tobabarte xirfadeed *(nom)* apprentice
a good apprentice
toban *(adj)* ten
toban dhaloonyinka *ten bottles*
toban sanno *(nom)* decade
this decade
toban xagal leh *(nom)* decagon
a decagon has ten angles
todoba qofood *(nom)* seven persons
seven persons are coming
todoba xagal leh *(nom)* heptagon
a heptagon has seven angles

todobaad *(nom)* week
this week
todobaatan *(adj)* seventy
seventy bottles
todobo *(adj)* seven
todobo dhaloonyinka *seven bottles*

todobo iyo toban *(adj)* seventeen
todobo iyo toban dhaloonyinka *seventeen bottles*
tolid *(act)* sew
sew cloth
toobad keenid *(nom)* repentance
love and repentance
Toogaaliis *(nom)* Togolese
the Togolese
toogasho *(act)* shoot
to shoot a gun
Toogo *(nom)* Togo
go to Togo
toonta *(nom, c1)* garlic

toorirayn *(act)* stab
to stab a man
tooriyam *(sci)* thorium
thorium (Th) has 90 protons
toosan *(adj)* straight
straight road
toosi *(act)* awaken
wake him up; awaken him
toosid *(act)* wake up

toosin *(act)* straighten
straighten your dress
tubaako *(nom)* tobacco
smoke tobacco
tufaax *(nom)* apple
eat the apple
tuke *(nom)* crow
a black crow
tuko *(act)* pray
to pray for my enemies
tumaal *(nom)* blacksmith
she is a blacksmith
tumaal *(nom)* smith
a smith makes tools
tumid *(nom)* pestle
pestle and mortar
Tunuusiya *(nom)* Tunisia
go to Tunisia
Tunuusiyaan *(nom)* Tunisian
the Tunisians
turaan-turoon *(act)* stumble
she stumbled
turjumaan *(nom)* interpreter
the man needs an interpreter
turjumid *(act)* translate

turjumid *(act)* stretch
stretch the cloth
Turki *(nom)* Turkey
go to Turkey
turki *(nom)* turkey
turkey meat

Turkimeenistaan *(nom)* Turkmenistan
go to Turkmenistan
Turkimen *(nom)* Turkmen
the Turkmen
Turkish *(nom)* Turk
the Turks
turub/qof kaftama *(nom)* joker

tusaale *(nom)* example
a good example
tuse *(nom)* directory
search the phone directory
tuubada *(nom)* tap
open the tap
tuug *(nom)* thief
he is not a thief
tuugso *(act)* beg
to beg for something
tuujin *(act)* squeeze
squeeze the orange
tuuliyam *(sci)* thulium
thulium (Tm) has 69 protons
tuulo *(nom)* hamlet

tuurid *(act)* throw
*the food is spoilt so I have thrown it
away*

U

u dhexeeeya *(pre)* between
between A and B

u doodid *(nom)* advocate
four advocates
u eekaan *(act)* resemble
you resemble your sibling
u khusuucsanaan xad dhaaf ah *(nom)* adulation
she deserves adulation
u maleyn *(nom)* thought
your thoughts
u maqsuud *(act)* appreciate
you do not appreciate this
u qalan *(act)* deserve
God deserves thanksgiving
u qushuuc *(act)* admire
to admire someone
u rajeyn safar wacan *(exc)* godspeed
I wish you godspeed
u xiis *(act)* miss
I miss home
u xiisid *(nom)* miss
lady and young lady
u xoogsheegte *(nom)* bully
he is a bully
u yeel *(act)* let
let us found a group
ubax *(nom)* flower
ubax qurux badan pretty flower
ubax *(nom)* rose
a rose is a flower
ugaadhsade *(nom)* hunter
five hunters
ugu dambee *(act)* be last

you are last
ugu hor dhashay *(nom)* firstborn
my firstborn
ugu horeeya *(nom)* first
his first day
ugu muhiimsan *(adj)* main

ugu wanaagsan *(adj)* best

ugu yar *(adj)* smallest
his smallest child
ugxan *(nom)* ovary
women have two ovaries
ujeeddo *(nom)* aim
life's aim
ujeedo *(nom)* intent

ujeedo *(nom)* purpose
your purpose
ukunta beerta *(nom)* garden egg
garden egg stew
ul *(nom)* stick
break the stick
ul doon ku wadid *(nom)* paddle
canoe and paddle
unug *(nom)* cell

unug dhalid *(act)* bud
the maize is budding
unug dhalid *(nom)* bud

flower bud

unuunbetiyam *(sci)* ununpen-tium
ununpentium (Uup) has 115 protons

unuunsebtiyam *(sci)* ununsep-tium
ununseptium (Uus) has 117 protons

unuuntiriyam *(sci)* ununtrium
ununtrium (Uut) has 113 protons

ur *(nom)* smell
I sense a smell

uraya *(adj)* smelly
smelly armpit

Urdun *(nom)* Jordan
go to Jordan

Urduniyaan *(nom)* Jordanian
the Jordanians

urin *(act)* smell
to smell the flowers

urur *(nom)* association
come to the men's association meet-ing

ururi *(act)* gather
gather everyone

uruuri *(act)* collect
to collect money

USA *(nom)* USA

Usbaakistaan *(nom)* Uzbekistan
go to Uzbekistan

Usbeek *(nom)* Uzbek

the Uzbeks

usha mafiiqda *(nom)* broom-stick
ten broomsticks

uskag *(nom)* dirt
dirt and disease

Ustaraaliya *(nom)* Australia
go to Australia

uumi *(nom)* heat
the heat has arrived

uur *(nom)* pregnancy
my pregnancy is easy

uur qaad *(act)* be pregnant
I am pregnant

uuri *(act)* impregnate
You have impregnated my sister

uurka da' yarta *(nom)* teenage pregnancy
teenage pregnancy creates suffering

W

waa *(pro)* its
its house

waabberi *(nom)* dawn
we will leave here at dawn

waad mahadsan tahay *(exc)* thank you
thank you very much

waadixi *(act)* clear
clear your throat

waah *(exc)* waah
  cry waah like a baby
waalidin *(nom)* parents
  his parents
waalo *(act)* go mad
  you have gone mad
waan ka xumay *(exc)* sorry
  sorry sorry!
waan kuu xiisay *(exc)* i miss you
  I miss you
waawayn *(adj)* major
  a major town
waax *(nom)* sector

waayo *(adv)* why
  why so?
Wabriis *(nom)* July
  July has 31 days
wacdiye *(nom)* preacher
  she is a preacher
wada sahqeyn leh *(nom)* co-operative

wada shaqeyn *(nom)* cooperation
  Ghana and Togo cooperation
wadaad *(nom)* priest, pastor

wadaad *(nom)* priest, pastor

wadaad masiixi ah *(nom)* bishop
  she is a bishop

wadaag *(nom)* share
  where is my share?
wadaagid *(act)* share
  share the food
wadajir *(adv)* together
  they went together
wadan *(nom)* country
  your country
wadaninimo *(nom)* patriotism
  he has patriotism
wadanka oo dhan *(adj)* nationwide

wadar ah *(adj)* total
  the total amount
wadarta *(nom)* sum

waddo *(nom)* avenue

wadid *(act)* steer
  to steer the boat
wadiiqo *(nom)* path
  follow the path
wadne *(nom)* heart
  good heart
wado *(nom)* road
  new road
wado *(nom)* street
  new street
wado *(nom)* way
  the way
wado tareen *(nom)* railway
  a railway passes through my town

112

wado tareen *(nom)* spoor
the spoor of an animal
wado weyn *(nom)* highway
cars on a highway
waji *(nom)* face
look at my face
wakhti *(nom)* moment
the moment is up
wakhti *(nom)* time
the time is up
wakhtiga firaaqda ah *(nom)*
leisure
you have leisure?
wakhtiga lagu jiro *(nom)* duration
forty-hour duration
wakhtigii kale *(adv)* the other
time
she came the other time
wakhtiyadii hore *(nom)* ancient times
in ancient times this here was a road

wakthiga nolosha *(nom)* lifetime
in my lifetime
walaac *(nom)* concern

walaal *(nom)* brother
my only brother
walaal *(nom)* sibling
my mother's child is my sibling
walaaqid *(act)* stir

stir the porridge
walaasha *(nom)* sister
my only sister
wali *(adv)* still
still doing
walwalsan *(adj)* nervous
a nervous person
wanaag *(nom)* goodness
goodness and mercy
wanaagsan *(nom)* good
good and evil
wanagsan *(adj)* good
a good gift
waqooooyi *(nom)* north
go north
Waqooyi Kuuriyaan *(nom)* North
Korean
the North Koreans
Waqooyiga Kuuriya *(nom)* North
Korea
go to North Korea
war bixin *(nom)* report
make a report
waraabe *(nom)* hyena
two hyenas
waraaqda musqusha *(nom)* toilet roll
to buy toilet roll
waran *(nom)* spear
they pierced him with a spear
warar *(nom)* news
news of the realm
wareer *(nom)* confusion

plenty of confusion

wargeys *(nom)* newspaper
I am reading the newspaper

warwar *(nom)* worry
many worries

was *(act)* fuck

wasaarad *(nom)* ministry
ministry of education

wasakheysan *(adj)* dirty
dirty dress

wasakheysan *(adj)* filthy
the place is filthy

waw *(exc)* wow
wow! thank you!

wax *(nom)* thing
the thing; the things

wax *(pro)* something
show me something

**wax ay bini aadamku sameey-
een** *(nom)* artefact

wax cunid shanqadh sare leh
(act) slurp
she is slurping the soup

wax kamid ah *(pro)* some
give me some

wax macno daro ah *(nom)* nonsense
he talks nonsense

wax qabad *(nom)* activity
there are many activities there

wax qof loo eekaysiiyay oo

**beeraha la dhexdhigo si ay
xawayaanka uga baqadsiiso**
(nom) scarecrow
a scarecrow in a farm

wax sii sheeg *(act)* prophesy
prophesy prosperity

wax uun *(nom)* something
to hold something firmly

wax yar *(adv)* a little
wait a little

wax yeelayn *(nom)* affect

waxa *(pro)* the thing
the thing she does

waxaa *(pro)* that thing
what is that thing I got

waxaaga *(pro)* yours
Kofi, this thing is yours

waxayaga *(pos)* our
our house

waxayaga *(pro)* ours
I and Kofi, this thing is ours

waxba *(nom)* nothing
I have nothing

waxbarashada jinsigaga *(nom)*
sex education
I complet sex education

waxbarasho *(nom)* education
health and education

waxeeda *(pos)* her
her house

waxeeda *(pro)* her
show her

waxeyga *(pro)* mine
  this thing is mine
waxkasta *(pro)* everything
  everything has gone well
waxna *(adj)* any

waxooda *(pos)* their
  their house
waxooda *(pro)* theirs
  this thing is theirs
waxoogaa *(nom)* mouthful
  two morsels
waxyaabaha madaxa lagu xidho
  (nom) headgear
  put on headgear
waxyaalaha *(nom)* things
  your things
wayso *(nom)* basin
  nine basins
webi *(nom)* river
  a river goes into a sea
webi yar *(nom)* brook
  to drink from the brook
weedh *(nom)* sentence
  words join to make sentences
weli *(cjn)* yet
  the book is big yet I read all of it
weydii *(act)* ask
  to ask Kofi
weydiin *(nom)* demand
  demand and supply
weydiiye *(nom)* inquirer

weyn *(adj)* big
  Big Adae
weyn *(adj)* great
  a great name
weyn *(adj)* huge
  a huge building
wifi-da interneetka *(nom)* wifi
  my phone sees the wifi
wiil *(nom)* boy
  wiilku halkan ayuu joogaa the boy
  is here
wiil *(nom)* son
  my son
wiil aad adeer *(nom)* nephew
  my father's nephew
wiil yar *(nom)* young boy
  young boy, come here!
wiilka saxiibka ah *(nom)* boyfriend

wixiina *(pro)* youes
  the two of youes
wixiisa *(pro)* his
  this thing is his
wiyil *(nom, c1)* rhino, rhinoceros
  *maybe the aforementioned person
  has sent him*
Wolof *(nom)* Wolof
  Wolof language
wuhu *(exc)* whoa
  whoa, this man!
wuu *(pro)* he
  wuu cunaa he eats

X

xaaji *(nom)* alhaji
 he is an alhaji
xaako *(nom)* phlegm
 wipe the phlegm
xaalad *(nom)* circumstance
 my circumstances are difficult
xaas *(nom)* wife
 my wife and my children
xaas *(nom)* missus
 Missus Clinton
xaasid ah *(act)* mean
 kasahorow means "many languages"

xabsi *(nom)* prison
 go to prison
xabuub *(nom)* tomato
 laba xabuub two tomatoes
xad dhaafid *(act)* overflow
 the lake has overflowed
xad korid *(act)* overgrow
 the backyard is overgrown
xad la'aan *(nom)* infinity
 *if you divide any number by zero,
 you get infinity*
xadhig *(nom)* rope
 a long rope
xadi *(nom)* amount

xadid *(act)* steal
 steal and destroy
xafajo *(nom)* sleep crust
 wash the sleep crust from under your

eyes
xafidaad *(nom)* memorization
 some memorization is good
xafiis *(nom)* office
 the office of my mother
xaflad *(nom)* party
 I am going to a party
xaga hoose *(adv)* downward
 to go downward
xaga hoose *(pre)* under
 she will sweep under the table
xaga hore *(nom)* front
 the front of the book
xagaa *(nom)* summer
 I spend summer in Canada
xagan *(nom)* here
 go from here
xagtin *(adj)* scary
 it is scary
xagtin *(nom)* scar
 her cheek has a scar
xamaal *(nom)* porter
 the porter carries a box
xamaam *(nom)* woodpigeon
 a tiny woodpigeon
xameeti *(nom)* gall

xamo *(act)* goessip
 goessip about her
xan *(nom)* goessip
 goessip is not good
xanaaq *(nom)* anger
 calm your anger

xanaaq *(nom)* annoyance
it is an annoyance
xangulaha *(nom)* spinal cord
my spinal cord
xanuun *(nom)* pain
the pain is here
xanuun ah *(adj)* painful
illness is painful
xanuun leh *(nom)* sore
the dog is licking its sore
xanuunso *(act)* be ill
I am ill
xaqiiq ah *(adj)* real

xaqiiqdii *(cjn)* in fact
in fact it is yours
xaqiraad *(nom)* contempt
stop the contempt
xaraash *(act)* auction
to auction the house
xarig *(nom)* string
string and needle
xariif *(adj)* intelligent
an intelligent person
xariif ah *(adj)* smart

xariijimo loo sameeyay *(adj)*
striped
striped sheep
xariir *(nom)* silk
white silk
xasaasiyad *(nom)* allergy
groundnut allergy

xasaasiyad leh *(adj)* allergic
allergic skin
xasad *(nom)* envy
gred and envy
xashiish *(nom)* trash
throw away the trash
xasil *(nom)* daybreak
daybreak and nightfall
xasillan *(adj)* quiet
be quiet
xawaash kaluun bi'isaa *(nom)*
stinking fish seasoning
*add some stinking fish seasoning to
the soup*
xawayan badeed *(nom)* shrimp
four shrimps
xayasiis *(nom)* advertisement

xayawaan badeed *(nom)* porpoise
three porpoises
xayawaan dabjoog ah *(nom)*
pet
my pet
xayaysii *(act)* advertise
to advertise a product
xayaysiin *(nom)* advertisement

xeeb *(nom)* beach
beach sand
xeeb *(nom)* coast
gold coast
xeenoon *(sci)* xenon

xenon (Xe) has 54 protons
xero *(act)* pound
I pound fufu
xero *(nom)* camp
go to the camp
xero *(nom)* pound
ten pounds
xiddig *(nom)* star
 xiddigo badan *plenty of stars*
xidh *(act)* close
to close the door
xidh *(act)* shut
shut the door
xidh *(adv)* tightly
hold it tightly
xidhasho *(act)* wear
wear clothes
xidhid *(act)* switch off
switch off the light
xidid *(nom)* root
root of a tree
xidid *(nom)* vein
blood passes through veins
xidig-dhul *(nom)* hedgehog
seven hedgehogs
xifdi *(act)* memorize
to memorize
xigtada dhanka guurka *(nom)*
in-law

xigtada dhanka guurka *(nom)*
inlaw
our inlaws

xijaab *(nom)* headscarf
tie a headscarf
xilli jiilaal *(nom)* dry season
the dry season has arrived
xilli robaad *(nom)* rainy season
the rainy season has arrived
xilli roobaad *(nom)* wet season
the wet season has arrived
xiniin *(nom)* testicle
testicles of a dog
xirfad *(nom)* skill
she has good skills
xirfadoole kaftan *(nom)* jester
she is a jester
xisaab *(nom)* mathematics, maths
she teaches mathematics
xisaab *(nom)* math

xisaabaadka *(nom)* accounting

xisaabaadka *(nom)* mathematics, maths
she teaches mathematics
xisaabi *(act)* calculate

xisaabin *(nom)* computing
a computer does computing
xisaabin lacag *(nom)* account
bank account
xishonaya *(nom)* shyness

he has no shyness
xishood *(act)* be shy
　I am shy
xishoonaya *(adj)* shy
　a shy woman
xoog *(nom)* force
　he took it by force
xoog *(nom)* power
　strength and power
xoog *(nom)* strength
　strength and power
xoog leh *(adj)* strong
　a strong woman
xoog sarid *(exc)* emphasis
　I am coming!
xoog u sheegasho *(nom)* bullying
　stop the bullying
xoog u xanuujin *(act)* pinch
　stop pinching me
xoqad *(nom)* telescope
　a black telescope
xoqid *(act)* scrub
　scrub the floor well
xoriyad *(nom)* liberty
　we have liberty
xubin gollaha kamid ah *(nom)* councillor
　she is a councillor
xuddun *(nom)* navel, belly button

xudun *(nom)* navel, belly button

xudun *(nom)* umbilicus

xujo *(nom)* puzzle
　puzzles and riddles
xukun *(act)* govern
　govern Ghana
xukun *(nom)* judgement
　which judgement?
xumaan-fale *(nom)* evildoer
　we are all evildoers
xumaansho *(nom)* wickedness
　your stinginess and your wickedness

xun *(adj)* bad
　bad dog
xuquuq *(nom)* rights
　rights of humankind
xushmeyn *(act)* respect
　I respect you very much
xusuus *(nom)* memory
　computer memory
xusuusin *(act)* remind
　to remind someone
xusuuso *(act)* remember
　you remember me?
xuub caaro *(nom)* web
　the web of a spider

Y

yaanbo *(nom)* hoe
hoe and cutlass
Yaman *(nom)* Yemen
go to Yemen
Yamani *(nom)* Yemeni
the Yemenis
yar *(adj)* little
pour a little liquor
yar *(adj)* minor
a minor town
yar *(adj)* small
a small thing
yar *(nom)* little
a little is better than nothing
yaraan *(nom)* scarcity
scarcity of water
Yaraansho *(nom)* Peter
read 1 Peter 2:1
yaraant booratiinka *(nom)* kwashiorkor
kwashiorkor is a disease
yarad *(nom)* dowry
a large dowry
yaxaas *(nom)* alligator
yaxaasku wuxuu leeyahay dabo
an alligator has a tail
yaxaas *(nom)* crocodile
a crocodile likes water
Yeey *(nom)* wolf
two wolves
Yitriyam *(sci)* yttrium
yttrium (Y) has 39 protons
Yugaandha *(nom)* Uganda

go to Uganda
Yugaandhaan *(nom)* Ugandan
the Ugandans
Yuhuudi *(nom)* Israeli
the Israelis
Yukray *(nom)* Ukraine
go to Ukraine
Yukrayniyaan *(nom)* Ukrainean
the Ukraineans
yuroniyam *(sci)* europium
europium (Eu) has 63 protons
Yurub *(nom)* Europe
Europe is a continent
Yuruba *(nom)* Yoruba
Yoruba language
yuuraaniyam *(sci)* uranium
uranium (U) has 92 protons

English - Somali

A

a little *(adv)* wax yar
wait a little
abdomen *(nom)* coloosha
abdomen of a dog
Abena *(nom)* Abena - magac
Abena is my daughter
able *(adj)* awoodid
an able woman
abochi *(nom)* abochi - magaca
we are very good friends
abomination *(nom)* karaahiyo
it is an abomination
aborigine *(nom)* nin asal ah
we are the aborigines
abortion *(nom)* ilmo iska so ri-did
the doctor performs abortion
about *(pre)* ku saabsan
I think about you
above *(pre)* ka sareeya
above the house
abroad *(nom)* dibada
she goes abroad
abundant *(adj)* barwaaqaysam

academy *(nom)* akadami

accept *(act)* aqbal
accept her
acceptance *(nom)* ogolaansho
love, acceptance and forgiveness

access *(nom)* awood isticmaal
give me access
accident *(nom)* shil
car accident
accomplish *(act)* dhamee

account *(nom)* xisaabin lacag
bank account
accountability *(nom)* la xisaab-tan
responsibility and accountability

accounting *(nom)* xisaabaadka

accounts *(nom)* akoonada
she made accounts
Accra *(nom)* Akra
I am going to Accra
accusation *(nom)* ashtako
lay an accusation
accuse *(act)* eedee
they accused him
achieve *(act)* gaadh
to achieve something
achievement *(nom)* guul
your achievement is appreciated

acidic *(adj)* asiidh leh
acidic water
act *(nom)* fal
Act 1 of the play
act *(act)* matal
to act now

actinium *(sci)* aktaaniyam
 actinium (Ac) has 89 protons
action *(nom)* talaabo
 show me the action
active *(adj)* firfircoon
 an active lifestyle
activity *(nom)* wax qabad
 there are many activities there
actual *(adj)* dhabta ah

ad *(nom)* xayaysiin

add *(act)* ku dar
 add sugar
addition *(nom)* isku gayn
 1 + 1 = 2; this is addition
address *(nom)* ciwaan
 your address
adequate *(adj)* ku filan

adjective *(nom)* sifeeye
 three adjectives
adjust *(act)* hagaaji
 to adjust the door
administration *(nom)* maamul
 her administration brought progress

admire *(act)* u qushuuc
 to admire someone
admit *(act)* qir

adopt *(act)* korso
 to adopt a child

adoption *(nom)* la qabsasho
 give her up for adoption
adulation *(nom)* u khusuucsanaan
 xad dhaaf ah
 she deserves adulation
adult *(nom)* hanaqaad
 he is an adult
adultery *(nom)* sino
 adultery and divorce
advance *(adj)* heer sare
 give me an advance warning
advantage *(nom)* faa'iido
 they have an advantage
advent *(nom)* dhalasho

adverb *(nom)* fal-kaabe
 ten adverbs
advert *(nom)* xayaysiin

advertise *(act)* xayaysii
 to advertise a product
advertisement *(nom)* xayaysiin

advice *(nom)* tallo
 a priest has advice
advise *(act)* tallo bixi
 Samia advises Olu
advocate *(nom)* u doodid
 four advocates
aeroplane *(nom)* diyaarad
 two aeroplanes laba diyaaradood

affair *(nom)* arrin

123

affect *(nom)* wax yeelayn

affluent *(adj)* nolol heer sare ah

Afghan *(nom)* Afgaan
the Afghans
Afghanistan *(nom)* Afgaanistaan
go to Afghanistan
Africa *(nom)* Afrika
visit Africa
African *(nom)* Afrikaan
I am an African (person)
African *(adj)* Afrikaan
African soccer team
African *(nom)* Afrikaan
I am an African (person)
African Union *(nom)* Midowga Africa
African Union troops
afternoon *(nom)* galab
I will come in the afternoon
again *(adv)* mar labaad
see her again
age *(nom)* da'da
your age
age group *(nom)* da'aha isku dhow
your age group
aggression *(nom)* dagaal gar daro ah
too much aggression

agree *(act)* ogolow
do you agree?
ah *(exc)* ah
ah yes!
aid *(nom)* gargaar

aim *(nom)* ujeeddo
life's aim
air *(nom)* hawo
the air is blowing
airport *(nom)* garoon diyaradeed
I'm going to the airport
Ajoa *(nom)* ajoya - magac
Ajoa is my daughter
Akan *(nom)* Akaan - dad ku nool Gaana
I speak Akan
Akuapem *(nom)* Akubeen - dad ku nool koonfur bari Gaana
Akuapem is an Akan language
alert *(act)* digniin u diyaari
alert them
Algeria *(nom)* Aljeeriya
go to Algeria
Algeria *(nom)* Aljeeriya
go to Algeria
algorithm *(nom)* Algooriisam - nidaam xisaabiye oo koombuyuuter
a new algorithm
alhaji *(nom)* xaaji
he is an alhaji
all *(det)* dhamaan

all things
all *(pro)* dhamaan
all came
allergic *(adj)* xasaasiyad leh
allergic skin
allergy *(nom)* xasaasiyad
groundnut allergy
alligator *(nom)* yaxaas
*an alligator has a tail yaxaasku
wuxuu leeyahay dabo*
alligator pepper *(nom)* nooc
basbaaska kamida
*add some alligator pepper to the
food*
allow *(act)* ogolow
allow them
almighty *(adj)* awood oo dhan
leh
almighty god
Almighty *(nom)* qaadir
The Almighty
alone *(adv)* kali ah
he will go alone
alphabet *(nom)* alfabeeto
I know all the alphabet
also *(adv)* sidoo kale
he will also come
aluminium *(sci)* alumuuniyam
aluminium (Al) has 13 protons
always *(adv)* badana
he is always here
am *(tdy(je(act)* ahowaa

amazing *(adj)* yaab leh
amazing story
ambassador *(nom)* safiiir
ambassador of Kenya
ambition *(nom)* hammi

America *(nom)* Ameerika
America is a continent
American *(nom)* Mareykan
she is an American
americium *(sci)* amiriikiyam
americium (Am) has 95 protons

Amharic *(nom)* Amxaar
Amharic and Oromo
among *(pre)* ka mid ah
among people
amongst *(pre)* ku jira

amount *(nom)* xadi

ampay *(nom)* Ambaay - Buur ku
taala wadan Beeruu
let's play ampay
amuse *(act)* madadaali

amusing *(adj)* farxad leh

ancestor *(nom)* tafiir
my ancestors
anchor *(nom)* baroosin
anchor of a ship
ancient *(adj)* qadiimi ah

ancient house
ancient times *(nom)* wakhtiyadii hore
in ancient times this here was a road
and *(cjn)* iyo
Kofi and Ama Kofi iyo Ama
and *(cjn)* iyo
Kofi and Ama Kofi iyo Ama
anger *(nom)* xanaaq
calm your anger
angle *(nom)* dhinac
two angles
Angola *(nom)* Angoola
go to Angola
Angolan *(nom)* Angoolaan
the Angolans
anguish *(nom)* cidhiidhi

ankle *(nom)* canqow
your ankles
announce *(act)* ku dhawaaq
announce that
announcement *(nom)* ogeysiis
read the announcement
annoy *(act)* ka xanaaji
you are annoying me
annoyance *(nom)* xanaaq
it is an annoyance
annoying *(adj)* caro leh
it is annoying to you
annual *(adj)* sannadle ah

annul *(act)* tirtir
annul a marriage
anoint *(act)* saliid isku shub
she anointed my head with oil
answer *(act)* ka jawaabid
answer me
answer *(nom)* jawaab
give me an answer
ant *(nom)* qudhaanjo
thousands of ants
Antartica *(nom)* Antaraatiga
Antartica is a continent
antelope *(nom)* biciid
a lion likes antelope meat
anthill *(nom)* guri quraanjo
a tall anthill
antimony *(sci)* midabyo
antimony (Sb) has 51 protons
antiquity *(nom)* taariikh hore
they have been here from antiquity
ants *(nom)* qudhaanjooyin
the ants are thriving
anvil *(nom)* dubbe
hammer and anvil
any *(adj)* waxna

apathy *(nom)* arxan-darro
apathy kills good things
ape *(nom)* daanyeer
an ape and a monkey
apparition *(nom)* muuqaal
fear an apparition

appellation *(nom)* darajo
　proclaim her appellations
apple *(nom)* tufaax
　eat the apple
application *(nom)* codsi
　job application
appreciate *(act)* u maqsuud
　you do not appreciate this
apprentice *(nom)* tobabarte xir-
　fadeed
　a good apprentice
approach *(act)* ku dhawow
　to approach quickly
apricot *(nom)* khudaar
　two apricots
April *(nom)* Soonfur
　April has 30 days
are *(tdy(tu(act)* ahowtaa

area *(sci)*
　area (rectangle) = length x width

area *(nom, c2)* derisnimo

argon *(sci)* argoon
　argon (Ar) has 18 protons
argue *(act)* muran
　argue with him
argument *(nom)* dood
　many arguments
arm *(nom)* cudud
　lift up your arm
Armenia *(nom)* Armeeniya

　go to Armenia
Armenian *(nom)* Armeeniyaan
　the Armenians
armpit *(nom)* kilkilo
　smelly armpit
arrange *(act)* habee
　arrange the chairs
arrive *(act)* kaalay/imaw
　when you arrive, call me
arrogant *(adj)* iskibriya/cawaandi
　arrogant man
arrow *(nom)* falaar
　bow and arrow
arse *(nom)* dameer

arsenic *(sci)* arseenik
　arsenic (As) has 33 protons
art *(nom)* farshaxan
　food and art
artefact *(nom)* wax ay bini aadamku
　sameeyeen

artery *(nom)* halbowle dhiig
　a large artery
article *(nom)* maqaal

as *(adv)* sida
　as it is
ash *(nom)* dambas
　charcoal and ashes
Asia *(nom)* Aasiya
　Asia is a continent
ask *(act)* weydii

to ask Kofi

aspiration *(nom)* doonid
good aspirations

asset *(nom)* hanti
a good asset

assist *(act)* caawimo

assistance *(nom)* gargaaar

assistant *(nom)* caawiye
my assistant

association *(nom)* urur
come to the men's association meet-ing

astatine *(sci)* astantiin
astatine (At) has 85 protons

at *(pre)* ag
meet me at home

athlete *(nom)* orodyahan
she is an athlete

atom *(sci)* atam
an atom has a nucleus and elec-trons

attach *(act)* ku lifaaq
attach to wall

attire *(nom)* labis
your attire is beautiful

auction *(act)* xaraash
to auction the house

August *(nom)* Safar
August has 31 days

aunt *(nom)* eedo/habaryad
Aunt Ama

auntie *(nom)* eedo/habaryad

aunty *(nom)* eedo/habaryad

Australia *(nom)* Ustaraaliya
go to Australia

authoritative *(nom)* awood
she is authoritative

authority *(nom)* ammar

autism *(nom)* Ootiisam
autism is a disease

Autumn *(nom)* dayr
I spend Autumn in France

avenue *(nom)* waddo

awaken *(act)* toosi
wake him up; awaken him

award *(nom)* abaal marin
give her an award

awesome *(adj)* aad u cajiib ah
awesome God

axe *(nom)* faas
four axes

aye *(exc)* haa
Aye! Silence!

Azerbaijan *(nom)* Asarbijaan
go to Azerbaijan

Azerbaijani *(nom)* Asarbijaani
the Azerbaijanis

azonto *(nom)* jaas - laga ciyaaro Gaana
I know how to dance azonto

B

baby *(nom)* ilmo
  I have a baby waxaan leeyahay ilmo

back *(nom)* dib
  the back of the door
backyard *(nom)* daarada danbe
  the backyard is overgrown
bad *(adj)* xun
  bad dog
badge *(nom)* calaamad
  a white badge
bag *(nom)* shandad
  look at the bag
Bahrain *(nom)* Baxrayn
  go to Bahrain
Bahraini *(nom)* Baxrayni
  the Bahrainis
bake *(act)* dub
  bake bread
balderdash *(nom)* iska hadal -
maalaayacni

ball *(nom)* kubad
  play ball
balloon *(nom)* biibiile
  two balloons laba biibiile
banana *(nom)* muus
  a monkey likes bananas daany-
eerku wuxuu jecelyay muuska
Bangladesh *(nom)* Bangaaladhish
  go to Bangladesh

Bangladeshi *(nom)* Bangaaladhishi
  the Bangladeshis
bank *(nom)* bangi
  my money is at the bank
banku *(nom)* banku - cunto lagu
cuno Gaana
  you eat banku?
baptise *(act)* baabtiis
  baptise John
baptise *(act)* baabtiis
  baptise John
baptism *(nom)* babtiisam
  repentance and baptism
barb *(act)* kalluunka - sanduuqa
biyaha lagu rido
  barb hair; cut hair
bargain *(act)* gorgortan
  bargain over price
barium *(sci)* baariyam
  barium (Ba) has 56 protons
bark *(nom)* qaylo eey
  bark of a tree
barrel *(nom)* foosto
  fill up the barrel
barren *(adj)* madhalays
  barren woman
basic *(adj)* aasaasi ah

basin *(nom)* wayso
  nine basins
basket *(nom)* sallad
  carry a basket

bat *(nom)* fiidmeer
 three bats
bathe *(act)* qubayso
 to bath each morning
bathroom *(nom)* musqul
 go to the bathroom
battery *(nom)* baytariyo
 a new battery
battle *(act)* dagaalan
 we are going to battle them
battle *(nom)* dagaal
 we are going to battle
be *(act)* ahow
 You are an important person
be able to *(act)* Awoodo inuu
 I am able to climb a tree
be beautiful *(act)* noqdo mid
qurux badan
 a butterfly is beautiful
be big *(act)* noqo mid weyn
 you are big and you are high
be cooked *(act)* in la kariyo
 food is cooked
be defeated *(act)* in la jabiyo
 you were defeated
be drunk *(act)* sakhraan
 you are drunk
be emotionally charged *(act)*
noqoshada mid dareen adag
 today will be emotionally charged

be evil *(act)* noqoshada shaydaan

 abusing drugs is evil
be finished *(act)* in la dhameeyo
 the oil is finished
be fitting *(act)* inuu haboonaado
 it is fitting that
be good *(act)* In la wanaagsanaado
 prayer is good
be guilty of *(act)* in la dareemo
eed
 we are guilty
be high *(act)* in la sakhraamo
 you are big and you are high
be ill *(act)* xanuunso
 I am ill
be jealous *(act)* hinaas
 be jealous over her husband
be last *(act)* ugu dambee
 you are last
be lengthy *(act)* dheerow
 your story is lengthy
be pregnant *(act)* uur qaad
 I am pregnant
be relevant to *(act)* khusee
 it is not about me
be satisfied *(act)* qanacsanoow
 I am satisfied
be shy *(act)* xishood
 I am shy
be trivial *(act)* dhayal
 working is not trivial
be wrong *(act)* khaldanaw
 am I wrong?

beach *(nom)* xeeb
 beach sand
bead *(nom)* kuul
 good beads
beaker *(nom)* masaf
 there is water in the beaker
bean *(nom)* digir
 rice and beans bariis iyo digir
bear fruit *(act)* miro soo saar
 the tree has borne fruit
beard *(nom)* gadh
 long beard
beat *(act)* garaac
 beat someone
beautiful *(adj)* qurxoon
 it is beautiful
beauty *(nom)* qurux
 beauty and love
because *(cjn)* maxaa yeelay
 because I like you
become famous *(act)* noqo caan
 Nkrumah has become famous
bed *(nom)* sariir
 sleep on the bed Ku seexo sariirta

bedbug *(nom)* dhilqaha
 to kill bedbugs
bedroom *(nom)* qolka hurdada
 the house has two bedrooms
bedstead *(nom)* shaxda sariirta
 to buy a bedstead
bee *(nom)* shinni
 many bees shinni badan

beef *(nom)* lo'
 eat beef
beer *(nom)* khamri
 we are drinking beer
beetle *(nom, c1)* duqsiyo

befit *(act)* ku haboonow
 it befits you
before *(pre)* ka hor
 eat before (you) sleep
befriend *(act)* la saaxiib
 befriend me
beg *(act)* tuugso
 to beg for something
begin *(act)* bilaw
 start eating
beginning *(nom)* bilow
 the beginning
behaviour *(nom)* dhaqan
 normal behaviour
behind *(pre)* ka danbeeya
 go behind
behind *(nom)* danbe
 the end has neared
being *(nom)* ahaansho
 human being
belch *(act)* daac
 eat then belch
belief *(nom)* aaminsanaan

believe *(act)* rumeyso
 believe Kofi
bell *(nom)* jalas/ dawan

school bell
belly *(nom, c3)* calool

belly button *(nom, c1)* xudun

beloved *(nom)* la jecelyahey

belt *(nom)* suun
black belt
Bemba *(nom)* Bemba - dad ku nool Saambiya
Bemba language
bench *(nom)* kayd
to sit on the bench
bend *(act)* qalooci
bend it a bit
benevolence *(nom)* kalgacayl

Benin *(nom)* Biniin
go to Benin
Beninois *(nom)* Biniinoos
the Beninois
berkelium *(sci)* beerkiliyam
berkelium (Bk) has 97 protons
beryllium *(sci)* beerliyam
beryllium (Be) has 4 protons
best *(adj)* ugu wanaagsan

betray *(act)* khiyaamee
do not betray me
better *(adj)* ka wanaagsan

between *(pre)* u dhexeeeya

between A and B
bewitch *(act)* sixir
your love has bewitched me
Bhutan *(nom)* Fuutaan
go to Bhutan
Bhutann *(nom)* Fuutaani
the Bhutanns
bias *(nom)* eexasho

bible *(nom)* buug masiixi ah
the Bible and the Koran
bicycle *(nom)* baaskiil
new bicycle baaskiil cusub
big *(adj)* weyn
Big Adae
bile *(nom)* cadho
green bile
bill *(nom)* biilka

billhook *(nom)* faash
three billhooks
billion *(adj)* bilyan
a billion bottles
billy *(adj)* lab

biology *(nom)* bayoolaji
we are learning biology
bird *(nom)* shimbir
a bird flies shimbirtu way duushaa

birth *(act)* dhal
to birth twins
birth *(nom)* dhalasho

place of birth
birthday *(nom)* maalinta dhalashada
today is my birthday
bishop *(nom)* wadaad masiixi
ah
she is a bishop
bismuth *(sci)* bismat
bismuth (Bi) has 83 protons
Bissau-Guinean *(nom)* Bisow-
Giniyaan
the Bissau-Guineans
bite *(act)* qaniin
the dog can bite
bitter *(adj)* qadhaah
bitter medicine
black *(adj)* madow
black cloth
blacksmith *(nom)* tumaal
she is a blacksmith
blame *(act)* eed saar

blanket *(nom)* buste
wet blanket buste qoyan
blazing *(adj)* ololaysa
blazing fire
bleach *(act)* is cadee
*some women bleach their skins
to become fairer*
bleed *(act)* dhiig bax
he is bleeding
bleeding *(nom)* dhiigbax
stop the bleeding

bless *(act)* ducee
bless me
blessing *(nom)* barako
God's blessing
blindness *(nom)* indhoolnimo
blindness is a disease
block *(act)* jooji
to block the way
blog *(nom)* qorid/bolog gareyn
food blog
blood *(nom)* dhiig
water and blood
blow *(act)* dhirbaax
blow air
blow *(nom)* dhabar jab
give him a blow
blowfly *(nom)* cayayaan duula
blowflies are annoying
blue *(adj)* buluug
blue dress
boat *(nom)* doon
red boat doon cas
bodice *(nom)* dharka dumarka
ee qaarka sare marka laga reebo
gacmaha
she wears a bodice
body *(nom)* jidh
a person is body, soul and spirit

bohrium *(sci)* bahriyum
bohrium (Bh) has 107 protons
boil *(act)* kari
the soup is boiling

boil *(nom)* karkarin
 a boil is painful
boiled herbs *(nom)* geedo la karkariyay
 drink the boiled herbs
bold *(adj)* geesi
 a bold man
bolt *(nom)* bool

bomb *(nom)* qarax
 the bomb exploded
bone *(nom)* laf
 my hand has bones
book *(act)* is diiwaangeli
 book a ticket
book *(nom)* buug
 this book buugan
borehole *(nom)* ceel
 dig a borehole
boron *(sci)* boroon
 boron (B) has 5 protons
borrow *(act)* amaaho
 borrow money
boss *(nom)* maamule
 my boss
both *(adj)* labadaba
 both sides
bother *(act)* dhib
 you are bothering me
bother *(nom)* dhibid
 too much bother
Botswana *(nom)* Bootiswaana
 go to Botswana

bottle *(nom)* quruurad
 five bottles shan dhalooyinka
bountiful *(adj)* deeqsiya

bow *(nom)* madax foorarin
 bow and arrow
bow-legged *(adj)* cago kala baxsan
 bow-legged man
bowl *(nom)* madiibad
 a red bowl
box *(nom)* sanduuq
 box A is bigger than box B sanduuqa A ayaa ka weyn sanduuqa B

boxing *(nom)* feedh
 boxing is a sport
boy *(nom)* wiil
 the boy is here wiilku halkan ayuu joogaa
boyfriend *(nom)* wiilka saxiibka ah

brain *(nom)* maskax
 my brain
brake *(act)* jooji
 the driver has braked
brake *(nom)* joojin
 brake of a car
branch *(act)* laan
 branch here
branch *(nom)* laan
 family branch
branch *(nom)* laan

family branch

brave *(adj)* geesi
brave man

Brazzaville-Congolese *(nom)* Baraasfile-Koongaaliis
the Brazzaville-Congolese

bread *(nom)* rooti
soft bread rooti jilicsan

breadth *(nom)* baladh
breadth and width

break *(act)* jabi
break the stick

breakfast *(nom)* quraac
he will eat breakfast

breast *(nom)* naas
breast milk

breastmilk *(nom)* caanaha naaska
drink the breastmilk

breath *(nom)* neefsasho
collect your breath; rest

breathe *(act)* neefso
breathe a little; take a breather

breathe *(act)* neefso
breathe a little; take a breather

bribe *(nom)* laaluush
he wants a bribe

bribery *(nom)* laaluushid
bribery and corruption

brick *(nom)* leben
red bricks

bride *(nom)* aroosad

bride's husband; groom

bridge *(nom)* biriij
cross the bridge

brief *(adj)* kooban
let your story be brief

bright *(adj)* dhalaalaya
bright room

bring *(act)* keen
he will bring a book wuu buug keeni doonaa

broad *(adj)* balaadhan

bromine *(sci)* boromiin
bromine (Br) has 35 protons

brook *(nom)* webi yar
to drink from the brook

broom *(nom)* mafiiq
broom and dustpan mafiiq iyo jaqaf

broomstick *(nom)* usha mafi-iqda
ten broomsticks

brother *(nom)* walaal
my only brother

brown *(adj)* buni
brown bird

bruise *(act)* nabar
you swat the fly in anger and you bruise your wound

Brunei *(nom)* Burunaay
go to Brunei

Bruneian *(nom)* Buruniyaan
the Bruneians

brush *(nom)* burush garee
a black brush
bucket *(nom)* baaldi
the bucket leaks baaldigu wuu darrooraa
bud *(act)* unug dhalid
the maize is budding
bud *(nom)* unug dhalid
flower bud
budget *(nom)* miisaniyad
this year's budget
buffalo *(nom)* dibi-dibaded
one buffalo
build *(act)* dhisid
build a house
bullet *(nom)* rasaas
two bullets
bully *(nom)* u xoogsheegte
he is a bully
bully *(act)* cagajuglee
they are bullying him
bullying *(nom)* xoog u sheegasho
stop the bullying
bum *(nom)* darbi-jiif
large bum
bumblebee *(nom)* nac-naclayn
a fat bumblebee
bump into *(act)* ka hor imaansho
the car has bumped into something
bungalow *(nom)* aqal
three bungalows

burden *(nom)* culeys
very heavy burden
burglary *(nom)* jabsi
burglary is increasing
burgle *(act)* jabso
they burgled me
Burkina Faso *(nom)* Burkiina Faaso
go to Burkina Faso
Burkinabe *(nom)* Burkiinaabe
the Burkinabes
burn *(act)* gub
burn papers
burn *(act)* gub
burn papers
Burundi *(nom)* Burundi
go to Burundi
Burundian *(nom)* Burundiyaan
the Burundians
bury *(act)* aas
to bury a corpse
bus conductor *(nom)* kirishboyga baska
he's a bus conductor
bush *(nom)* baadiyaha
go into the bush
business *(nom)* ganacsi
business and politics
busy *(adj)* mashquul

but *(cjn)* laakiin
I like it, but
butcher *(nom)* hilib qale

she is a butcher
butter *(nom)* subag
bread and butter
butterfly *(nom)* balanbaalis
a butterfly is beautiful balanbaalistu way qurux badantahay
buttocks *(nom)* badhida
big buttocks
button *(nom)* butoon
press the button
buy *(act)* iibso
to buy something
buyer *(nom)* iibsade
buyers and sellers
by *(pre)* ka hor
written by a teacher
by any chance *(adv)* fursad
kasta
have you seen her by any chance?

bye *(nom)* nabadgalyeyn

C

cadmium *(sci)* kandhiyam
cadmium (Cd) has 48 protons
caesium *(sci)* kasiyam
caesium (Cs) has 55 protons
cake *(nom)* keeg
we will eat the cake
calabash *(nom)* kalabaash - geed
ka baxa maraykanka

drink from the calabash
calcium *(sci)* kalshiyam
calcium (Ca) has 20 protons
calculate *(act)* xisaabi

calculus *(nom)* kalkulas
I am learning calculus
calendar *(nom)* Jadwal taari-
ikheed/kaalandar
a new calendar
calf *(nom)* kub
every leg has a calf
calf *(nom)* kub
every leg has a calf
California *(nom)* Kaalifoorniya

californium *(sci)* kaliforniyam
californium (Cf) has 98 protons
calm *(act)* is daji
calm your anger
Cambodia *(nom)* Kaamboodhiya
go to Cambodia
Cambodian *(nom)* Kaamboodhiyaan
the Cambodians
came *(ydy(f(act)* way ... kaalay-
tay

camel *(nom)* geel
six camels
camera *(nom)* kamarad
lens of a camera

Cameroon *(nom)* Kamaruun
 go to Cameroon
camisole *(nom)* garanka dumarka

camp *(nom)* xero
 go to the camp
can *(act)* awood
 I can read
can *(act)* awood
 I can read
Canada *(nom)* Kanada
 I spend the summer in Canada
cancel *(act)* jooji
 cancel the meeting
cancer *(nom)* kansar
 the cancer has disappeared
candle *(nom)* shamac

candy *(nom)* nacnac

cane *(nom)* bakoorad
 bring the cane
cannon *(nom)* madfac
 shoot the cannon
canoe *(nom)* huudhi
 canoe and paddle
canvas *(nom)* shiraac
 a large canvas
capable *(adj)* awoodi kara
 a capable woman
capital *(nom)* caasimad
 Accra is the capital of Ghana
capital *(nom)* caasimad

Accra is the capital of Ghana
capsid *(nom)* kaabsid - galka booratiinka ee fayraska
 capsids eat cocoa trees
captain *(nom)* kabtan
 she is a captain
car *(nom)* baabuur
 drive a car kaxee baabuur
carbon *(sci)* kaarbon
 carbon (C) has 6 protons
carcass *(nom)* raq
 the carcass is rotting
card *(nom)* kaadh
 a white card
care *(act)* daryeel

careful *(adj)* taxadir leh
 a careful person
carefully *(adv)* si taxadir leh
 to walk carefully
carefulness *(nom)* taxadirnimo
 too much carefulness
caress *(act)* salaaxid
 her hand caresses it
Caribbean *(nom)* Kaaribiyaan
 go to the Caribbean
carpenter *(nom)* njiaar
 he is a carpenter
carpentry *(nom)* nijaarnimo
 she knows carpentry
carpet *(nom)* roog
 new carpet
carrot *(nom)* kaarood

four carrots
carry *(act)* qaadid
carry the book
cartoon *(nom)* kartoon
new cartoons
carve *(act)* goo
carve the wood
cash *(nom)* lacag kaash ah
I have cash
cassava *(nom)* baradho macaan
plantain and cassava
cast *(nom)* qanid
cast of a film
castanet *(nom)* shugux shugux
play the castanets
castle *(nom)* qalcad
the white castle
cat *(nom)* bisad
a cat has a tail bisadu waxay leeda-hay dabo
catarrh *(nom)* axal
I have catarrh
catch *(act)* qabo
catch the ball
category *(nom)* qeyb
five categories
caterpillar *(nom)* dirindir
a caterpillar becomes a butterfly

cause itchiness *(act)* sababid
cuncun
the medicine causes itchiness
cedi *(nom)* halbeeg - lacageed

oo laga isticmaalo Gaana
hundred pesewas make one cedi

cedi *(nom)* halbeeg - lacageed
oo laga isticmaalo Gaana
hundred pesewas make one cedi

celery *(nom)* khudaar laamo leh
eat the celery
cell *(nom)* unug

cement *(nom)* sibidh
stones and cement
census *(nom)* tirakoob

centipede *(nom)* dirxi lugo badan leh
look at the centipede
Central African *(nom)* Afrikaan Dhexe
the Central Africans
Central African Republic *(nom)* Jamhuuriyada Afrikada Dhexe
go to Central African Republic
centre *(nom)* dhexe
be in the centre
century *(nom)* qarni
this century
cerium *(sci)* seeriyam
cerium (Ce) has 58 protons
certificate *(nom)* shahaado
when you complete school you get a certificate

139

Chad *(nom)* Jaad - wadan Afrikaan
ah
go to Chad
Chadian *(nom)* Jaadiyaan
the Chadians
chain *(nom)* silsilad
she has broken my chains
chair *(nom)* kursi
arrange the chairs habbee Kuraasta

chairman *(nom)* gudoomiye

chairperson *(nom)* qofka gudoomiyaha ah
she is the chairperson
chairwoman *(nom)* gabadha
gudmooyaha ah

chalk *(nom)* tamaashiir
white chalk
challenge *(nom)* caqabad
a good challenge
chameleon *(nom)* maansalugaleyda
I see the chameleon
chamomile *(nom)* jaamomayl -
geed yuribiyaan ah oo ubax soo
saara
chamomile tea
champion *(nom)* qof/koox horyaal ah
she is a champion
change *(act)* badal

*if time changes, change with the
times*
change *(nom)* badal
do you have change?
chaotic *(adj)* nidaam daran
the place is chaotic
chapter *(nom)* cutub
chapter 12
character *(nom)* qof/dabeecad
her character
characteristic *(adj)* sifooyinka

charcoal *(nom)* dhuxul
sack of charcoal
charge *(sci)* lacag bixin
*electricity has positive charge and
negative charge*
chariot *(nom)* jaariyot
chariot of iron
chase *(act)* eryasho
no one is chasing him
cheap *(adj)* jaban
be cheap
cheat *(act)* khiyaamee
don't cheat me
cheater *(nom)* khiyaame
they are cheaters
check *(nom)* hubi

cheek *(nom)* dhaban
fat cheeks
cheese *(nom)* burcad
blue cheese

cheetah *(nom)* haramcad
a cheetah is an animal
chef *(nom)* kuug
a good chef
cheque *(nom)* hubin
write a cheque
chest *(nom)* shaf/xabad
chest hair
chew *(act)* calaali
to chew groundnuts
Chewa *(nom)* Jeewa - luqad lagaga hadlo wadano badna oo Afrikaan
ah
Chewa language
chicken *(nom)* digaagad
chicken meat hilib digaag
chickenpox *(nom)* bus-buska
chickenpox is a disease
chief *(nom)* hogaamiye
she is a chief
chieftain *(nom)* qofka hogaamiyaha
dad ama qabiil

child *(nom)* ilmo
my mother's child is my sibling
childbirth *(nom)* dhalashada
ilmo
a childbirth brings joy
childhood *(nom)* carruurnimo
my childhood
children *(plural(nom)* ilmo

chimpanzee *(nom)* daanyeer

I saw a chimpanzee
chin *(nom)* gar
hold your chin
China *(nom)* Jayna
go to China
Chinese *(nom)* Sheyniis
the Chinese
chisel *(nom)* qalab wax lagu jaro
hammer and chisl
chives *(nom)* jayfis - geed yar
oo ka baxa Yuuroraashiya
chives and onions
chloride *(sci)* koloraydh
sodium chloride
chlorine *(sci)* koloriin
chlorine (Cl) has 17 protons
chocolate *(nom)* Jokolaynt
the chocolate has become cheap

choice *(nom)* doorasho

choose *(act)* dooro

Christ *(nom)* Masiix
Jesus Christ!
Christian *(nom)* Masiixi
a Christian and a Muslim
Christianity *(nom)* Masiixin-
imo
Christianity and Islam
Christmas *(nom)* Ciida masiix-
iga
Christmas is coming

chromium *(sci)* koromiyam
chromium (Cr) has 24 protons
chronic *(adj)* raaga

church *(nom)* kiniisad
go to church
cigarette *(nom)* sigaar
smoke a cigarette
cilantro *(nom)* Koryaander
cilantro is a plant
cinema *(nom)* shaneemo
I am going to a cinema
cinnamon *(nom)* qorfe
cinnamon is fragrant
circle *(nom)* goobo
three circles
circumstance *(nom)* xaalad
my circumstances are difficult
citizen *(nom)* muwaadin
I am a citizen
civil war *(nom)* dagaal sokeeye
stop the civil war
civilized *(adj)* ilbaxay
a civilized world
claim *(act)* sheego

clap *(act)* sacabi
to clap for Yaa
class *(nom)* fasal
he is in class 2
clay *(nom)* dhoobo
clay vase
clean *(act)* nadiifi

clean your teeth
clear *(act)* waadixi
clear your throat
clearly *(adv)* si cad
you see it clearly
clever *(adj)* xariif ah

click *(act)* guji
click here
clinic *(nom, c1)* cusbitaal

clock *(nom)* saacad
tell me the time on the clock
close *(act)* xidh
to close the door
cloth *(nom)* dhar
wear cloth
clothes *(nom)* dhar
buy clothes libso dhar
cloud *(act)* daruur
the sky has clouded
cloud *(nom)* daruur
a white cloud daruur cad
cloudy *(adj)* daruuro leh
a cloudy day
clove *(nom)* dhego yare
add some cloves to the food
clown *(nom)* qof dadka ka qosliya

coach *(nom)* tobabare
a football team coach
coast *(nom)* xeeb
gold coast

coat *(nom)* koodh
she is putting on a coat
cobalt *(sci)* kobalt
cobalt (Co) has 27 protons
cobra *(nom)* kubra
black cobra
cockerel *(nom)* diig yar
a cockerel is crowing
cockroach *(nom)* baranbaro
I see a cockroach
cocoa *(nom)* geed shukulaato ah
cocoa tree
coconut *(nom)* qumbe
two coconuts
code *(nom)* kood
to write code
coffee *(nom)* qaxwe
she drinks coffee
coin *(nom)* shilin
four coins afar shilin
cold *(adj)* qabow
cold water
collander *(nom)* shaandho miir
use the collander to drain the rice

colleague *(nom)* qof aad wada shaqeysaan
your colleagues
collect *(act)* uruuri
to collect money
college *(nom)* kulliyad
where is the college?

color *(nom)* midab

colour *(act)* midabee
colour and learn
colour *(nom)* midab
seven colours
comb *(nom)* garfeedh
use a comb to comb your hair
comb *(act)* feedh
use a comb to comb your hair
combine *(act)* isku dar

come *(act)* kaalay
to come here
come *(act)* kaalay
to come here
come *(cmd(tu(act)* kaalay

comfort *(nom)* raaxo
give me comfort
coming *(nom)* imanaya
the second coming
comma *(nom)* hakad
comma and fullstop
command *(act)* ammar
to command a soldier
command *(nom)* amrid
give him a command
commend *(act)* ammaan
commend her
commerce *(nom)* ganacsi

community *(nom)* bulsho

to integrate a new family into the community

Comoran *(nom)* shimbir biy-eed
the Comorans

company *(nom)* shirkad
a small company

compassion *(nom)* naxariis
she has compassion

compensation *(nom)* magdhow
have you received your compensation?

competent *(adj)* awood xirfadeed leh

competition *(nom)* tartan
football competition

computer *(nom)* kuumbuyu-uter
computer keyboard kiiboodhka kuumbuyuuterka

computing *(nom)* xisaabin
a computer does computing

concern *(nom)* walaac

conclude *(act)* gabagabee

conclusion *(nom)* soo gebogabayn

concubine *(nom)* adoon
Yaa is my concubine

condom *(nom)* kondhom
wear a condom

conference *(nom)* shir
we are going to the conference

conference *(nom)* shir
we are going to the conference

confidence *(nom)* kalsooni
I have confidence

confusion *(nom)* wareer
plenty of confusion

congenial *(adj)* qof wacan
a congenial place

Congo *(nom)* Koongo
go to Congo

Congo-Brazzaville *(nom)* Koongo-Baraasifiile
go to Congo-Brazzaville

Congo-Kinshasa *(nom)* Koongo-Kinshaasa
go to Congo-Kinshasa

conjunctivitis *(nom)* daaf
conjunctivitis is a disease

conqueror *(nom)* guuleyste
she is a conqueror

conscience *(nom)* damiir
your conscience

consent *(act)* ogolaansho sii

consequence *(nom)* cawaaqib
its consequences

consist *(act)* ka koobnaw
water consists of hydrogen and oxygen

consolation *(nom)* gargaarid
love and consolation

construct *(act)* dhis
  he has constructed a new machine

contempt *(nom)* xaqiraad
  stop the contempt
continent *(nom)* qaarad
  African continent
continue *(act)* sii wad
  continue the work
controversy *(nom)* khilaaf

converse *(act)* sheekee
  I will converse with someone
cook *(act)* kari
  cook a little rice
cool *(act)* qabooji
  the food has cooled
cool *(act)* qabooji
  the food has cooled
cool *(act)* qabooji
  the food has cooled
cool *(adj)* qabow
  a cool beer
cooperation *(nom)* wada shaqeyn
  Ghana and Togo cooperation
cooperative *(nom)* wada sahqeyn
leh

copernicium *(sci)* kobarnishiyam
  copernicium (Cn) has 112 protons

copper *(sci)* kopar
  copper (Cu) has 29 protons

coriander *(nom)* Koryaander
  you can eat coriander
corn *(nom)* galley
  corn and groundnuts
corner *(nom)* dhinaca
  the table is in the corner
corners *(nom)* dhinacyada
  all corners of the world
corpse *(nom)* meyd
  the corpse is rotting
corpse *(nom)* meyd
  the corpse is rotting
corpse *(nom)* meyd
  the corpse is rotting
corruption *(nom)* musuq-maasuq
  bribery and corruption
cost *(nom)* qiime
  price = cost + profit
Cote d'Ivoire *(nom)* Ayfri Koost
  go to Cote d'Ivoire
cottage *(det, c1)*

cotton *(nom)* cudbi
  cloth of cotton
cotton *(nom)* cudbi
  cloth of cotton
couch *(nom)* fadhi
  the red couch
cough *(act)* qufac
  to cough profusely
cough *(nom)* qufac
  he has a cough
could *(ydy(f(act)* way ... awood-

tay

councillor *(nom)* xubin gollaha kamid ah
she is a councillor

count *(act)* tiri
count money

country *(nom)* wadan
your country

courage *(nom)* dhiirigelin
she has courage

courageous *(adj)* dhiirigelin badan

court *(nom)* maxkamad
I am going to court

courtship *(nom)* isjeclaansho laba qof
courtship and marriage

covenant *(nom)* axdi
a new covenant

cover *(act)* dabool
cover it up

cover *(act)* dabool
cover it up

cover *(nom)* jaldi

covetuousness *(nom)* hunguri
covetuousness is not good

cow *(nom)* lo'
cow meat; beef hilibka lo'da

cowhide *(nom)* haraga lo'da
waache and cowhide

cowhide *(nom)* haraga lo'da

waache and cowhide

cowry *(nom)* aleelaxay
five cowries

crab *(nom)* carsaanyo
crab soup

crawl *(act)* gurguuro
the child is crawling

create *(act)* abuur
create something new

creation *(nom)* abuuritaan
all creation

creative *(adj)* hal abuurnimo leh
a creative person

creator *(nom)* abuure
creator god

cripple *(nom)* curyaan
he is a cripple

crocodile *(nom)* yaxaas
a crocodile likes water

cross *(act)* ka gudub
cross the stream

cross *(nom)* ka gudbid
the cross of Christ

crow *(act)* cida diiga
a cockerel is crowing

crow *(nom)* tuke
a black crow

crowd *(nom)* tarabuun
noisy crowd

crown *(nom)* taaj

crown *(nom)* taaj

crumble *(act)* burburi
　the house crumbled
cry *(act)* ooy
　to cry each time
crystal *(nom)* qarsho dabiici ah
　a beautiful criestal
cube *(nom)* cunto jarjarid
　a cube of sugar
cubit *(nom)* dhudhun
　three cubits
culture *(nom)* dhaqan
　the culture of my school
cumin *(nom)* kamuun
　cumin grows in Asia
cunning *(adj)* soo jiidasho leh
　a cunning woman
cup *(nom)* koob
　tea cup koobka shaaha
cup *(act)* koob
　her hand is cupped over her mouth

curium *(sci)* kuraniyam
　curium (Cm) has 96 protons
currency *(nom)* lacag

curse *(act)* inkaar
　do not curse me
curse *(nom)* habaar
　a prayer and a curse
curse *(act)* inkaar
　do not curse me
curtain *(nom)* daah

　the window needs a curtain
custom *(nom)* caado
　love is a good custom
customer *(nom)* macmiil
　a good customer
cut *(act)* jar
　to cut the cake in two
cut ties *(act)* ka hadh
　he and I have cut ties
cutlass *(nom)* seex yar
　give me the cutlass
cymbal *(nom)* saxan muusik
　play the cymbals
Cypriot *(nom)* Saybiiriyot
　the Cypriots
Cyprus *(nom)* Qubrus
　go to Cyprus

D

daily *(adv)* malin kasta
　he comes here daily
damsel *(nom)* gabadh aan gu-ursan
　this damsel is pretty
dance *(act)* jaas
　to dance with joy
dancing *(nom)* jaas
　singing and dancing
danger *(nom)* khatar
　I see danger
danger *(nom)* khatar
　I see danger

dangerous *(adj)* khatar ah
 a dangerous game
dark *(adj)* madow
 dark night
darkness *(nom)* madow
 night brings darkness
darmstadtium *(sci)* darmastiyam
 darmstadtium (Ds) has 110 pro-
 tons
date *(nom)* taariikh
 which date is today?
date *(act)* la haasow
 will you date me?
daughter *(nom)* gabadh
 my daughter
dawn *(nom)* waabberi
 we will leave here at dawn
dawn *(nom)* waabberi
 we will leave here at dawn
day *(nom)* maalin
 the day has arrived
daybreak *(nom)* xasil
 daybreak and nightfall
dead *(adj)* dhintay
 a dead tree
dear *(nom)* gacaliye/gacaliso
 don't worry dear
death *(nom)* dhimasho
 place of death
debate *(nom)* dood
 the debate is starting
debt *(nom)* deyn

 he has many debts
decade *(nom)* toban sanno
 this decade
decagon *(nom)* toban xagal leh
 a decagon has ten angles
deceive *(act)* khiyaameyn

December *(nom)* Rajalood sedex
 December has 31 days
deception *(nom)* khiyaamid
 deception and discord
decision *(nom)* go'aan
 a good decision
deduct *(act)* ka jar
 deduct one from two
deep *(adj)* qoto dheer
 a deep hole
deer *(nom)* deero
 a lion likes deer meat
defeat *(nom)* jabin
 victory and defeat
defecate *(act)* saxarood
 the chicken has defecated every-
 where
defect *(nom)* cillad
 the building has many defects
defile *(act)* nijaasee
 do not defile yourself
definition *(nom)* qeexitaan
 a good definition
deflate *(act)* naqaska kasii daa
 your tyre is deflating
delay *(act)* dib u dhig

you have delayed

delightful *(adj)* rayrayn leh
delightful work

deliver *(act)* keen
deliver money to me

delivery *(nom)* ka dhalin/keenid
the delivery has arrived

demand *(nom)* weydiin
demand and supply

democracy *(nom)* dimuqraadiyad
peace and democracy

deny *(act)* beeni
you cannot deny the truth

depart *(dtv)* ka tag
depart from here

dependable *(adj)* la isku aamini karo
dependable god

deplete *(act)* baabii
the water is deplet

depth *(nom)* baaxad
the depth of a well

descend *(act)* dag
descend to the ground

desert *(nom)* lama degaan
water is scarce in the desert

deserve *(act)* u qalan
God deserves thanksgiving

desirable *(adj)* la rabi karo
it is desirable

desire *(act)* rab
I desire a banana

desire *(nom)* rabitaan

your heart's desire

desperation *(nom)* quus

destiny *(nom)* qadar
a good destiny

destroy *(act)* burburi
destroy everything

determination *(nom)* go'aansasho
we will do it with determination

development *(nom)* horumar
good development

device *(nom)* aalad
a phone is a device

devil *(nom)* shaydaan
don't fear devils

devour *(act)* si degdeg ah u cun

dew *(nom)* dhado
morning dew

dewdrop *(nom)* dhibic dhado ah
many dewdrops

diamond *(nom)* dheeman
a white diamond

diarrhoea *(nom)* shuban
I have diarrhoea

dick *(nom)* gus

dictionary *(nom)* qaamuus
picture dictionary

did *(ydy(i(act)* wuu ... sameeay

die *(act)* dhimo
 to die young in the play
different *(adj)* ka duwan
 different things
difficult *(adj)* adag
 the exam is difficult
difficulty *(nom)* adkaansho

dig *(act)* qod
 to dig a hole
dimwit *(adj)* qof nacas ah
 Fool! Dimwit!
dine *(act)* cun casho

Dinka *(nom)* Dinka - dadka ku nool Suudaan
 cmd(tu(act:write)) nom:Dinka
directory *(nom)* tuse
 search the phone directory
dirt *(nom)* uskag
 dirt and disease
dirty *(adj)* wasakheysan
 dirty dress
disappear *(act)* tirtiran
 she has disappeared
disappoint *(act)* niyad jab
 my lover has disappointed me
disappointment *(nom)* niyad-jab
 love has disappointment
discard *(act)* ka reebid
 discard the ball
disciple *(nom)* qof masiix raa-

cay nolishiisa

discipline *(act)* edbin
 discipline your child
discord *(nom)* fasir
 lies and discord
discreet *(adj)* digtoon

disease *(nom)* cudur
 heal disease
disgrace *(act)* ceebayn
 you are disgracing yourself
disgrace *(nom)* sharaf dhac
 shame and disgrace
disgusting *(adj)* karaahiyo ah
 the place is disgusting
dish *(nom)* bileedh
 meydh bileedhkaaga
dishevelled *(adj)* qof aan nadiif ahayn
 dishevelled self
dishonor *(act)* sharaf rid

dishonour *(act)* sharaf rid
 you have dishonoured me
disorder *(nom)* cudur

disposition *(nom)* ku wareejin
 a person's disposition
dispute *(act)* khilaaf
 dispute him
diss *(act)* dhaleecayn
 diss someone

diss *(nom)* cay
 it is not a diss
distinguished *(adj)* kala garasho
 a distinguished frog
distinguished *(nom)* kala saaray
 a distinguished frog
distress *(nom)* saxariir
 shame and distress
distressed *(adj)* dhibaateysan
 a distressed mind
ditch *(nom)* booraan
 there is water in the ditch
diverse *(adj)* kala duduwan
 a diverse group
diversity *(nom)* kala duwanaan
 diversity gives a group strength

divide *(act)* qeybi
 divide the bread
divine *(adj)* Rabaani ah
 divine power
division *(nom)* qeyb
 2/1 = 2; this is division
divorce *(nom)* isfuris (laba isqaba)
 marriage and divorce
divorce *(nom)* isfuris (laba isqaba)
 marriage and divorce
Djibouti *(nom)* Jabuuti
 go to Djibouti
Djiboutian *(nom)* Jabuutiyaan
 the Djiboutians
do *(act)* samee
 she is doing something

doctor *(nom)* dhakhtar
 she is a doctor
doctor *(act)* dhakhtar
 they have doctored the thing
document *(nom)* dhokumenti

dog *(nom)* eey
 a dog barks
doll *(nom)* caruusad
 my doll caruusadayda
dollar *(nom)* doolar
 ten dollars
donate *(act)* ku tabaruc
 let us donate to them
done *(done$_t$ dy(i(act) samee*

donkey *(nom)* dameer
 ten donkeys
door *(nom)* albaab
 close the door xidh albaabka
doubt *(nom)* shaki
 she has doubts
doubt *(act)* ka shaki

dough *(nom)* cajiin
 he pressed the dough
dove *(nom)* qoolley
 white dove
down *(adv)* hoos
 go down
downstairs *(adv)* dabaqa hoose
 he is downstairs
downward *(adv)* xaga hoose*

to go downward

dowry (nom) *yarad*
  a large dowry

doze (act) *casayso*
  you are dozing

drain (act) *dareeri*
  use the collander to drain the rice

drama (nom) *riwaayad*
  I like drama films

drank (ydy(i(act) *wuu ... cabay*

draughts (nom) *qoraal qabyo ah*
  play draughts

draw (act) *sawir*
  draw a bird

drawers (nom) *khaanado*
  are you wearing drawers?

drawing (nom) *sawir*
  my new drawing

dream (act) *riyood*
  to dream a lot

dream (nom) *riyo*
  many dreams

dress (nom) *dhar*
  blue dress

drink (act) *cab*
  to drink water

drive (act) *kaxee*
  drive a car

driver (nom) *darawal*
  the driver has braked

drop (nom) *dhibic*

drop by drop a chicken drinks water

drown (act) *qarqan*
  to drown quickly

drowsiness (nom) *hurdo heyso*

drum (nom) *durbaan*
  I hear the drums

drummer (nom) *durbaan tume*
  she is a drummer

drunkard (nom) *sakhraan*
  he is a drunkard

drunkenness (nom) *sakhraanimo*
  drunkenness and pain

dry (act) *qalal*
  to dry clothes

dry (adj) *qalalan*
  dry land

dry season (nom) *xilli jiilaal*
  the dry season has arrived

dubnium (sci) *dubniyam*
  dubnium (Db) has 105 protons

duck (nom) *boolonboolo*
  white duck

dumb (adj) *aan hadli karin/doqon*

dump (nom) *qashin qub*
  rubbish dump

dumpling (nom) *cunto cajiin ka sameysan*
  we are eating Chinese dumplings

dung (nom) *digo*

cow dung
duration *(nom) wakhtiga lagu jiro*
 forty-hour duration
durbar *(nom) maxkamada hindiyaan*
 ah
 we will go to the durbar
dust *(nom) dhas*
 red dust
dustpan *(nom) jaqaf*
 broom and dustpan
dwarf *(nom) cilin*
 seven dwarves
dye *(nom) midabeyn*
 black dye
dysmenorrhoea *(nom) caado cal-*
 lool xun wadata
 I have dysmenorrhoea
dysprosium *(sci) dhisoboriyam*
 dysprosium (Dy) has 66 protons

E

each and everyone *(pro) mid*
 kasta iyo qofkasta
 each and everyone came
eagle *(nom) gorgor*
 two eagles
ear *(nom) dhag*
 ear and nose
early *(adv) hore*
 come early

early *(adj) hore*
 early morning
earpiece *(nom) dhag la gashto*
 new earpiece
earring *(nom) dhago la gashto -*
 sida dahabka
 he wears earrings
earth *(nom) dhulka*
 people of the earth
earthenware *(nom) jalxad*

earthquake *(nom) dhul gariir*
 big earthquake
east *(nom) dhulalka bariga*
 go east
East Timor *(nom) Bariga Taymor*
 go to East Timor
East Timorese *(nom) Bariga Tay-*
 moriis
 the East Timorese
easy *(adj) fudud*
 the exam is easy
eat *(act) cun*
 to eat everything *si aad wax kasta*
 u cunto
eaten $(done_t dy(i(act, c3)cun$

ebola *(nom) cudurka ebola*
 ebola is a disease
ebony *(nom) qof madow*
 black ebony
economy *(nom) dhaqaale*
 the economy of Africa

eczema (nom) *cambaar*
  eczema is a skin disease
education (nom) *waxbarasho*
  health and education
eel (nom) *kalluun*
  seven eels
effect (nom) *saamayn*

effort (nom) *dadaal*
  a good effort
Efua (nom) *magac hableed - laga
  isticmaalo Gaana*
  Efua is my daughter
egg (nom) *beed*
  chicken egg beedka digaaga
eggplant (nom) *miro ukun u eeg
  oo la cuno*
  eggplant stew
Egypt (nom) *Masar*
  go to Egypt
Egyptian (nom) *Masaari*
  the Egyptians
Eid (nom) *Ciid*
  Eid is a holiday
eight (adj) *sideed*
  Eight bottles sideed dhaloonyinka

eight days (nom) *sideed maalmood*
  wait eight days
eight persons (nom) *sideed qofood*
  eight persons are coming
eighteen (adj) *siddeed iyo toban*

*eighteen bottles siddeed iyo toban
  dhaloonyinka*
eighty (adj) *sideetan*
  80 bottles
einsteinium (sci) *iinseetiniyam*
  einsteinium (Es) has 99 protons
Ekua (nom) *magac hableed - laga
  isticmaalo Gaana*
  Ekua is my daughter
elastic (adj) *laastiig*
  elastic string
elbow (nom) *suxul*
  elbows and knees
elder (adj) *duq*
  my elder sibling
elder (nom) *qof weyn*
  the elders
electric (adj) *koronto*
  electric light
electricity (sci) *koronto*
  *electricity is when charges go from
  one place to a new place*
electron (sci) *koronto*
  an electron has a charge of -1
elephant (nom) *maroodi*
  *an elephant is very big marood-
  igu aadbuu u weyn yahay*
eleven (adj) *kow iyo toban*
  eleven bottles kow iyo toban dhaloonyinka

eleventh (adj) *koob iyo tobnaad*
  eleventh house
email (nom) *iimayl*

print the email

embrace *(act)* hab sii

  embrace me

emotion *(nom)* shucuur

empathy *(nom)* u damqasho

  she has such empathy

emphasis *(exc)* xoog sarid

  I am coming!

empty *(adj)* madhan

  empty bucket

encourage *(act)* dhiiri geli

  encourage her

encouragement *(nom)* dhiirigelin

  encouragement and joy

end *(nom)* dhamaad

  the end has come

end *(act)* dhamee

  you will end the war

enema *(nom)* hanaanka gelinta hawo

  ama dareere malawadka

  I need an enema

enemy *(nom)* cadow

  enemies will tire

energetic *(adj)* firfircoon

  an energetic dog

energy *(sci)* tamar

  you can change mass into energy

engine *(nom)* injiin

  a new engine

engineer *(nom)* injineer

  an engineer makes tools

England *(nom)* Ingiriiska

  I spend spring in England

English *(nom)* Ingiriis

  I speak English

enmity *(nom)* colnimo

  great enmity

enter *(act)* gal

  enter into the room

entertain *(act)* maweeli

  entertain yourself

entertaining *(adj)* madadaalo leh

  it is entertaining

entire *(adj)* gebi ahaanba

  the entire house

entry *(nom)* gelitaan

  a new entry in the book

envy *(nom)* xasad

  gred and envy

equal *(adj)* lamid ah

Equatorial Guinea *(nom)* Iqwaatooriyaal Gini

  go to Equatorial Guinea

erbium *(sci)* eerbiyasm

  erbium (Er) has 68 protons

Eritrea *(nom)* Ereteriya

  go to Eritrea

Eritrea *(nom)* Ereteriya

  go to Eritrea

Eritrean *(nom)* Ereteriyaan

  the Eritreans

err *(act)* qaldan

  I have erred

espionage *(nom)* basaasnimo
  espionage films
essential *(adj)* muhiim ah

estimate *(act)* qiyaas
  estimate your height
eternity *(nom)* daa'in
  from now to eternity
Ethiopia *(nom)* Itoobiya
  go to Ethiopia
Ethiopian *(nom)* Itoobiyaan
  the Ethiopians
Europe *(nom)* Yurub
  Europe is a continent
europium *(sci)* yuroniyam
  europium (Eu) has 63 protons
evening *(nom)* fiid
  evening meal; dinner
event *(nom)* dhacdo
  the event has started
everlasting *(adj)* jiraya/waaraya

every *(adj)* kasta

everything *(pro)* waxkasta
  everything has gone well
everywhere *(pro)* meel kasta
  everywhere is hot
evil *(nom)* shaydaan
  which evil is this?
evildoer *(nom)* xumaan-fale
  we are all evildoers
Ewe *(nom)* lax dhedig ah

Ewe language
exam *(nom)* imtixaan
  the exam is easy
example *(nom)* tusaale
  a good example
except *(cjn)* marka laga reebo
  except God
except that *(cjn)* marka laga reebo
taas
  except that I want salt
exchange *(act)* kala badal

excuse me *(exc)* iga rali ahaw
  Sorry. Excuse me.
excuse my language *(cjn)* ka rali
ka noqo luqadayda
  excuse my language, shit smells
  but someone collects it
executioner *(nom)* dile - qofka dila
dadka dil tooagsho lagu xukumo
  the king's executioner
exit *(act)* ka bax
  pass here to exit
expand *(act)* balaari

expensive *(adj)* qaali ah
  it is expensive
experience *(nom)* khibrad
  she has experience
explain *(act)* sharax
  to explain to me
explanation *(nom)* sharaxaad
  the explanation is clear

explode (act) *qarxi*
the bomb exploded
extend (act) *kordhi*
extend your palms
extension (nom) *kordhin*
house extension
extinguish (act) *bakhtii*
extinguish the flame
exult (act) *farax*
exult her
exult (act) *farax*
exult her
exultation (nom) *aad u faraxsan*
songs of exultation
eye (nom) *il*
eye and eyebrow *il iyo sunayaal*
eyeball (nom) *bu'da isha*
eye and eyeball
eyebrow (nom) *suniyaasha isha*
eye and eyebrow

F

fabric (nom) *dhar*
buy fabric for me
face (nom) *waji*
look at my face
fade (act) *qarsoon*
the cloth has faded
faeces (nom) *saxaro*

faith (nom) *iimaan*
faith and peace

falcon (nom) *galayr*

fall (act) *dhac*
a rope fell from the roof of the
house
fall down (act) *hoos u dhac*
the egg has fallen down
fall into (act) *ku dhac*
fall into a pit
falsification (nom) *been abuur*
lies and falsifications
familiar (adj) *la yaqaan*
a familiar animal
family (nom) *qoys*
new family
famous (adj) *caan ah*
famous person
fan (nom) *taageere/maraxawad*
electric fan
farm (nom) *beer*
cocoa farm
farmer (nom) *beerwale*
she is a farmer
fart (act) *dhuus*
someone has farted
fart (nom) *dhuuso*
her fart smells badly
fast (act) *soon*
fast and pray
fast (adj) *si dhakhso ah*
a fast horse
fast (adv) *si dagdag ah*

fasten (act) *giiji*

fasting (nom) *soomid*
 prayer and fasting
fat (adj) *buuran*
 fat cheeks
father (nom) *aabe*
 my father's child is my sibling
fatigue (nom) *daal*
 tiredness and fatigue
favor (nom) *eex*

favoritism (nom) *eexsasho*

favour (nom) *eex*
 favour and kindness
favouritism (nom) *eexsasho*
 stop the favouritism
fear (act) *baqo*
 fear an apparition
fear (nom) *baqdin*
 fear has filled her heart
feather (nom) *baal*
 bird's feathers
February (nom) *Sabuux*
 February has 28 or 29 days
feces (nom) *saxaro*

feel (act) *dareen*
 I am feeling good
feeling (adj) *dareemaya*
 your mind and your feelings
fees (nom) *lacag*

 school fees
fell (ydy(i(act)) *wuu ... dhacay*

female (nom) *dhedig*
 female's womb
female (adj) *dhedig*
 a female child
fence (nom) *bowd*
 behind a fence
fermium (sci) *ferminam*
 fermium (Fm) has 100 protons
fertile (adj) *bacrin ah*
 fertile land
festival (nom) *dabaaldeg*
 a yearly festival
fetish (nom) *caado ama walax la
 caabudo*
 this town has a fetish
fever (nom) *qandho*
 she has a fever
field (nom) *garoon*
 they are on the field
fifteen (adj) *shan iyo toban*
 fifteen bottles *shan iyo toban dhaloonyinka*

fifty (adj) *konton*
 fifty bottles
fight (act) *dagaalan*
 Ali and Frazier fought
figure (act) *sawir*
 you figure it is hard?
figure of speech (nom) *jismiga
 hadalka*

every language has figures of speech

file (nom) *feyl*
  computer file
Filipino (nom) *Filibiino*
  the Filipinos
fill (act) *buuxi*
  fill it
fill up (act) *buuxi*
  fill up the barrel
film (nom) *filim*
  cast of a film
filthy (adj) *wasakheysan*
  the place is filthy
find (act) *baadh*
  find the word
fine (adj) *fiican*
  grind it finely
finger (nom) *far*
  how do you me sr finger
fingernail (nom) *cidida farta*

fingertip (nom) *caarada farta*
  lick your fingertips
finish (act) *dhamee*
  they will finish the food
fire (nom) *dab*
  light the fire
fire (act) *eri/ceyri*
  fire him; sack him
firewood (nom) *rash*
  pickup firewood
firmly (adv) *adag*

to stand firmly
first (nom) *ugu horeeya*
  his first day
firstborn (nom) *ugu hor dhashay*
  my firstborn
fish (act) *kalluumayso*
  let's go and fish
fish (nom) *kalluun*
  fried fish *kalluun la shiilay*
fish-hook (nom) *jillaab kalluun*
  two fish-hooks
fisherman (nom) *kalluumeyste*
  he is a fisherman
fishing-net (nom) *shabaga kallu-umeysiga*
  a new fishing-net
fist (nom) *tantooyo*
  your fist
five (adj) *shan*
  Five bottles *shan dhaloonyinka*
five persons (nom) *shan qofood*
  five persons are coming
fixer (nom) *hagaajiye*
  she is a fixer
flag (nom) *calan*
  yellow flag
flat (adj) *siman*
  flat table
flatulate (act) *dhuusid*
  he flatulated
flee (act) *cararid*
  he fled
flerovium (sci) *filaromiyam*

flerovium (Fl) **has 114 protons**
flesh (nom) *hilib*
 flesh and blood
flexible (adj) *dabacsan*
 a flexible stick
flicker (act) *dhaqaaq yar*
 the light is flickering
flint (nom) *dhagax madow*
 use the flint to light the fire
flood (nom) *daad*
 Accra flood
flood (nom) *daad*
 Accra flood
floor (nom) *sagxad dhul/dabaq*
 on the floor
flour (nom) *daqiiq/bur*
 corn flour
flower (nom) *ubax*
 pretty flower *ubax qurux badan*
fluorine (sci) *foloriin*
 fluorine (F) **has 9 protons**
flute (nom) *siin baar*
 play the flute
flute (nom) *siin baar*
 play the flute
fly (act) *duul*
 to fly into the sky
fly (nom) *duulid*
 a fly flies
focus (nom) *diirad saarid*
 my focus
fog (nom) *ceeryaan*
 dark fog

fold (act) *laalaab*
 to fold mother's cloth
foliage (nom) *caleen*
 cut the foliage
follow (act) *raac*
 follow me
folly (nom) *nacasnimo*
 it is just folly
food (nom) *cunto*
 eat food *cun cunto*
fool (nom) *nacas*
 Fool! Dimwit!
foolish (adj) *nacasnimo*
 a foolish story
foolishness (nom) *nacasnimo*

football (nom) *kubad*
 football competition
footstep (nom) *tallaabo cageed*
 follow in your mother's footsteps

for (pre) *loogu talogaly*
 for ourselves
forbid (act) *mamnuuc*
 forbid her
force (act) *qasab*
 you are forcing me
force (nom) *xoog*
 he took it by force
forehead (nom) *fooda madaxa*
 look at her forehead
foreigner (nom) *shisheeye*
 the foreigners have arrived

foresee (act) saadaali
  I foresee victory
forest (nom) kayn
  animals in the forest
forever (adv) abid
  she lives forever
forget (act) ilow
  I have forgotten
forgetfulness (nom) ilowshiiyo
  her forgetfulness
forgive (act) cafi
  forgive me my wrong
forgiveness (nom) saamaxaad
  love, acceptance and forgiveness

fork (nom) farageeto
  fork and knife farageeto iyo midi
fortress (nom) qalcad
  God is my fortress
forty (adj) afartan
  forty bottles
found (act) helay
  let us found a group
foundation (nom) aasaas
  foundation of the house
four (adj) afar
  There are four bottles on the wall
  afar dhaloonyinka
four persons (plural(adj) afar

fourteen (adj) afar iyo toban
  fourteen bottles afar iyo toban dhaloonyinka

fox (nom) dacawo
  three foxes
fraction (nom) jajab
  three fractions
fragrance (nom) caraf/udug
  the fragrance of sheabutter
fragrant (adj) carfoon
  cinnamon is fragrant
framework (nom) qaab
  the framework of the house
France (nom) Faransiiska
  go to France
francium (sci) farkaniyam
  francium (Fr) has 87 protons
frankly (adv) daacadnimo ah
  say it frankly
free (act) bilaash
  she will free the dog
free (adj) bilaash
  free food
freedom (nom) madax banaani
  freedom and justice
freezing (adj) qaboojin
  night is freezing
French (nom) Faransiis
  she speaks French
fresh (adj) cusub
  fresh leaves
friction (nom) isxoqid
  friction came between us
Friday (nom) Jimca
  Friday children
fridge (nom) tallaagad

open the fridge

fried-fish (nom) *kalluun la shi-ilay*

  I am eating fried-fish

friend (nom) *saaxiib*

  my friend

friendly (adj) *saxiibtinimo*

  a friendly child

friendship (nom) *saaxiibtinimo*

  friendship is good

frighten (act) *argagaxi*

  frighten evil people

frighten (act) *argagaxi*

  frighten evil people

frightening (adj) *cabsi leh*

  it is frightening

frog (nom) *rah*

  a frog likes water *rahu wuxuu je-cel yahay biyaha*

from (pre) *ka*

  go from here *ka tag halkan*

frond (nom) *caleen*

  to cut the fronds

front (nom) *xaga hore*

  the front of the book

fruit (nom) *miro*

  pluck fruit

fruitful (adj) *barwaqaysan*

fry (act) *shiil*

  use vegetable oil to fry fish

fuck (act) *was*

fufu (nom) *fuufuu - cunto laga is-ticmaalo galbeedka afrika*

  eat fufu

full (adj) *buuxa*

  full bucket

full stop (nom) *joogsi*

  add a full stop after the word

fun (adj) *madadaalo*

  today is a fun day

funeral (nom) *aas*

  I am going to a funeral

funny (adj) *maad leh*

  funny story

future (nom) *mustaqbalka*

  I see luxury in your future

G

Gabonese (nom) *Gabooniis*

  the Gabonese

GaDangme (nom) *Gadagme - luqad lagaga hadlo meelo kamida Afrika*

  I speak GaDangme

gadolinium (sci) *gadoloniyam*

  gadolinium (Gd) has 64 protons

gain (act) *hel*

  if I have life, I have gained everything

gall (nom) *xameeti*

gallium (sci) *galadiyam*

  gallium (Ga) has 31 protons

gallon (nom) *gallaan*
 a gallon of water
Gambia (nom) *Gaambiya*
 go to Gambia
Gambian (nom) *Gaambiyaan*
 the Gambians
game (nom) *ciyaar*
 play a game
gap (nom) *farqi/dallool*
 she has a beautiful gap between
 her teeth
garage (nom) *geerash*
 car garage
garden (nom) *beer*
 our garden
garden egg (nom) *ukunta beerta*
 garden egg stew
gari (nom) *gari - cunto laga cuno*
 meelo kamida Galbeedka Afrika
 beans and gari
garlic (nom, c1) *toonta*

garment (nom) *dhar*
 wear a garment
gas (nom) *gaas/hawo*
 gas stove
gaseous (adj) *gaaseysan*
 gaseous water
gate (nom) *albaab*
 open the gate
gather (act) *ururi*
 gather everyone
gaudy (adj) *dhaasheer*

 gaudy necklace
gave (ydy(i(act) *wuu ... siay*

Gaza (nom) *Qasa*
 go to Gaza
Gazan (nom) *Qasaan*
 the Gazans
genealogy (nom) *abtirsashada*
 the genealogy of Nkruma
generation (nom) *jiil*
 five generations
generosity (nom) *deeqsinimo*
 your generosity
gentle (adj) *jilicsan*
 a gentle tongue
gentleman (nom) *mudane*
 senior gentleman
gently (adv) *si jilicsan*
 to shake gently
Georgia (nom) *Joorjiya*
 go to Georgia
Georgian (nom) *Joorjiyaan*
 the Georgians
germanium (sci) *jeermaniyam*
 germanium (Ge) has 32 protons
Germany (nom) *Jarmalka*
 I spend the winter in Germany
germinate (act) *gaagaab*
 the corn is germinating
get (act) *hel*
 get the book
get lost (act) *tag*
 to get lost in town

get wet *(act)* qoy
  the place has gotten wet
Ghana *(nom)* Gaana
  people from Ghana are called Ghanaians
Ghanaian *(nom)* Gaaniyaan
  the Ghanaians
ghost *(nom)* reer-aakhiraad
  I see a ghost
giant *(adj)* cimlaaq
  he is a giant man
giant *(nom)* cimlaaq
  four giants
gift *(nom)* hadiyada
  a good gift hadiyad wanaagsan
giggle *(act)* qosol

Gikuyu *(nom)* Gikuuyu - luqad lagaga hadlo Kiiniya
  I can read Gikuyu
ginger *(nom)* sinjibiil
  ginger soup
ginseng *(nom)* Ginseen - geed ka
baxa Aasiya
  ginseng is a plant
giraffe *(nom)* geri
  a giraffe is an animal gerigu waa
xayawaan
girl *(nom)* gabar
  tall girl gabar dheer
girlfriend *(nom)* saaxiibad

give *(act)* sii

  give the water to him
glass *(nom)* quruurad/muraayad
  a glass of water
glorify *(act)* ammaan

glory *(nom)* ammaan
  glory of humankind
glossy *(adj)* dhalaalaya
  a glossy magazine
glutton *(nom)* qof cir weyn
  he is a glutton
go *(act)* tag
  to go to school
go mad *(act)* waalo
  you have gone mad
go to the toilet *(act)* musqul
  to go to the toilet weekly
goal *(nom)* gool
  score a goal
goat *(nom)* ri'
  a goat and a sheep ri' iyo ido
god *(nom)* Eebbe
  dependable god
godspeed *(exc)* u rajeyn safar wacan
  I wish you godspeed
gold *(nom)* dahab
  fragrance and gold
gold *(sci)* dahab
  gold (Au) has 79 protons
gone $(done_t \, dy(i(act) \, samee$

gong gong *(nom)* goon-goon - waa

wax biyaha ku jira oo ay caabudaan Jeyniiisku

play the gong gong

good (nom) *wanaagsan*

good and evil

good (adj) *wanagsan*

a good gift

good afternoon (exc) *duhur wanagsan*

good afternoon Esi

good evening (exc) *fiid wanagsan*

good evening Kofi

good job (exc) *shaqo wanagsan*

good morning (exc) *subax wanagsan*

good morning Kofi

goodbye (exc) *nabad galiyo*

say goodbye

goodness (nom) *wanaag*

goodness and mercy

goosebumps (nom) *jiriirico*

I have got goosebumps

gospel (nom) *injiil*

the goespel of Jesus

gossip (act) *xamo*

goessip about her

gossip (nom) *xan*

goessip is not good

got (ydy(i(act) *wuu ... helay*

govern (act) *xukun*

govern Ghana

governance (nom) *maamulid*

good governance

government (nom) *dawlad*

Nkrumah's government

governor (nom) *maamule*

she is the governor

grab (act) *cusko*

grab his hand

grace (nom) *bilic*

the grace of God

gracious (adj) *asluub leh*

a gracious person

graduate (nom) *qalinjabiye*

she is a graduate

gram (nom) *garaam*

gram (nom) *garaam*

gramme (nom) *garaam*

ten grammes

grandfather (nom) *awoow*

my grandfather

grandma (nom, c1) *ayeey*

grandmother (nom) *ayeey*

grandpa (nom, c1) *awoow*

my grandfather

grape (nom) *canab*

eat the grapes

grapevine (nom) *kutiri-kuteenka suuqa dhexmaraysa*

grasp (act) *qabso*

grasp my hand

grass *(nom)* caws
  a cow chews grass
grasshopper *(nom)* jiriqaa
  ant and grasshopper
grave *(nom)* qabri/xabaal
  four graves
grease *(nom)* dufan
  grease in a pan
great *(adj)* weyn
  a great name
greed *(nom)* damac
  gred and envy
greedy *(adj)* damaaci
  greedy fool
green *(adj)* cagaaran
  green leaf
greenish *(adj)* cagaar ah
  greenish house
greet *(act)* salaan
  greet Ama
greeting *(nom)* salaan
  a new greeting
grief *(nom)* caloool xumo
  grief is killing me
grieve *(act)* murugo
  my soul grieves
grind *(act)* il jabi
  to grind corn
groin *(nom)* gumaar
  groin of a man
groom *(nom)* aroos
  groom's friends
ground *(nom)* dhulka

groundnut *(nom)* rooti
  corn and groundnuts
group *(nom)* koox
  let us found a group
grove *(nom)* dhir yar
  grove of spirits
grow *(act)* kori
  the child has grown
guard *(act)* ilaali
  guard the house
guava *(nom)* saytuun
  the guava is sweet
guess *(act)* garo

guest *(nom)* marti
  I am a guest
guest room *(nom)* qolka martida
  sleep in the guest room
guide *(act)* hag
  to guide people
guide *(nom)* hagid
  she is our guide
Guinea *(nom)* Gini
  go to Guinea
guinea grain *(nom)* badarka gini

Guinea-Bissau *(nom)* Gini-Bisow
  go to Guinea-Bissau
guinea-fowl *(nom)* haadka-gini
  three guinea-fowls
Guinean *(nom)* Giniyaan
  the Guineans

gun *(nom)* *qori*
  a soldier has a gun
gunpowder *(nom)* *baaruud*
  I smell gunpowder
gutter *(nom)* *biyomareen*
  there is water in the gutter
guy *(adj, c1)* *lab*

H

habitat *(nom)* *degaanka*
  habitat of animals
had *(ydy(i(act)* *wuu … heysoay*

hafnium *(sci)* *haafniyam*
  hafnium (Hf) has 72 protons
hair *(nom)* *timo*
  chest hair
haircut *(nom)* *tima-jarasho*
  I need a haircut
hall *(nom)* *qol weyn*
  we are sitting in the hall
hallelujah *(exc)* *halleluuya - erey*
  ay idhaahdaan kiristanku
  sing hallelujah
hamlet *(nom)* *tuulo*

hammer *(nom)* *dube*
  hammer and nail
hammock *(nom)* *leexo*
  sleep in the hammock

hand *(nom)* *gacan*
  lift up your hand
handkerchief *(nom)* *fastaleeti*
  do you have a handkerchief?
handsome *(adj, c2)* *qurxoon*
  it is beautiful
hang *(act)* *sur*
  hang it there
happen *(act)* *dhicid*
  let it happen
happiness *(nom)* *farxad*
  happiness has arrived
happy *(adj)* *faraxsan*
  today is a happy day
harbour *(nom)* *deked*
  Takoradi has a harbour
harbour *(nom)* *deked*
  Takoradi has a harbour
hard *(adj)* *adag*
  it is hard
hard *(adv)* *adag*
  to work hard
hardship *(nom)* *adkaansho*
  great hardship
hardship *(nom)* *adkaansho*
  great hardship
hare *(nom)* *bakayle*
  to run like a hare
harmattan *(nom)* *dabey qalalan*
  harmattan winds
harvest *(nom)* *miro goosasho*
  a plentiful harvest
has *(tdy(f(act)* *heysotaa*

hashtag (nom) *haashtaag*
 Twitter hashtag
hassium (sci) *hasiyam*
 hassium (Hs) has 108 protons
hassle (act) *dhibaatee*
 hassle him so that he pays
hat (nom) *koofiyad*
 he is wearing a hat
hate (act) *nac*
 to hate laziness
hatred (nom) *naceyb*
 hatred has no cure
Hausa (nom) *Hausa - luqad*
 Hausa language
have (act) *heyso*
 she has money
have a hold on (act) *mamul*
 hunger has a hold on me (I am hungry)
having (pro) *isagoo haysta*
 tea with sugar (literally, tea having sugar)
hawk (act) *dafo*
 hawk things
hawk (nom) *dafo*
 a hawk and a chicken
he (pro) *wuu*
 he eats *wuu cunaa*
head (nom) *madax*
 your big head
headache (nom) *madax xanuun*
 headache medicine

headgear (nom) *waxyaabaha madaxa lagu xidho*
 put on headgear
heading (nom) *ku socda*
 book headings
headscarf (nom) *xijaab*
 tie a headscarf
heal (act) *bogso*
 heal disease
healing (nom) *bogsasho*
 he brought healing
health (nom) *caafimaad*
 food gives health
heap (nom) *taallo*
 a heap of books
hear (act) *maqal*
 she heard the whistle
heard (ydy(i(act) *wuu ... maqalay*

heart (nom) *wadne*
 good heart
heartburn (nom) *laab-qarrar*
 I have heartburn
hearth (nom) *girgire*
 there is fire in the hearth
heat (nom) *uumi*
 the heat has arrived
heavy (adj) *culus*
 it is heavy
hedgehog (nom) *xidig-dhul*
 seven hedgehogs
heel (nom) *cidhib*
 toe and heel

heh (exc) *heh*
  sorry, heh
height (nom) *dherer*
  height and width
helicopter (nom) *helikobtar*
  two helicopters
helium (sci) *hilyam*
  helium (He) has 2 protons
hello (exc) *ma nabad baa*
  hello sir
helmsman (nom) *qofka wada doon/maaxas*
  helmsman of a boat
help (act) *caawi*
  you are helping everyone
help (nom) *caawimo*
  everyone needs help
helper (nom) *caawiye*
  my helper
heptagon (nom) *todoba xagal leh*
  a heptagon has seven angles
her (pos) *waxeeda*
  her house
her (pro) *waxeeda*
  show her
herb (nom) *dhir*
herbalist (nom) *qofka dhirta yaqaana*
  she is a herbalist
here (nom) *xagan*
  go from here
here (adv) *halkan*
  click here
hero (nom) *geesi*

  she is a hero
herpes (nom) *cuncun*
  herpes is a disease
herring (nom) *kalluunka la cuno*
  a herring is a fish
hers (pro) *kuweeda*
  this thing is hers
herself (pro) *nafteeda*
  she respects herself
hexagon (nom) *lix xagal leh*
  a hexagon has six angles
hey (exc) *aryaa*

hi (exc) *nabadeey*

hiccups (nom) *hingo*
  he has got the hiccups
hide (nom) *qari*
  animal hide
highway (nom) *wado weyn*
  cars on a highway
hill (nom) *taag*
  hill top
him (pro) *isaga*
  show him
himself (pro) *naftiisa*
  he respects himself
hindrance (nom) *carqalad*

hip (nom) *misig*
  my hips
hippo (nom) *jeer*

hippopotamus *(nom)* jeer
  a hippopotamus has a big stomach jeertu waxay leeday calool weyn

his *(pos)* kiisa
  his house
his *(pro)* wixiisa
  this thing is his
history *(nom)* taariikh
  learn history
hit *(act)* ku dhufo
  do not hit me
hoe *(nom)* yaanbo
  hoe and cutlass
hold *(act)* qabso
  to hold something firmly
hold *(act)* qabso
  to hold something firmly
hold *(act)* qabso
  to hold something firmly
hole *(nom)* god
  small hole
holiday *(nom)* fasax
  today is a holiday
holmium *(sci)* holmiyam
  holmium (Ho) has 67 protons
holy *(adj)* barakaysan
  holy book
home *(nom)* guriga
  your home
homeless *(adj)* bilaa hoy ah
  a homeless person
hometown *(nom)* magalada hooyo

  I'm going to my hometown
honey *(nom)* malab
  honey is sweet
honeycomb *(nom)* awllalada malabka
  honey in a honeycomb
honor *(nom)* sharaf

honour *(act)* sharaf
  honour the Lord
honour *(nom)* sharaf
  honour and love
hope *(nom)* rajo
  I have hope
horn *(nom)* geesi
  horn music
horn *(nom)* geesi
  horn music
horse *(nom)* faras
  white horse faras cad
hospital *(nom)* cusbitaal

hot *(adj)* kulayl
  hot water
hotel *(nom)* hudheel la seexdo
  she sleeps at a hotel
hour *(nom)* saacad
  ten hours
house *(nom)* guri
  the house guriga
housefly *(nom)* dukshi
  a housefly can carry disease
how *(adv)* sidee

how to eat
how are you *(exc)* *sidee tahay*
  how do you are ?
how much *(adj)* *immisa*
  how much is it?
however *(cjn)* *hasa yeeshee*

hug *(act)* *hab sii*
  embrace me
huge *(adj)* *weyn*
  a huge building
human *(nom)* *insaan*
  we are humans
humankind *(nom)* *insi*
  we are humankind
humble *(adj)* *aan kibir badnayn*
  humble person
humiliation *(nom, c1)* *sharaf dhac*
  shame and disgrace
humility *(nom)* *hooseysiin*
  you show humility
hundred *(adj)* *boqol*
  hundred bottles
hunger *(nom)* *gaajo*
  hunger and thirst
hungry *(adj)* *gajoonaya*

hunter *(nom)* *ugaadhsade*
  five hunters
husband *(nom)* *say'i*
  I love my husband
hut *(nom)* *aqal*
  ten huts

hydrogen *(nom)* *haydarojiin*
  hydrogen car
hydrogen *(sci)* *haydorojiin*
  hydrogen (H) has 1 proton
hyena *(nom)* *waraabe*
  two hyenas
hypocrisy *(nom)* *munaafaqnimo*
  hypocrisy and lies

I

i miss you *(exc)* *waan kuu xiisay*
  I miss you
ice-cream *(nom, c1)* *jellaato*
  One evening, he told them a story

idea *(nom)* *fikrad*
  I have an idea
ideal *(adj)* *horyaal*
  an ideal woman
idiot *(nom)* *nacas*

idol *(nom)* *sanam/qof lagu daydo*

if *(cjn)* *haddii*
  if someone loves you
if ... then *(cjn)* *haddii... ka dibna*
  if A then B
Igbo *(nom)* *Igo - luqad*
  Igbo language
image *(nom)* *sawir*

imbecile (nom, c1) *nacas*

immediately (adv) *isla markiiba*
  cut off immediately

immerse (act) *quusi*
  immerse him in the water

immigrant (nom) *haajire*
  we are immigrants

impact (nom) *saameyn*
  learning has great impact

imperfection (nom) *cillad lahaan*

impertinence (nom) *bilaa qadarin*
  stop the impertinence

important (adj) *muhiim ah*
  you are an important person

impregnate (act) *uuri*
  You have impregnated my sister

improvement (nom, c1) *horumar*

in advance (adv) *ka hor*
  eat in advance

in fact (cjn) *xaqiiqdii*
  in fact it is yours

in front (pre) *horteeda*
  go in front

in that case (adv) *haddi ay dhacdo*
  taasi
  in that case come

in-law (nom) *xigtada dhanka gu-*
  urka

inactive (nom) *aan shaqeynayn*
  he is inactive

incinerate (act) *baabii*
  incinerate all the papers

increase (act) *kordhi*
  burglary is increasing

independence (nom) *madax ba-*
  naani
  independence day

India (nom) *Hindiya*
  go to India

Indian (nom) *Hindi*
  the Indians

indictment (nom) *eedayn*
  nine indictments

indigent (nom) *faqiir*
  an indigent has nothing

indigent (nom) *faqiir*
  an indigent has nothing

indigo (adj) *soosali*
  indigo cloth

indium (sci) *indhiyam*
  indium (In) has 49 protons

Indonesia (nom) *Indooniisiya*
  go to Indonesia

Indonesian (nom) *Indooniisiyaan*
  the Indonesians

infect (act) *qaadsii*
  the disease has infected me

infertile (adj) *ma dhalays*
  infertile land

infinite (adj) *aan dhamaad lahayn*

infinity *(nom)* xad la'aan
  if you divide any number by zero,
  you get infinity
influence *(nom)* faragelin

Inglish *(nom)* Ingiriisi
  I can read Inglish
inheritance *(nom)* dhaxaltoyo
  claim your inheritance
inject *(act)* duri
  inject me
injection *(nom)* duris
  an injection is painful
injure *(act)* dhaawac
  I am injured
ink *(nom)* khad
  ink in a pen
inlaw *(nom)* xigtada dhanka guurka
  our inlaws
inquirer *(nom)* weydiiye

insect *(nom)* cayayaan
  a cockroach is an insect
insect *(nom)* cayayaan
  a cockroach is an insect
inside *(adv)* gudaha
  go inside
insinuate *(act)* si dahsoon u hadal
  they insinuate that
insult *(act)* cay
  stop insulting her
insult *(act)* cay

  stop insulting her
insult *(nom)* cay
  many insults
insults *(nom)* caytinta
  unnecessary insults
integrate *(act)* isku dar
  to integrate a new person into the
  family
intelligent *(adj)* xariif
  an intelligent person
intent *(nom)* ujeedo

interest *(nom)* dan
  loan interest
internet *(nom)* interneet
  internet link
interpreter *(nom)* turjumaan
  the man needs an interpreter
interrupt *(act)* ka dhex gal
  interrupt him
intersection *(nom)* bar-kulan, is
  goys

investment *(nom)* maalgashi
  I need an investment
iodine *(sci)* ayodhiin
  iodine (I) has 53 protons
Iran *(nom)* Iraan
  go to Iran
Iranian *(nom)* Iraani
  the Iranians
Iraq *(nom)* Ciraaq
  go to Iraq

Iraqi (*nom*) *Ciraaqi*
  the Iraqis
iridium (*sci*) *iridhiyam*
  iridium (Ir) has 77 protons
iron (*sci*) *ayron*
  iron (Fe) has 26 protons
irritation (*nom*) *cuncun*

is (*tdy(f(act*) *ahowtaa*

Islam (*nom*) *Islaam*
  Christianity and Islam
Islamic (*adj*) *Islaami ah*
  Islamic holiday
island (*nom*) *jasiirad*
  Seychelles island
Israel (*nom*) *Israa'iili*
  go to Israel
Israeli (*nom*) *Yuhuudi*
  the Israelis
issue (*nom*) *arrin*
  new issue
it (*pro*) *iyada*
  it falls
Italy (*nom*) *Itaaliiya*
  to visit Italy
its (*pos*) *iyada*
  its house
its (*pro*) *waa*
  its house
Ivoirian (*nom*) *Ayforiyaan*
  the Ivorians
ivory (*nom*) *fool maroodi*

ivory necklace

J

jail (*nom*) *jeel*
  go to jail
jama (*nom*) *jama*
  sing jama
James (*nom*) *James - magac*
  my name is James
January (*nom*) *Sadataal*
  January has 31 days
Japan (*nom*) *Jabaan*
  go to Japan
Japanese (*nom*) *Jabaaniis*
  the Japanese
jar (*nom*) *dhalo*
  seven jars
jaw (*nom*) *daan*
  my jaw
jealousy (*nom*) *hinaase*

jeans (*nom*) *jinis*
  blue jeans
jest (*act*) *kaftan hadal*
  who is the one jesting?
jester (*nom*) *xirfadoole kaftan*
  she is a jester
Jesus (*nom*) *Ciise*
  Jesus Christ!
jewelry (*nom*) *dahab*
  pretty jewelry

job (nom) shaqo
  I need a job
John (nom) John - magac
  to baptise John
join (act) ku biir
  words join together to make sentences
joint (nom) kala goys
  stretch your joints
joke (nom) kaftan
  tell me a joke
joker (nom) turub/qof kaftama

jollof (nom) bariis jollof
  jollof is food
jollof (nom) bariis jollof
  jollof is food
Jordan (nom) Urdun
  go to Jordan
Jordanian (nom) Urduniyaan
  the Jordanians
journalist (nom) saxafi
  we are journalists
journey (nom) socdaal
  a long journey
joy (nom) farxad

judge (nom) garsoore
  seven judges
judgement (nom) xukun
  which judgement?
July (nom) Wabriis
  July has 31 days

jump (act) bood
  to jump a wall
junction (nom) bar-kulan, is goys

June (nom) Mawliid
  June has 30 days
junk (nom) qashin
  there is junk in the room
just (adj) immika
  it is just folly
just (pre) kaliya
  just as he got there
just (adv) kaliya
  just see!
justice (nom) cadaalad
  freedom and justice

K

Kazakhstani (nom) Kasakhasitani
  the Kazakhstanis
keep (act) hay
  keep the change
kenkey (nom) kinkee - cunto cajiin
  ah oo lagu cuno Waqooyiga Africa
  kenkey and stew
kente (nom) kinte - walxdo midabo
  leh oo lagu sameeyo Gaana
  kente cloth
Kenya (nom) Kiiniya
  go to Kenya
kept (ydy(i(act) wuu ... hayay

kerosene *(nom)* *gaasta la shito*
  bottle of kerosene
key *(nom)* *fure*
  door and key
khakhi *(nom)* *kaaki*
  khakhi shorts
khebab *(nom)* *kabaab*
  khebabs and beer
kidnapping *(nom)* *afduubasho*
  kidnapping is evil
kidney *(nom)* *kalida*
  a cat has a kidney
kill *(act)* *dil*
  to kill a goat
killer *(nom)* *dille*

kilogram *(nom)* *kiiloogaraam*
  ten kilograms
kilogramme *(nom)* *kiiloogaraam*
  ten kilogrammes
kilometer *(nom)* *kiiloomitir*
  ten kilometers
kilometer *(nom)* *kiiloomitir*
  ten kilometers
kilometre *(nom)* *kiiloomitir*
  ten kilometres
kind *(nom)* *naxariis leh*
  he and his kind
kindle *(act)* *shid*
  kindle a fire
kindness *(nom)* *naxariis*
  favour and kindness
king *(nom)* *boqor*

  he is a king
kingdom *(nom)* *boqortooyo*
  the kingdom of God
kiss *(act)* *dhunko*
  kiss my lips
kitchen *(nom)* *kijin/madbakh*
  I am in the kitchen
knee *(nom)* *jilib*
  my knees
knife *(nom)* *mindi*
  sharpen a knife *afee midi*
knot *(nom)* *gunti*
  tie the knot
know *(act)* *ogow*
  I know her
Kobina *(nom)* *Kobiina - magac*
  Kobina is my son
Kofi *(nom)* *Koofi - magac*
  Kofi is my son
Kojo *(nom)* *Koojo - magac*
  Kojo is my son
Komoros *(nom)* *Komoroos - jasi-irad*
  go to Komoros
Kongo *(nom)* *Kongo - dadka ku nool*
  wadanka Koongo
  Kongo language
koran *(nom)* *Quraanka*
  the Bible and the Koran
krypton *(sci)* *karaybton*
  krypton (Kr) has 36 protons
Kuwait *(nom)* *Kuwayt*
  go to Kuwait

Kuwaiti (nom) Kuwayti
  the Kuwaitis
Kwame (nom) Kiwame - magac
  Kwame is my son
kwashiorkor (nom) yaraant booratiinka
  kwashiorkor is a disease
Kweku (nom) Kiweku - magac
  My son is Kweku
Kwesi (nom) Kiwesi - magac
  my son is called Kwesi
Kyrgyzstan (nom) Kirigistaan
  go to Kyrgyzstan
Kyrgyzstani (nom) Kirigistaani
  the Kyrgyzstanis

L

laboratory (nom) sheybaadh
  hospital laboratory
ladder (nom) sallaan
  long ladder
ladle (act) malqaacad
  ladle some for her
ladle (nom) malqaacad weyn
  soup ladle
lady (nom) gabadh
  Lady Danso
lagoon (nom) haro bada
  Elmina lagoon
lake (nom) haro
  the lake has overflowed

lameness (nom) cuyaanimo
  her lameness is improving
lamentation (nom) baroorasho
  many lamentations
land (nom) dhul
  buy land
land (act) dhul
  the aeroplane has landed
language (nom) af
  many languages afaf badan
lantern (nom) siraad
  turn on the lantern
lanthanum (sci) lantaanum
  lanthanum (La) has 57 protons
Lao (nom) la'o - luqada wadanka
  La'oos
  the Laos
Laos (nom) La'oos - wadan ku yaala
  aasiya
  go to Laos
lapse (nom) inta u dhaxeysa laba
  wakhti
  too many lapses
large (adj) balaadhan
  a large tiger
lastborn (nom) guri danbays
  your lastborn
late (adv) goor danbe ah
  to come late
later (adv) hadhow
  they will eat later
latrine (nom) musqul
  where is the latrine?

laugh (act) *qosol*
  he is laughing
lavatory (nom) *musqusha*

law (nom) *sharci*
  the law says
lawrencium (sci) *lawrensiyam*
  lawrencium (Lr) has 103 protons

lawyer (nom) *qareen*
  four lawyers
laziness (nom) *caajisnimo*
  laziness is not good
lazy (adj) *caajis ah*
  lazy man
lead (act) *hogaami*
  lead us
lead (sci) *ledh*
  lead (Pb) has 82 protons
leader (nom) *hogaamiye*
  this is our leader
leaf (nom) *caleen*
  green leaf *caleen cagaaran*
leak (act) *sii dayn*
  the bucket leaks
lean on (act) *ku tiirso*
  lean on me
learn (act) *baro*
  they learn a language
learner (nom) *barte*
  we are learners
leave (act) *tag*
  leave it behind

Lebanese (nom) *Lubnaani*
  the Lebanese
Lebanon (nom) *Lubnaan*
  go to Lebanon
ledge (nom) *tiir*
  sleep on the ledge
left (adj) *bidix*
  go left
left (ydy(i(act) *wuu ... tagay*

leg (nom) *lug*
  swollen leg
leisure (nom) *wakhtiga firaaqda ah*
  you have leisure?
lemon (nom) *liin*
  three lemons
lend (act) *amaahi*
  lend me this book
length (nom) *dherer*
  height, width and length
leniency (nom) *naxariisasho*
  show him leniency
lens (nom) *bikaaco*
  lens of a camera
leopard (nom) *haramcad*
  a leopard has a tail
leper (nom) *qof baras leh*
  ten lepers
leprosy (nom) *baras*
  leprosy is a disease
Lesotho (nom) *Lisooto*
  go to Lesotho

lesson (nom) *cashar*
  learn the lesson
let (act) *u yeel*
  let us found a group
let's go (exc) *inakeen*
  let's go home
let's go (exc) *ina keen*

levy (nom) *aasaasid cashuur*
  pay a levy
liar (nom) *beenaale*
  three liars
liar (nom) *beenaale*
  three liars
Liberia (nom) *Laybeeriya*
  go to Liberia
Liberian (nom) *Laybeeriyaan*
  the Liberians
liberty (nom) *xoriyad*
  we have liberty
library (nom) *maktabad*
  we will go to the library
Libya (nom) *Liibiya*
  go to Libya
Libyan (nom) *Liibiyaan*
  the Libyans
lick (act) *leef*
  to lick the spoon
lick (act) *leef*
  to lick the spoon
lid (nom) *dabool*
  lid of a cup
lie (nom) *been*

lies and discord
lie (nom) *been*
  lies and discord
life (nom) *nolol*
  live your life well
lifestyle (nom) *qaab nololeed*
  an active lifestyle
lifetime (nom) *wakthiga nolosha*
  in my lifetime
lift (act) *qaad*
  to lift higher
lift (act) *qaad*
  to lift higher
lift up (act) *kor u qaadid*
  lift yourself up!
light (nom) *iftiin*
  light of the sky
lightning (nom) *hilaac*
  lightning and thunder
lightweight (adj) *fudud*
  the book is lightweight
like (adv) *ka helid*
  it feels like fufu
like (act) *ka hel*
  a frog likes water
like (pre) *sida*
  to think like a human
likeness (nom) *isu ekaan*

lily (nom) *Lili - magac*
  a lily is a flower
lime (nom) *nuurad*
  lime juice

line (nom) *layn/xariiq*
  the ball has crossed the line
Lingala (nom) *Lingaala - luqad la-gaga hadlo meelo kamida Afrika*
  I speak Lingala
link (nom) *liinki/xidhiidh*
  Internet link
lion (nom) *libaax*
  a lion eats flesh
lip (nom) *dibin*
  red lips
liquid (adj) *dareere*
  liquid water
liquor (nom) *nooc khamriga kamid ah*
  pour a little liquor
listen (act) *dhageyso*
  to listen to music
listener (nom) *dhageyste*
  hello listeners
literature (nom) *suugan*

lithium (sci) *lityam*
  lithium (Li) has 3 protons
litigant (nom) *qofka ku lugelh dacwad maxkamadeed*
  she is a litigant
litigate (act) *dacwee*
  we are litigating
litigation (nom) *dacwo maxkameed*
  he likes litigation
little (nom) *yar*
  a little is better than nothing

little (adj) *yar*
  pour a little liquor
little (nom) *yar*
  a little is better than nothing
little by little (adv) *inyar inyar*
  little by little a chicken drinks water
live (act) *noolow*
  we live here
liver (nom) *beer*
  a dog has a liver
livermorium (sci) *lifermooriyam*
  livermorium (Lv) has 116 protons

living (adj) *noloosho*
  living god
living-room (nom) *qolka fadhiga*

lizard (nom) *mulac*
  a lizard eats grass
loan (nom) *amaah*
  I need a loan
loan (act) *amaahi*
  loan me money
lobster (nom) *daba-qalooc*
  I eat lobster
location (nom) *goob*
  from here to a new location
lock (nom) *quful/xidh*
  five locks
locust (nom) *ayax*
  locusts and honey
lodge (nom) *buul*

stay at the lodging for a while
logo *(nom)* summad
  church logo
loin *(nom)* libaax
  my loins
London *(nom)* Londhon
  I am going to London
long *(adj)* dheer
  long beard
longevity *(nom)* nolol dheeraan-sho
  wealth and longevity
look *(act)* fiirin
  look at the boy
look away *(act)* fiiri dhinac kale
  I look away
loosen *(act)* is dabci
  to loosen the belt
Lord *(nom)* suldaan
  my soul bless The LORD
lorry *(nom)* baabuur
  lorry stop
lose *(act)* khasaar
  He lost his way home
lost *(ydy(i(act)* wuu ... khasaaray

lot *(nom)* inbadan
  a lot of hard work
loud *(adj)* cod dheer
  loud siren
louse *(nom)* injir
  chicken lice
love *(act)* jeclah

I love you
lover *(nom)* jecle
  my lover has tricked me
loyal *(adj)* daacad ah
  my loyal friend
loyalty *(nom)* daacadnimo
  loyalty and love
luck *(nom)* nasiib
  luck and success
lucky *(adj)* nasiib badan
  lucky girl
Luganda *(nom)* Lugandha-luqad lagaga hadlo Yugaandha
  Luganda language
lump *(nom)* kuus/buro
  a lump of gold
lutetium *(sci)* luteetiyam
  lutetium (Lu) has 71 protons
Luwo *(nom)* Luwo-dad ku nool waqooyiga Suudaan
  I can read Luwo
Luxembourg *(nom)* Lugsembeeg
  go to Luxembourg
Luxembourger *(nom)* Lugsem-beeger
  the Luxembourgers
luxury *(nom)* raaxo
  I see luxury in your future

M

Madagascar *(nom)* Madagaskar
  go to Madagascar

madam *(nom)* marwo
  madam Mary
made *(ydy(i(act)* wuu ... sameeay

made up *(act)* ka sameysan

magazine *(nom)* majalad
  a new magazine
maggot *(nom)* dirxi
  many maggots
magnesium *(sci)* magniisiyam
  magnesium (Mg) has 12 protons

maid *(nom)* adeegto
  she is a maid
maiden *(nom)* gabadh weyn oo aan
  guursan
  beautiful maiden
main *(adj)* ugu muhiimsan

maize *(nom)* galley
  corn and groundnuts
maize *(nom, c3)* galley
  corn and groundnuts
major *(adj)* waawayn
  a major town
make *(act)* samee
  make food
Malagasy *(nom)* Malagasi - luqada
  wadanka Madagaskar
  Malagasy language
malaria *(nom)* cudurka duumada
  malaria is a disease

Malawi *(nom)* Malawi
  go to Malawi
Malawian *(nom)* Malaawiyaan
  the Malawians
Malaysia *(nom)* Malayshiya
  go to Malaysia
Malaysian *(nom)* Malayshiyaan
  the Malaysians
Maldives *(nom)* Maldhifees
  go to Maldives
Maldivian *(nom)* Maldhafiyaan
  the Maldivians
male *(nom)* lab
  Mandela is male
male *(adj)* lab

Mali *(nom)* Maali
  go to Mali
Malian *(nom)* Maaliyaan
  the Malians
man *(nom)* nin
  a tall man nin dheer
manage *(act)* maamul
  to manage someone
manager *(nom)* maamule
  a good manager
manganese *(sci)* maanganiis
  manganese (Mn) has 25 protons

mango *(nom)* cambe
  the mango has ripened cambuhu
  wuu bislaaday
manner *(nom)* hab wax u dha-

caan
his manner is amusing
many (adj) badan
many vehicles
map (nom) khariirad
read the map
March (nom) Soon
March has 31 days
marijuana (nom) maruwaana -
maandooriye
she smokes marijuana
Mark (nom) Mark - magac
my name is Mark
mark (nom) Mark - magac
my name is Mark
market (nom) suuq
go to market
marriage (nom) guur
good marriage
marry (act) guurso
marry me
mass (sci) cuf
you can change mass into energy

massive (adj) balaadhan

master (nom) sayid
Master Kofi
masticate (act) calaali
a cow masticates grass
mat (nom) salli
spread out a mat
math (nom) xisaab

mathematics (nom) xisaabaadka
she teaches mathematics
maths (nom) xisaabaadka
she teaches mathematics
Matthew (nom) Mathew - magac
read Matthew 19:14
mattress (nom) furaash
a new mattress
Mauritania (nom) Murutaaniya
go to Mauritania
Mauritanian (nom) Murutaaniyaan
the Mauritanians
Mauritian (nom) Maaritiyaan
the Mauritians
Mauritius (nom) Maaritiyuus
go to Mauritius
maximum (adj) inta ugu badan
maximum amount
May (nom) Sako
May has 31 days
maybe (adv) laga yabee
maybe he will come
maybe (adv) laga yabee
maybe he will come
me (pro) anniga
me and you
mean (act) xaasid ah
kasahorow means "many languages"

meaning (nom) micno
seek meaning
measles (nom) jadeeco

measles *is a disease*
measure *(act)* *qiyaas*
 measure two spoonfuls
measure *(nom)* *cabir*
 three measures of flour
meat *(nom)* *hilib*
 goat meat *hilibka riyaha*
medicine *(nom)* *daawo*
 bitter medicine
meet *(act)* *la kulan*
 meet me at home
meeting *(nom)* *kulan*
 cancel the meeting
meitnerium *(sci)* *meetreeniyam*
 meitnerium (Mt) has 109 protons

melon *(nom)* *qare*
 green melon
melon seed *(nom)* *siidh*
 melon sed stew
melt *(act)* *mil*
 the sheabutter is melting
memorization *(nom)* *xafidaad*
 some memorization is good
memorize *(act)* *xifdi*
 to memorize
memory *(nom)* *xusuus*
 computer memory
men *(plural(nom)* *nin*

mendelevium *(sci)* *mendaliiniyam*
 *mendelevium (Md) has 101 pro-
 tons*

menses *(nom)* *caadada*

mercury *(sci)* *meerkuri*
 mercury (Hg) has 80 protons
mercy *(nom)* *naxariis*
 goodness and mercy
mere *(adj)* *aan ka badnayn*
 mere fool
message *(nom)* *fariin*
 when the message arrived
messenger *(nom)* *nebi*
 the messengers arrived
messengers *(nom)* *nebiyo*
 the messengers have come
messiah *(nom)* *masiixa*
 are you the messiah?
met *(ydy(i(act)* *wuu ... laay kulan*

metal *(nom)* *bir*
 hat of metal
metaphor *(nom)* *sarbeeb*
 a good metaphor
meter *(nom)* *halbeega dhererka*
 ten meters
metre *(nom)* *halbeega dhererka*
 ten metres
microorganism *(nom)* *noole yar*

microwave *(nom)* *maeekrowevu*
 $pro{:}my_n om : mothertdy(f(act : want))det : a_n om : microwave$

middle *(nom)* *dhexda*

mile (nom) *mayl*
  ten miles
milestone (nom) *guul*
  an important milestone
milk (nom) *caano*
  to drink milk
millet (nom) *masago*
  millet porridge
million (adj) *milyan*
  a million bottles
mind (nom) *maskax*
  her mind
mine (pro) *waxeyga*
  this thing is mine
minimum (adj) *inta ugu yar*
  minimum quantity
ministry (nom) *wasaarad*
  ministry of education
minor (adj) *yar*
  a minor town
mint (nom) *reexaan*
  mint and water
minute (nom) *daqiiqad*
  five minutes
mirror (nom) *muraayad*
  big mirror *muraayad weyn*
miser (nom) *qofka kaydiya han-*
  tida ee isticmaala inyar
  he is a miser
miserly (adj) *bakhalynimo*
  he is miserly
misfortune (nom) *nasiib daro*

  many misfortunes
miss (act) *u xiis*
  I miss home
miss (nom) *u xiisid*
  lady and young lady
miss (nom) *u xiisid*
  lady and young lady
mission (nom) *hawlgal*

missionary (nom) *qof u shaqeeya*
  din faafin
  they are missionaries
missus (nom) *xaas*
  Missus Clinton
mist (nom) *ceeryaamo*
  morning mist
mistake (nom) *khalad*
  everyone makes mistakes
mister (nom) *mudane*
  Mister Annan
mistress (nom) *marwo*
  master and mistress
mix (act) *isku dar*
  to mix tomatoes and pepper
mix (act) *isku dar*
  to mix tomatoes and pepper
modern (adj) *cusub /casri*
  modern language
molybdenum (sci) *molibednum*
  molybdenum (Mo) has 42 protons

mom (nom) *hooyo*

moment (nom) *wakhti*
 the moment is up
Monday (nom) *Isniin*
 Monday children
money (nom) *lacag*
 money helps
Mongolia (nom) *Moongooliya*
 go to Mongolia
Mongolian (nom) *Moongooliyaan*
 the Mongolians
monitor (nom) *kormeer*
 heart monitor
monkey (nom) *daanyeer*
 a monkey likes bananas *daany-eerku wuxuu jecelyay muuska*
month (nom) *bil*
 one month
moon (nom) *dayax*
 moon and stars *dayax iyo xiddigo*

more (adj) *badan*
 more food
more than (pre) *in ka badan*
 she eats more than me
morning (nom) *subax*
 early morning
Moroccan (nom) *Morookaan*
 the Moroccans
Morocco (nom) *Marooko*
 go to Morocco
morsel (nom) *waxoogaa*
 two morsels
mortar (nom) *hoobiye*

 pestle and mortar
Mosotho (nom) *Mosoto*
 the Basotho
mosquito (nom) *kaneeco*
 a mosquito has bitten me
mother (nom) *hooyo*
 my mother's child is my sibling
Motswana (nom) *Motiswaana*
 the Batswana
mountain (nom) *buur*
 mountain peak
mourner (nom) *baroorte*
 many mourners
mouse (nom) *jiir*
 a big mouse *jiir weyn*
mouse (sci) *jiir*
 computer mouse
mouth (nom) *af*
 my mouth *afkayga*
mouthful (nom) *waxoogaa*
 two morsels
move (act) *guur*

Mozambican (nom) *Musaabiqiyaan*
 the Mozambicans
Mozambique (nom) *Musaambiqiyuu*
 go to Mozambique
mud (nom) *dhoobo*
 wash the mud
mudfish (nom) *kalluunka dhoobada hoos gala*
 catch the mudfish
multiplication (nom) *isku dhu-*

fasho
2 x 1 = 2; this is multiplication
murder (*nom*) dilaa
goessip and murder
murderer (*nom*) gacankudhiigle
he is a murderer
mushroom (*nom*) boqoshaa
mushroom soup
music (*nom*) hees
play music
musician (*nom*) muusikiiste
the musicians
muslim (*nom*) muslim
a Christian and a Muslim
mute (*nom*) ammusan
a mute cannot speak
mute (*adj*) aan hadli karin/doqon

my (*pos*) kayga
my house gurigayga
Myanma (*nom*) Maynaama
the Myanmas
Myanmar (*nom*) Maynamaar
go to Myanmar
myself (*pro*) naftayda
I love myself

N

Nairobi (*nom*) Nayroobi
go to Nairobi
name (*nom*) magac
my name magacayga

Namibia (*nom*) Naamiibiya
go to Namibia
Namibian (*nom*) Naamiibiyaan
the Namibians
nation (*nom*) qaran
your nation
national (*adj*) qaran
a national bank
nationwide (*adj*) wadanka oo dhan

nausea (*nom*) lallabo
she has nausea
navel (*nom*) xudun

near (*adv*) dhow
pull near to me
neck (*nom*) qoor
the tie hangs on his neck
necklace (*nom*) silsilad
ivory necklace
need (*act*) baahi
to need family
needle (*nom*) irbad
string and needle
negative (*adj*) diidmo ah
negative one
neighbor (*nom*) deris

neighborhood (*nom*) derisnimo

neighbour (*nom*) deris
my neighbour
neighbourhood (*nom*) derisnimo

we live in the same neighbour-hood
neodymium *(sci)* *neofhmiyam*
 neodymium (Nd) has 60 protons

neon *(sci)* *niyoon*
 neon (Ne) has 10 protons
Nepal *(nom)* *Niibaal*
 go to Nepal
Nepali *(nom)* *Niibaali*
 the Nepalis
nephew *(nom)* *wiil aad adeer*
 my father's nephew
neptunium *(sci)* *nibtiiniyam*
 neptunium (Np) has 93 protons
nerve *(nom)* *dareemayaasha*
 brain and nerves
nervous *(adj)* *walwalsan*
 a nervous person
nest *(nom)* *buul shimbireed*

net *(nom)* *shabaq*
 a fisherman's net
network *(nom)* *shabakad*
 the network light is on
neutron *(sci)* *niyutoron*
 a neutron has a charge of 0
nevertheless *(cjn)* *laakiin*
 I like it, but
new *(adj)* *cusub*
 new family
news *(nom)* *warar*
 news of the realm

newspaper *(nom)* *wargeys*
 I am reading the newspaper
nice *(adj)* *fican*
 make it nice
nickel *(sci)* *niikal*
 nickel (Ni) has 28 protons
niece *(nom)* *inanta aad abti/adeer*
 u tahay
 my nieces
Niger *(nom)* *Nayjar*
 go to Niger
Nigeria *(nom)* *Nayjeeriya*
 go to Nigeria
Nigerian *(nom)* *Nayjeeriyaan*
 the Nigerians
Nigerien *(nom)* *Nayjeriyeen*
 the Nigeriens
night *(nom)* *habeen madoobaad*
 8 o'clock in the night
nightfall *(nom)* *galab*
 daybreak and nightfall
nine *(adj)* *sagaal*
 Nine bottles *sagaal dhaloonyinka*
nine persons *(nom)* *sagaal qo-food*
 nine persons are coming
nineteen *(adj)* *sagaal iyo toban*
 nineteen bottles *sagaal iyo toban*
 dhaloonyinka
ninety *(adj)* *sagaashan*
 ninety bottles
niobium *(sci)* *niibiyam*
 niobium (Nb) has 41 protons

nitrogen *(sci)* naytarojin
 nitrogen (N) has 7 protons
no *(exc)* maya
 I say no
Noah *(nom)* Nuux
 Noah is a man
nobelium *(sci)* noobeeliyam
 nobelium (No) has 102 protons
noise *(nom)* sawaxan
 stop making noise
nominate *(act)* magacow
 name a time
nonagon *(nom)* sagaal xagale
 a nonagon has nine angles
nonsense *(nom)* wax macno daro
ah
 he talks nonsense
noon *(nom)* duhur
 noon has arrived
normal *(adj)* caadi ah
 normal behaviour
north *(nom)* waqoooyi
 go north
North Korea *(nom)* Waqooyiga
Kuuriya
 go to North Korea
North Korean *(nom)* Waqooyi Ku-
uriyaan
 the North Koreans
Norway *(nom)* Noorway
 go to Norway
nose *(nom)* san
 ear and nose

not *(adv)* maya
 it is not a snake
not have *(act)* ma haysto
 *I don't have money but I have prop-
erty*
nothing *(nom)* waxba
 I have nothing
noun *(nom)* magac
 four nouns
November *(nom)* Rajalood labaad
 November has 30 days
novice *(nom)* barbarad
 he is a novice
now *(adv)* hadda
 go now
now *(cjn)* immika
 so what now?
nub *(nom)* kuus yar
 nub of a pen
nucleus *(sci)* nukliyas
 *a nucleus contains protons and
neutrons*
number *(nom)* tiro
 number 5
nurse *(nom)* kalkaaliso
 she is a nurse
nut *(nom)* laws
 they eat nuts

O

obedience *(nom)* addeecid
 obedience and love

obey *(act)* adeec
　obey your parents
obstacle *(nom)* caqabad
　many obstacles
obviously *(adv)* sida cad

occupational *(adj)* shaqada

ocean *(nom)* bad
　a large ocean
octagon *(nom)* sideed xagale
　an octagon has eight angles
October *(nom)* Rajalood kow
　October has 31 days
offering *(nom)* soo bandhigaya
　we will receive an offering
office *(nom)* xafiis
　the office of my mother
often *(adv)* inta badan
　she often comes here
oh *(exc)* oh
　oh my sister!
oil *(nom)* saliid
　the oil
okay *(exc)* haye
　okay let's go
okra *(nom, c1)* baamiye

okro *(nom)* baamiye

old *(adj)* da' ah
　old pan
old lady *(nom)* gabadh weyn

　my old lady
old man *(nom)* nin weyn
　he is an old man
Olympics *(nom)* Ciyaaraha Olom-
　bikada
　Olympics competition
Oman *(nom)* Cumaan
　go to Oman
Omani *(nom)* Cumaani
　the Omanis
on *(pre)* dulsaara
　sleep on the table
one *(adj)* hal
　There is one bottle standing on
　top of the house hal dhalo
one *(pro)* hal
　one does not believe fables
one by one *(adv)* mid mid
　they came one by one
one person *(nom)* hal qof
　one person is coming
onion *(nom)* basal

only *(adj)* kaliya
　only you
open *(act)* fur
　I open the door
oppose *(act)* khilaaf
　we will oppose evil
oppress *(act)* dulmi
　you are oppressing me
oppression *(nom)* dulmi
　such oppression!

option *(nom)* doorasho
  five options
or *(cjn)* mise
  Kofi or Ama Kofi mise Ama
orange *(adj)* liimi
  wear the orange cap
orange *(nom)* araanjo
  three oranges araanjo saddex
order *(act)* habee/dalbo
  to order food
order *(act)* habee/dalbo
  to order food
ordinance *(nom)* qaynuun

organism *(nom)* noole

orient *(nom)* dhulalka bariga
  go east
Oromo *(nom)* Oromo
  Oromo language
orphan *(nom)* agoon
  we are orphans
osmium *(sci)* oosmiyam
  osmium (Os) has 76 protons
ostentatious *(adj)* soo jiidasho leh
  an ostentatious dress
ostrich *(nom)* goroyo
  an ostrich is a bird
other side *(adv)* dhinaca kale
  let us go to the other side
ouch *(exc)* ax
  Ouch! It hurts
our *(pos)* waxayaga

  our house
ours *(pro)* waxayaga
  I and Kofi, this thing is ours
ourselves *(pro)* naftayada
  for ourselves
out *(adv)* baxay
  he is coming out of the house
outdated *(adj)* dhacay
  outdated lorry
outdoors *(nom)* banaan
  go outdoors
outside *(adv)* dibada
  stroll outside
outside *(nom)* ka baxsan
  go outside
outskirt *(nom)* duleed
  I live in the outskirts
ovary *(nom)* ugxan
  women have two ovaries
oven *(nom)* foorno
  the bread is in the oven
overflow *(act)* xad dhaafid
  the lake has overflowed
overgrow *(act)* xad korid
  the backyard is overgrown
overturn *(act)* kala wareeg
  the pan has overturned
oware *(nom)* jees
  can you play oware?
owe *(act)* ku yeelo
  I owe you
owl *(nom)* guumeys
  an owl is a bird guumeystu waa

shimbir
owner (nom) mulkiile
 the owner of the car
ox (nom) dibi
 I see an ox
oxygen (nom) Ogsajiin
 oxygen is in air
oxygen (sci) ogsijin
 oxygen (O) has 8 protons
oyster (nom) lohod
 I eat oysters

P

paddle (nom) ul doon ku wadid
 canoe and paddle
padlock (nom) quful
 padlock and key
page (nom) bog
 open page twenty-two
pail (nom) baaldi
 pail and soap
pain (nom) xanuun
 the pain is here
painful (adj) xanuun ah
 illness is painful
paint (nom) rinji
 white paint
Pakistan (nom) Bakistaan
 go to Pakistan
Pakistani (nom) Bakistaani
 the Pakistanis

pal (nom) saxiib

palace (nom) qasri/madaxtooyo
 new palace
Palestine (nom) Falastiin
 go to Palestine
Palestinean (nom) Falastiiniyaan
 the Palestineans
palladium (sci) balaadhiyam
 palladium (Pd) has 46 protons
palm (nom) sacab
 open out your palms
palm (nom) sacab
 open out your palms
palmwine (nom) nooc khamriga
 kamid ah
 drink palmwine
pap (nom) cunto carruureed
 eat the pap
papaya (nom, c1) ciddiyaha aroosada

parable (nom) masaal
 the parables of Jesus
paraesthesia (nom) shucuur aan
 caadi ahayn

paralysis (nom) curyanimo
 paraliesis is a disease
parched (adj) la dubay
 parched skin
parents (nom) waalidin
 his parents
paresthesia (nom) shucuur aan

caadi ahayn

parliament *(nom)* baarlaman
 elect her to go to parliament
parrot *(nom)* baqbaaq
 two parrots
parsley *(nom)* kimsir
 parsley is a plant
part *(nom)* qayb
 the book has three parts
partner *(nom)* lamaane
 she is my partner
party *(nom)* xaflad
 I am going to a party
pass *(act)* dhaaf
 if you are passing, call me
pass by *(act)* ka gudbid

passport *(nom)* basaboor/dal ku
 gal
 your passport
password *(nom)* ereyga sirta ah
 change password
paste *(act)* koollo
 to paste it on the wall
pastor *(nom, c1)* wadaad

path *(nom)* wadiiqo
 follow the path
patience *(nom)* samir
 love and patience
patient *(nom)* bukaan
 the patients sleep here

patriotism *(nom)* wadaninimo
 he has patriotism
pawpaw *(nom)* ciddiyaha aroosada

pay *(act)* bixi
 I will pay
peace *(nom)* nabad
 I want peace
peacock *(nom)* daa'uus
 three peacocks
peck *(act)* qaniinyo shimbireed
 the chicken is pecking corn
pedestrian *(nom)* lugeyn
 nine pedestrians
pedophile *(nom)* faro xumeyn
 he is a pedophile
peel *(act)* diir
 to peel plantain
peel off *(act)* diirka ka qaad
 peel off the plaster
peer *(nom)* iskufil
 your peers
pen *(nom)* qalin
 ink in a pen
pencil *(nom)* qalin
 pencil and pen qalin iyo qalin
pencil *(nom)* qalin
 pencil and pen qalin iyo qalin
penis *(nom)* gus
 you don't say 'penis' in public
pentagon *(nom)* shan geesle
 a pentagon has five angles
people *(nom)* dad

some people

pepper (nom) basbaas
the pepper burns

perfect (adj) kaamil ah
a perfect ending

perfume (nom) cadar
what perfume is that?

period (nom) muddo
my period came early

perjury (nom) been sheeg
perjury in court

permanent (adj) joogto ah
a permanent job

permission (nom) ogolaansho

person (nom) qof
important person

pesewa (nom) halbeeg lacageed oo
laga isticmaalo Gaana
one cedi makes a hundred pesewas

pestle (nom) tumid
pestle and mortar

pet (nom) xayawaan dabjoog ah
my pet

Peter (nom) Yaraansho
read 1 Peter 2:1

petition (nom) codsi

pharmacist (nom) farmasiile

philanderer (nom) nin mararka
sameeya xiriirada jinsiga ee aan joog-

tada ahayn
you have made yourself a philan-
derer

philanthropist (nom) deeq bixiye
she is a philanthropist

Philippines (nom) Filibiinees
go to Philippines

philosopher (nom) faylasoof
she is a philosopher

philosophy (nom) falsafad
I am learning philosophy

phlegm (nom) xaako
wipe the phlegm

phone (act) telefoon
you phone me

phone (nom) telefoon
her phone telefoonkeeda

phosphorus (sci) fosfooras
phosphorus (P) has 15 protons

photograph (nom) sawir
take a photograph

physics (nom) fiisigis
we are learning physics

piano (nom) biyaano
play the piano

pick (nom) qaad
to break rocks with a pick

pick up (act) qaad
pick up the stones

pick up (act) qaad
pick up the stones

picture (nom) sawir
beautiful picture sawir qurux badan

pie (nom) *doolshe*
  three pies
pierce (act) *daloolin*
  pierce your ear
pig (nom) *doofaarka*
  some pigs are pink
pigeon (nom) *qoolley*
  a pigeon is a bird
pigfeet (nom) *cagaha dofaarka*
  pigfeet soup
piglet (nom) *doofaar yar*
  piglets
pillar (nom) *tiir*
  build the pillars
pillow (nom) *birkin*
  pillow and bed *birkin iyo sariir*
pimple (nom) *fin*
  I have a pimple
pinch (act) *xoog u xanuujin*
  stop pinching me
pineapple (nom) *canaanas*
  pineapple juice
pink (adj) *basali*
  some pigs are pink
pins and needles (nom) *musabiir iyo cirbado*
  pins and needles is not a disease

pioneer (nom) *horyaal*
  they are pioneers
pipe (nom) *biibiile*
  pipe water

pipe (nom) *biibiile*
  pipe water
pit (nom) *bohol*
  dig a pit
pitch black (adj) *dib u dhisitaan*
  pitch black darkness
pitiable (adj) *ka nixitaan*
  pitiable child
pitiful (adj) *naxdin leh*
  pitiful child
pito (nom) *siidhi*
  drink pito
pizza (nom) *biisa*
  five pizzas
place (nom) *meel*
  which place?
plague (nom) *cudur*
  no plagues there
plan (act) *qorshee*
  one head does not plan
plan (nom) *qorshe*
  a pot and a plan
plane (nom) *diyaarad*
  board a plane
planet (nom) *caalam*
  Earth is a planet
plank (nom) *banaan*
  plank and nail
plant (act) *beer*
  to plant a tree
plant (nom) *dhir*
  red plant
plantain (nom) *muuska balaan-*

tayn
plantain and cassava
plaster *(nom)* *salaaxid*
 remove the plaster
plastic *(adj)* *caag ah*
 plastic cup
plate *(nom)* *bileedh*
 meydh bileedhkaaga
platinum *(sci)* *ballaatiyam*
 platinum (Pt) has 78 protons
play *(nom)* *ciyaar*
 watch a play
play *(act)* *ciyaar*
 we are playing
playing field *(nom)* *garoon*
 they are on the field
pleasant *(adj)* *raaxo leh*
 a pleasant person
please *(adv)* *fadlan*
 to say 'please'
pleasure *(nom)* *raaxeysi*
 how do you sr pleasure
pledge *(nom)* *balanqaadid*
 God's pledge has been fulfilled
pledge *(nom)* *balanqaadid*
 God's pledge has been fulfilled
plenteous *(adj)* *barwaqada*

plentiful *(adj)* *faro badan*
 a plentiful harvest
plenty *(adj)* *badan*
 plenty of issues
pluck *(act)* *rif*

pluck fruit
plutonium *(sci)* *buluutooniyam*
 plutonium (Pu) has 94 protons
pocket *(nom)* *jeeb*
 nothing inside my pocket
point *(nom)* *dhibic*
 1 point 5 (1.5) is one and a half.

pointer *(nom)* *tilmaame*
 use the pointer
poisonous *(adj)* *sun ah*
 a poisonous man like you
poke *(act)* *guji*
 poke me on Facebook
police *(nom)* *boolis*
 five police
politician *(nom)* *siyaasi*
 Mahama is a politician
politics *(nom)* *siyaasad*
 you like politics
polonium *(sci)* *boloniyam*
 polonium (Po) has 84 protons
pomade *(nom)* *cadar madaxa lamarsado*
 fragrant pomade
poop *(nom)* *saxaro*

poor *(adj)* *fakhri ah*
 a poor country
porcupine *(nom)* *caanaqubta*
 three porcupines
pork *(nom)* *doofaarka*
 pork and beef
pork *(nom)* *doofaarka*

pork and beef
porpoise *(nom)* *xayawaan badeed*
 three porpoises
porridge *(nom)* *boorash*
 millet porridge
port *(nom)* *dekad*
 Takoradi has a port
porter *(nom)* *xamaal*
 the porter carries a box
porter *(nom)* *xamaal*
 the porter carries a box
Portugal *(nom)* *Boortugaal*

position *(nom)* *boos*
 a good position
possess *(act)* *lahow*

post office *(nom)* *boosto*
 I am going to the post office
pot *(nom)* *dheri*
 metal pot
potassium *(sci)* *botaashiyam*
 potassium (K) has 19 protons
pound *(act)* *xero*
 I pound fufu
pound *(act)* *xero*
 I pound fufu
pound *(nom)* *xero*
 ten pounds
pour *(act)* *shub*
 pour water
poverty *(nom)* *saboolnimo*
 poverty or wealth

powder-keg *(nom)* *qoriga*
 three powder-kegs
power *(nom)* *xoog*
 strength and power
powerful *(adj)* *awood leh*
 powerful prophet
praise *(act)* *ammaan*
 to praise God
praise *(nom)* *ammaanida*
 she deserves praise
praseodymium *(sci)* *barasodimiyam*
 praseodymium (Pr) has 59 protons
pray *(act)* *tuko*
 to pray for my enemies
prayer *(nom)* *salaad*
 prayer is good
preacher *(nom)* *wacdiye*
 she is a preacher
predict *(act)* *saadaali*

preface *(nom)* *gogoldhig*
 book preface
pregnancy *(nom)* *uur*
 my pregnancy is easy
prejudice *(nom)* *naceyb*
 fear and prejudice
preparation *(nom)* *diyaarin*
 make preparation
preparations *(nom)* *diyaarinta*
 make preparations
preschool *(nom)* *barbaarin*

present (nom) *hadiyada*
 a good gift *hadiyad wanaagsan*
preservation (nom) *ilaalin*
 the preservation of food
preservative (nom) *ilaalinta*
 it has no preservatives in it
preserve (act) *dhawr*
 to preserve the food
president (nom) *madaxweyne*
 the president has arrived
press (act) *riix*
 to press it seven times
pretend (act) *iska dhig*
 you are pretending
pretend (act) *iska dhig*
 you are pretending
pretty (adj) *qurxoon*
 a pretty woman
price (nom) *qiimaha*
 how much is the price?
pride (nom) *kibir*
 his pride
priest (nom) *wadaad*

prince (nom) *amiir*
 he is a prince
princess (nom) *amiirad*
 she is a princess
print (act) *daabac*
 they print books
print (act) *daabac*
 they print books
printer (nom) *daabace*

 book printer
priority (nom) *mudnaan*
 what is your priority?
prison (nom) *xabsi*
 go to prison
problem (nom) *dhibaato*
 many problems
proceed (act) *hore u wad*
 he proceeded to see
procession (nom) *socod*
 join the procession
proclamation (nom) *ogeysiis muhiim ah*
 proclamation of the rights of humankind
procrastination (nom) *dib u dhigis*
 procrastination is not good
product (nom) *badeeco*
 to advertise a product
profit (nom) *fa'iido*
 make profit
progress (nom) *horumar*

project (nom) *mashruuc*
 ten projects
promethium (sci) *boromiitiyam*
 promethium (Pm) has 61 protons

promise (act) *ballan qaad*
 promise me
promise (nom) *balan*
 give me a promise
pronoun (nom) *magac u yaal*

two pronouns

proof *(nom)* cadeyn
show me the proof

prop *(act)* ku tiiri
prop the door

property *(nom)* hanti
my property

prophesy *(act)* wax sii sheeg
prophesy prosperity

prophet *(nom)* nebi
powerful prophet

proposal *(nom)* hindise
a good proposal

proprietor *(nom)* mulkiile
she is a proprietor

prosperity *(nom)* barwaaqo
peace and prosperity

prostitute *(nom)* dhilo
a male prostitute

protactinium *(sci)* borotakaniyam
protactinium (Pa) has 91 protons

protect *(act)* ilaali
protect us

protection *(nom)* ilaalin
give me protection

proton *(sci)* borotoroon
a proton has a charge of +1

proverb *(nom)* maahmaah
quote a proverb

Proverbs *(nom)* maahmaayo
read Proverbs 27:17

provide *(act)* sii

prudence *(nom)* miyir
prudence and love

prudent *(adj)* si miyir leh
a prudent person

psychology *(nom)* cilmi nafsi
to learn pyschology

public *(nom)* dadweynaha
you don't say 'vagina' in public

puff-adder *(nom)* nooc masaska kamida
the puff-adder is dead

pull *(act)* soo jiid
to pull the rope

pungently *(adv)* si qaniinyo ah
smell pungently

punish *(act)* ciqaab
punish him

pupil *(nom)* arday
pupil and eyeball

puppet *(nom)* boonballo
red puppet

purchase *(act)* gado
purchase a few things

pure *(adj)* saafi ah
pure gold

purple *(adj)* buluug guduud ah
purple flower

purpose *(nom)* ujeedo
your purpose

pursue *(act)* eryo
pursue him

push *(act)* riix

to push the lorry
pussy (nom, c1) *bisad*
a cat has a tail *bisadu waxay leedahay dabo*
put (act) *dhig*

puzzle (nom) *xujo*
puzzles and riddles
python (nom) *mas weyn/luqada koombuyuuter ee bayton*
a python is a snake

Q

Qatari (nom) *Qadari*
the Qataris
quake (nom) *dhul gariir*
big earthquake
quake (act) *ruxruxid*

quantity (nom) *tirada*
quantity of the food
quarrel (nom) *muran*
a big quarrel
quarrel (nom) *muran*
a big quarrel
quarter (nom) *rubuc*
two quarters make half
queen (nom) *boqorad*
she is a queen
question (nom) *su'aal*
I have a question

quick (adj) *dhakso ah*

quickly (adv) *si dagdag ah*

quiet (adj) *xasillan*
be quiet
quran (nom) *Quran*

R

race (nom) *tartan*
run a race
radiation (sci) *shucaac*
the radiation of the sun
radio (nom) *raadiyow*
switch on the radio
radium (sci) *raadhiyam*
radium (Ra) has 88 protons
radon (sci) *raadon*
radon (Rn) has 86 protons
rag (nom) *calal*
old rag
railway (nom) *wado tareen*
a railway passes through my town

rainbow (nom) *qaanso-robaad*
I see a rainbow
rainy season (nom) *xilli robaad*
the rainy season has arrived
raise (act) *sare u qaad*
raise your hand

raisin *(nom)* sabiib
  eat the raisins
ran *(ydy(f(act)* way ... ordidtay

ransom *(nom)* madax furasho
  pay a ransom
rap *(nom)* raab
  rap music
rascal *(nom)* doqon
  she is a rascal
rat *(nom)* jiir
  a big rat
raucously *(adv)* sawaxan leh
  to laugh raucously
razor *(nom)* sheef
  sharpen the razor
reach a final milestone *(act)* gaar
  dhacdadii uu dambeysay
  if the time comes
read *(act)* akhri
  to read a book
reading *(nom)* akhris
  repeat the reading
ready *(adv)* diyaar ah
  I am ready
real *(adj)* xaqiiq ah

realm *(nom)* boqortoyadisi
  news of the realm
rear *(act)* gadaal
  rear animals
rear *(nom)* gadaal

rearguard *(nom)* gaadh
  they are the rearguard
reason *(nom)* sabab
  everything has a reason
rebel *(nom)* mucaarad
  the rebels won
rebellion *(nom)* caasinimo
  the rebellion has started
reconnaisance *(nom)* sahan

recover *(act)* ladnaansho
  a sick person recovers
rectangle *(nom)* afar xaglood/laydi
  a rectangle has four angles
recurring *(adj)* soo noqnoqosho
  recurring disease
red *(adj)* cas
  red lips bushimo cas
reduce *(act)* dhim
  reduce it by five
reflection *(nom)* milicsi
  his reflection
refrigerator *(nom)* tallaagad
  open the fridge
refuge *(nom)* qaxooti
  our refuge
regenerate *(act)* dib u cusbonaysii

region *(nom)* gobol
  three regions
regret *(act)* qoomamee
  I regret I said that
regret *(nom)* qoomameyn

pain and regret
reign (act) *boqor noqosho*
God reigns
reject (act) *diid*
I will reject fear
rejoice (act) *farxad geli*
rejoice, I say, rejoice
relative (nom) *qaraabo*
he is a relative
reliable (adj) *laguu kalsonaan karo*

remain (act, c1) *joogid*

remainder (nom) *ka dhiman/hadhaa*
the remainder of the food
remark (act) *tacliiq*

remember (act) *xusuuso*
you remember me?
remind (act) *xusuusin*
to remind someone
remorse (nom) *qoomamo*
he showed no remorse
remove (act) *ka saarid*
to remove the shoes from here
repeat (act) *ku celin*
repeat the reading
repent (act) *tawbad keenid*
they repented
repentance (nom) *toobad keenid*
love and repentance
replace (act) *beddelid*
replace me

replacement (nom) *bedel*

reply (act) *jawaab celin*

report (nom) *war bixin*
make a report
request (act) *codso*
to request food
request (nom) *codsi*
my request
requester (nom) *codsadaha*
who is the requester?
resemble (act) *u eekaan*
you resemble your sibling
reside (act) *degid*
I reside in Osu
resource (nom) *khayraad*
a good resource
respect (act) *xushmeyn*
I respect you very much
respect (nom) *ixtiram*
show respect
respond (act) *ka jawaabid*
he responded
response (nom) *jawaab*
song's response (i.e. chorus)
responsibility (nom) *mas'uuliyad*
it is your responsibility
responsible (adj) *masuul*
he is a responsible man
rest (act) *naso*

restaurant (nom) *makhaayad/hudheel*

laga cunteeyo
 a new restaurant
resurrection (nom) soo saarid
 the resurrection of Christ
retail (act) tafaariq

return (act) soo celi
 to return home
Reunion (nom) dib u kulan
 go to Reunion
reveal (act) muuji
 reveal the truth
revelation (nom) kashifaad
 he had a revelation
revival (nom) soo nooleyn
 revival has come to town
revive (act) dib u soo nolee
 revive yourself
rhenium (sci) heeniyam
 rhenium (Re) has 75 protons
rheumatism (nom) Ruumatiisamka
 rheumatism is a disease
rhino (nom, c1) wiyil
 maybe the aforementioned person has sent him
rhinoceros (nom, c2) wiyil
 maybe the aforementioned person has sent him
rhodium (sci) hoodiyam
 rhodium (Rh) has 45 protons
rice (nom) bariis
 rice and beans
rich (adj) maal leh

 a rich country
riddle (nom) hal xiraale
 puzzles and riddles
right (adj) midig
 go right
rights (nom) xuquuq
 rights of humankind
ring (nom) fargal
 put on the ring
ringworm (nom) fayada
 he has ringworm
ripen (act) bislee
 the mango has ripened
rise (act) kor u qaad
 to rise at six in the morning
rise (act) kor u qaad
 to rise at six in the morning
rival (nom) tartame
 she is my rival
rivalry (nom) tartan
 stop the rivalry
river (nom) webi
 a river goes into a sea
road (nom) wado
 new road
roam (act) mushaax
 roam everywhere
roast (act) dub
 roast a little corn
rock (act) dhagax
 I shall never be rocked
rock (nom) dhagax
 a big rock

roentgenium (sci) *rioonjiinayam*
  roentgenium (Rg) has 111 protons

Romans (nom) *roomaaniyiinta*
  read Romans 5:1
roof (nom) *saqaf*
  the house with the red roof
roof (act) *saqaf*
  roof the house
room (nom) *qol*
  she is sleeping in the room
roost (act) *meesha ay shimbruhu*
  u hoydaa
  if a bird does not fly, it roosts
root (nom) *xidid*
  root of a tree
rope (nom) *xadhig*
  a long rope
rose (nom) *ubax*
  a rose is a flower
rot (act) *qurmid*
  the mango is rotting
row (act) *safka/ taxid*
  row your boat
row (nom) *saf*
  three rows of chairs
royal (adj) *reer boqoreed ah*
  royal family
royalty (nom) *boqortoyada*
  you are royalty
rubbish (nom) *qashin*
  throw away the rubbish
rubidium (sci) *rubiidhiyam*

rubidium (Rb) has 37 protons
ruin (act, c1) *burburi*
  destroy everything
rule (nom) *sharci*
  she follows the rules
rum (nom) *raam*
  rum or vodka?
rump (nom) *saxgad taag ah*
  look at his rump
run (act) *ordid*
  to run like a hare
Russia (nom) *Ruush*
  go to Russia
Russian (nom) *Raashiyaan*
  the Russians
ruthenium (sci) *ruteeniyam*
  ruthenium (Ru) has 44 protons
rutherfordium (sci) *ruuteriind-hiyam*
  rutherfordium (Rf) has 104 pro-tons
Rwanda (nom) *Ruwaandha*
  go to Rwanda
Rwandan (nom) *Ruwaandhaan*
  the Rwandans

S

sabotage (act) *curyaamin*
  sabotage her
sabotage (nom) *curyaamin*
  this is sabotage

sack *(nom)* kiish
  sack of charcoal
sack *(nom)* kiish
  sack of charcoal
sacrifice *(nom)* hurid
  offer a sacrifice
sacrilege *(nom)* macbudyo
  what sacrilege is this?
sad *(adj)* murugsan
  a sad face
said *(ydy(i(act)* wuu ... dhihiday

salt *(nom)* cusbo

salted fish *(nom)* kalluun milix leh
  salted fish makes food tasty
salutation *(nom)* salaan

salvation *(nom)* badbaado
  our salvation
samarium *(sci)* samaariyam
  samarium (Sm) has 62 protons
same *(adj)* isku mid ah
  we are the same
sand *(nom)* ciid
  beach sand
sang *(ydy(i(act)* wuu ... heesiday

Santomean *(nom)* Saantoomiyaan
  the Santomeans
Sao Tome and Principe *(nom)* Sao Toome iyo Birinsayb

  go to Sao Tome and Principe
Saturday *(nom)* Sabti
  Saturday children
sauce *(nom)* suugo

saucepan *(nom)* digsi
  cook in the saucepan
Saudi Arabia *(nom)* Sucuudi Carabiya
  go to Saudi Arabia
Saudi Arabian *(nom)* Sucuudi Carabiyaan
  the Saudi Arabians
savant *(nom)* qof wax bartay
  they are savants
save *(act)* badbaadin
  save it
saviour *(nom)* baadbadiye
  my saviour
saw *(ydy(i(act)* wuu ... fiirashoay

saw *(nom)* mishaar
  the carpenter's saw
say *(act)* dhihid
  I say yes
say goodbye *(act)* dheh macaasalaama
  we take ten minutes to say goodbye
scald *(act)* biyo ku gubasho
  hot water scalds
scale *(nom)* qiyaas
  to measure with the scale
scale *(nom)* qiyaas

205

to measure with the scale
scandium (sci) *iskaandiyam*
scandium (Sc) has 21 protons
scar (nom) *xagtin*
her cheek has a scar
scarcity (nom) *yaraan*
scarcity of water
scare (act) *baqid*

scarecrow (nom) *wax qof loo eekaysi-iyay oo beeraha la dhexdhigo si ay xawayaanka uga baqadsiiso*
a scarecrow in a farm
scarlet (adj) *casaan*
a scarlet dress
scary (adj) *xagtin*
it is scary
scatter (act) *kala firdhid*
to scatter everywhere
scholarship (nom) *deeq waxbarasho*
I have a scholarship
school (nom) *dugsi/iskul*
I learn to read at school
science (nom) *saynis*
we are learning science
scissors (nom) *maqas*
give me the scissors
scoop (act) *qaadada*
scoop up sand
score (act) *dhibcaha*
to score a goal
scorn (nom) *quudhsi*
stop the scorn

scorpion (nom) *diba-qalooc*
a black scorpion
Scotland (nom) *Iskootlaan*
visit Scotland
scout (nom) *indheyn*

scrape (act) *nadiifin*
to scrape the fish scales
scream (act) *cabaadid*

scripture (nom) *kitaab*
to read the scriptures
scrub (act) *xoqid*
scrub the floor well
sea (nom) *bad*
a river goes into a sea
seaborgium (sci) *siiboorgiyam*
seaborgium (Sg) has 106 protons

search (act) *baadhid*
search his house
seat (nom) *kursi*
to sit on the seat
second (nom) *il biriqsi*
ten seconds
secret (nom) *sir*
I have a secret
sector (nom) *waax*

security (nom) *nabada ilaalin*
good security
see (act) *fiirasho*
to see ghosts

seed (nom) *iniin*
 three orange saws
seek (act) *doon doonid*
 to seek meaning
Sekondi (nom) *Sekondi*
 Sekondi and Takoradi
select (act) *doorasho*
 to select a book
selenium (sci) *seleeniyam*
 selenium (Se) has 34 protons
self (nom) *naf*
 myself, yourself
selfishness (nom) *daneystenimo*
 selfishness is not good
selfishness (nom) *daneystenimo*
 selfishness is not good
sell (act) *iibin*
 to sell houses
seller (nom) *iibiye*
 buyers and sellers
send (act) *dirid*
 send me
send (act) *dirid*
 send me
Senegal (nom) *Sinigaal*
 go to Senegal
Senegalese (nom) *Sinigaaliis*
 the Senegalese
sense (act) *dareemid*
 I sense we will score a goal
sense (nom) *dareen*

sentence (nom) *weedh*

 words join to make sentences
September (nom) *Carafo*
 September has 30 days
serious (adj) *dhab ah*
 a serious work
servant (nom) *adeege*
 my servant
servanthood (nom) *adeegenimo*
 our servanthood
serves you right (exc) *si sax ah
 u adeegid*
 *serves you right! come again to-
 morrow*
service (nom) *adeeg*
 thanksgiving service
Seselwa (nom) *Seseelwa*
 the Seselwas
set (nom) *bandhagid*

settle (act) *degid*
 settle there
seven (adj) *todobo*
 seven bottles todobo dhaloonyinka

seven persons (nom) *todoba qofood*
 seven persons are coming
seventeen (adj) *todobo iyo toban*
 *seventeen bottles todobo iyo toban
 dhaloonyinka*
seventy (adj) *todobaatan*
 seventy bottles
several (adj) *dhowr*

several people came
sew (act) *tolid*
 sew cloth
sex (nom) *jinsi*
 what is sex?
sex education (nom) *waxbarashada jinsigaga*
 I complet sex education
sexy (adj) *jinsi ahaan soo jiidasho leh*
 a sexy man
Seychelles (nom) *Seyjeelees*
 go to Seychelles
shade (nom) *hadh*
 I am sitting under the shade
shake (act) *ruxruxid*

shame (nom) *ceeb*
 shame and disgrace
shame (act) *ceeb*
 shame him
shape (nom) *qaab*
 the shape of the house
share (nom) *wadaag*
 where is my share?
share (act) *wadaagid*
 share the food
share bed with husband (act)
 la wadaag sarriirta sayiga
 Yaa will share a bed with her husband this night
sharpen (act) *afayn*
 sharpen a knife

she (pro) *iyada*
 she eats
sheabutter (nom) *subaga shiya*
 the fragrance of sheabutter
sheep (nom) *idaha*
 sheep meat (i.e. mutton) *hilibka idaha*
shell (nom) *qolof*
 shell of a crab
shield (nom) *dhufeys*
 He is my shield
shine (act) *iftiimin*
 sun is shining
ship (nom) *markab*
 a big ship
shirt (nom) *shaati/shaadh*
 she is wearing a shirt
shit (act) *saxaroon*
 the child is shitting
shoe (nom) *kabo*
 wear your shoes *xidho kabohaaga*

Shona (nom) *Shoona*
 I speak Shona
shoot (act) *toogasho*
 to shoot a gun
shop (nom) *dukaan*

shopping (nom) *dukaamaysi*
 my shopping
short (adj) *gaaban*
 short man
shorts (nom) *surwaal gaaban*

khakhi shorts

shoulder *(nom)* garab
  stand on my shoulders

shout *(act)* qaylin
  to shout for help

shovel *(nom)* majarafad

show *(act)* muujin

show ... pity *(act)* muuji ...u nixid
  show her pity

shower *(act)* qubayso
  to bath each morning

shower *(nom, c1)* musqul
  go to the bathroom

shrimp *(nom)* xawayan badeed
  four shrimps

shut *(act)* xidh
  shut the door

shut down *(act)* baqtii
  the shop shuts down in the evening

shy *(adj)* xishoonaya
  a shy woman

shyness *(nom)* xishonaya
  he has no shyness

shyness *(nom)* xishonaya
  he has no shyness

sibling *(nom)* walaal
  my mother's child is my sibling

sickness *(nom)* jirro
  what sickness have you?

side *(nom)* dhinac

love is on our side

Sierra Leone *(nom)* Si'eera Liy-oon
  go to Sierra Leone

Sierra Leonean *(nom)* Si'eera Liy-ooniyaan
  the Sierra Leoneans

sigh *(act)* guuxid
  he sighed

sighing *(nom)* taahid
  many sighings

sign *(nom)* saxiix
  a sign of hope

signify *(act)* tilmaamid

signpost *(nom)* boodh calaamadeed
  a tall signpost

silence *(nom)* aamusnaan
  silence, silence!

silent *(adj)* amuusan
  be silent

silicon *(sci)* silisoon
  silicon (Si) has 14 protons

silk *(nom)* xariir
  white silk

silk cotton tree *(nom)* geed suuf xariir ah
  cut the silk cotton tree

silver *(nom)* qallin
  silver and gold

silver *(sci)* silfer
  silver (Ag) has 47 protons

silver *(sci)* silfer

silver (Ag) has 47 protons
simple (adj) *fudud*

sin (nom) *dembi*
 sin and forgiveness
sing (act) *heesid*
  to sing a sweet song
sing jama (act) *hees jama*
  let us sing jama
Singapore (nom) *Singabuur*
  go to Singapore
Singaporean (nom) *Singabuuri*
  the Singaporeans
singing (nom) *heesid*
  I like her singing
singleton (nom) *hal qof*
  combine the singletons
sink (nom) *quusid*
  drain the sink
sink (act) *quusid*
  the boat is sinking
sir (nom) *mudane*
  I thank you sir
siren (nom) *firimbi*
  loud siren
sister (nom) *walaasha*
  my only sister
six (adj) *lix*
  six bottles *lix dhaloonyinka*
six persons (nom) *lix qofood*
  six persons are coming
sixteen (adj) *lix iyo toban*
  sixteen bottles *lix iyo toban dhaloonyinka*

sixty (adj) *lixdan*
  sixty bottles
skill (nom) *xirfad*
  she has good skills
skin (nom) *maqaar*
  dry skin
skirt (nom) *haaf - dharka hablaha*
  short skirt
skull (nom) *lafta madaxa*
  my skull
sky (nom) *cirka*
  to fly into the sky
slap (act) *dhirbaaxid*
  slap him
slate (nom) *nooc dhagaxa kamid ah*
  wipe the slate
slave (nom) *addoon*
  my slave
slavegirl (nom) *gabar adoon ah*
  six slavegirls
sleep (act) *seexasho*
  to sleep at night *si aad u seexato habeenkii*
sleep crust (nom) *xafajo*
  wash the sleep crust from under your eyes
sleep tight (exc) *si dagan u seexasho*

sleepiness (nom) *hurdo*
  food causes sleepiness

slept (ydy(i(act) wuu ... seexas-
hoay

slice (act) jar jarid
 slice the bread up
slim (adj) caato ah
 slim person
slip (act) siibasho
 she slipped and fell
slippers (nom) dacas
 you are wearing slippers waxaad
 xidhan tahay dacas
slow (adj) tartiib
 slow tortoise
slowly (adv) si tartiib ah
 a tortoise walks slowly
slowly (adv) si tartiib ah
 a tortoise walks slowly
sluggard (nom) caajis
 the sluggard is asleep
sluggard (nom) caajis
 the sluggard is asleep
slurp (act) wax cunid shanqadh
 sare leh
 she is slurping the soup
slut (nom) dhilo
 a male prostitute
small (adj) yar
 a small thing
smaller (adj) ka yar
 smaller house
smallest (adj) ugu yar
 his smallest child

smart (adj) xariif ah

smash (act) burburin
 the plate is smashed
smell (act) urin
 to smell the flowers
smell (nom) ur
 I sense a smell
smelly (adj) uraya
 smelly armpit
smile (act) dhoola caddayn
 to smile a bit
smith (nom) tumaal
 a smith makes tools
smoke (nom) qiiq
 belch smoke
smoothen (act) isku simid
 to smoothen the plank
snail (nom) ciddi
 I eat snails
snake (nom) mas
 a snake has no legs masku malaha
 cago
snatch (act) ka dhufasho
 snatched the phone
sneeze (act) hindhisid
 to sneeze loudly
snore (act) khuurin
 I snore
snoring (nom) khuurin
 loud snoring
snow (nom) baraf
 there is snow on the mountain

211

snuff (nom) *buuri*
  give me some snuff
so (cjn) *sidaa darteed*
  why so?
so there (exc) *daganaan u seex-asho*
  I say, "So there!"
soaked (adj) *la qooyay*
  soaked cloth
soap (nom) *saabuun*
  pail and soap *baag iyo saabuun*
sob (act) *ooy*
  to cry each time
soccer (nom) *kubada cagta*
  football competition
society (nom) *bulsho*

sock (nom) *sharabaad*
  you are wearing socks
sodium (sci) *soodiyam*
  sodium (Na) has 11 protons
sofa (nom) *fadhi*
  five sofas
soft (adj) *jilicsan*
  soft bread
soften (act) *jilcin*
  soften your voice
soil (nom) *dhulka*
  people of the earth
soldier (nom) *askari*
  the soldiers are marching
sole (adj) *kaliya*
  my sole child

sole (nom) *kaliya*
  how do you me sr soles
solemn (adj) *la sharfay*
  a solemn promise
solid (adj) *adke*
  solid water
Somali (nom) *Soomaali*
  Somali language *af Soomaali*
Somalia (nom) *Soomaaliya*
  go to Somalia
Somalian (nom) *Soomaaliyaan*
  the Somalians
some (pro) *wax kamid ah*
  give me some
some (det) *qaar ka mid ah*
  some food
someone (pro) *qof*
  someone is coming
something (nom) *wax uun*
  to hold something firmly
something (pro) *wax*
  show me something
somewhere (pro) *meel*
  we are going somewhere
son (nom) *wiil*
  my son
song (nom) *hees*
  play a song
soon (adv) *dhakho leh*
  she is coming soon
soot (nom) *danbas*
  black soot
sorcery (nom) *sixir*

practise sorcery
sore *(nom)* xanuun leh
  the dog is licking its sore
sorry *(exc)* waan ka xumay
  sorry sorry!
soul *(nom)* naf
  my soul exults
sound *(nom)* cod leh
  loud sound
soup *(nom)* maraq
  palm nut soup
south *(nom)* koonfur
  go south
South Africa *(nom)* Koonfurta Afrika
  go to South Africa
South African *(nom)* Koonfur Afrikaan
  the South Africans
South Korea *(nom)* Koonfur Ku-uriya
  go to South Korea
South Korean *(nom)* Koonfur Ku-uriyaan
  the South Koreans
South Sudan *(nom)* Koonfur su-udaan
  go to South Sudan
South Sudanese *(nom)* Koonfurta Sudaaniinta
  the South Sudanese
sow *(act)* beerin
  sow a tree
space *(sci)* hawada sare
  space is a vacuum

spade *(nom)* majarafad
  eight spades
Spain *(nom)* Isbayn
  we will go to Spain
Spanish *(nom)* Isbaanish
  I speak Spanish
spank *(act)* dhirbaaxid - gaar ahaan dabada
  I will spank you
spanner *(nom)* baanadd
  a big spanner
spatula *(nom)* malqaacad shaandho ah
three spatulas
speak *(act)* hadal
to speak the truth
spear *(nom)* waran
  they pierced him with a spear
special *(adj)* khaas ah
  special day
specific *(adj)* gaar ah
  show me the specific thing
spectacles *(nom)* muraayadaha indhaha
  she wears spectacles
spectator *(nom)* taageere
  the spectators
spider *(nom)* caaro
  spider's web xuubka caarada
spin-top *(nom)* qalab yar oo la wa-reejiyo si la isugu maaweeliyo
  five spin-tops
spinach *(nom)* isbiinaaj

spinach stew

spinal cord (nom) *xangulaha*
 my spinal cord
spine (nom) *dhabar*
 ear, nose and spine
spinning top (nom) *qalab yar oo*
 la wareejiyo si la isugu maaweeliyo
 Kofi plays with a spinning top
spirit (nom) *ruux*
 he has a strong spirit
spittle (nom) *candhuuf*
 wipe the spittle
split (act) *kala jabin*
 split in two
spoil (act) *kharibid*

spokesperson (nom) *afhayeen*
 the chieftain's spokesperson
sponge (nom) *isbuunyo*
 my sponge
sponsor (nom) *isku xayeysii*
 many sponsors
spoon (nom) *malqaacad*
 sixteen spoons *lix iyo toban malqaa-cadood*
spoor (nom) *wado tareen*
 the spoor of an animal
sport (nom) *ciyaaro*
 she likes sports
spread (act) *fidid*
 spread it
spread out (act) *kala fidid*
 spread out a mat

spring (nom) *guga*
 I spend Spring in England
springwater (nom) *biyaha guga*
 to drink springwater
sprout (act) *biqlid*
 the maize is sprouting
spy (nom) *sirdoon*
 he is a spy
spy (act) *jaajuusid*
 to spy on a country
squabbles (nom) *muran*
 squabbles and insults
squat (act) *fadhi-sare kac*
 hold your waist and squat
squeeze (act) *tuujin*
 squeeze the orange
squeeze drum (nom) *durbaanka*
 la cadaadiyo
 play the squeeze drum
squirrel (nom) *dabagaale*
 a squirrel likes palm nuts
Sri Lanka (nom) *Siira Laanka*
 go to Sri Lanka
Sri Lankan (nom) *Siira Laankaan*
 the Sri Lankans
stab (act) *toorirayn*
 to stab a man
staff (nom) *shaqaale*
 wooden staff
staff (nom) *shaqaale*
 wooden staff
stair (nom) *jaranjaro*
 climb the stairs

stamina (nom) *adkaysi*
  she has stamina
stamp (act) *calamad dhigid*
  Big Man, please stamp it for me

stamp (act) *calamad dhigid*
  Big Man, please stamp it for me

stand (act) *istaagid*
  to stand slowly
star (nom) *xiddig*
  plenty of stars *xiddigo badan*
start (act) *bilaabid*
  to start early
startle (act) *ka fiijin*
  I was startled
state (nom) *gobol*
  look at our pitiful state
state (act) *sheegid*
  he stated that
station (nom) *saldhig/xarun*
  train station
stay (act) *degid*
  I reside in Osu
steal (act) *xadid*
  steal and destroy
steer (act) *wadid*
  to steer the boat
step (act) *tallabayn*
  step on it
step-child (nom) *ilmo uu/ay dha-lay/dhashay sayigu/xaasku*
  my step-child

stew (nom) *fuud*
  make stew
steward (nom) *kirishboy*
  a good steward
stick (nom) *ul*
  break the stick
still (adv) *wali*
  still doing
stimulate (act) *kicin*
  to stimulate the wind
stinginess (nom) *bakheyl*
  stinginess or generosity
stink (act) *qurmuun*
  something is stinking
stinking fish seasoning (nom)
  xawaash kaluun bi'isaa
  add some stinking fish seasoning
  to the soup
stir (act) *walaaqid*
  stir the porridge
stomach (nom) *calool*

stomach-ache (nom) *calool xanuun*
  he has a stomach-ache
stone (nom) *dhagax*
  stones and cement
stool (nom) *saxaro*
  sit on the stool
stop (act) *joojin*
  stop making noise
stop (nom) *joojin*
  bus stop
store (nom) *keyd/bakhaar*

I will buy food from the store

storey building (nom) *dhismaha dabaq*

I am building a storey building

storm (nom) *duufaan*

storm with thunder

stove (nom) *kariyaha*

gas stove

straight (adj) *toosan*

straight road

straighten (act) *toosin*

straighten your dress

strainer (nom) *shaandho miir*

strange (adj) *cajiib ah*

stranger (nom) *qariib*

three strangers

stream (nom) *durdur*

cross the stream

street (nom) *wado*

new street

strength (nom) *xoog*

strength and power

stress (nom) *culayska maskaxda/cadaad*

stretch (act) *turjumid*

stretch the cloth

string (nom) *xarig*

string and needle

strip off (act) *is mudhxin*

strip off your shoes

stripe (nom) *karbaash*

many strips

striped (adj) *xariijimo loo sameeyay*

striped sheep

strive (act) *ku dadaalid*

she strives

stroll (nom) *socod tamashle*

take a stroll

stroll (act) *tamashleyn*

stroll outside

strong (adj) *xoog leh*

a strong woman

strongly (adv) *si xoog leh*

I warned them strongly

strontium (sci) *istaroontiyam*

strontium (Sr) has 38 protons

structure (nom, c1) *qaab*

the shape of the house

student (nom) *arday*

twenty students

study (act) *dhigasho*

stuff (nom) *alaab/walax*

stumble (act) *turaan-turoon*

she stumbled

stump (nom) *kurtin*

stump of a tree

submarine (nom) *gujis*

a new submarine

subtract (act) *kala jarid*

subtract one from two

subtraction (nom) *kala goyn*

2-1 = 1; this is subtraction

success *(nom)* guul
  success and happiness

such as this *(exc)* sida kan oo kale
  a person such as this!

suckle *(act)* nuugid
  suckle the breast

Sudan *(nom)* Suudaan
  go to Sudan

Sudanese *(nom)* Sudaaniis
  the Sudanese

suddenly *(adv)* si kadis ah
  it came suddenly

sue *(act)* dacwayn
  to sue someone

suffering *(nom)* ka cabasho
  fear with suffering

sugar *(nom)* sonkor

sugarcane *(nom)* aale sonkor
  to chew sugarcane

suicide *(nom)* banbo
  It is a suicide

suit *(nom)* suudh
  she wears a suit

suitcase *(nom)* shandad dhar
  a black suitcase

sum *(nom)* wadarta

summary *(nom)* koobitaan
  the summary of it is that you have done well

summer *(nom)* xagaa
  I spend summer in Canada

summit *(nom)* shirweyne
  mountain summit

sun *(nom)* cadceed
  the sun is shining cadceedu way dhalaalaysaa

Sunday *(nom)* Axad
  Kwasi and Akosua are Sunday children

sunny *(adj)* qorrax leh
  a sunny day

sunrise *(nom)* cad ceed soo bax
  from sunrise to sunset

sunset *(nom)* cad ceed dhac
  from sunrise to sunset

supplant *(act)* beddelid
  replace me

supply *(nom)* sahay
  demand and supply

support *(act)* taageerid
  I support him

supporter *(nom)* taageere
  hundred supporters

surf *(nom)* isticmalid
  look at the surf

surpass *(act)* ka sare marid
  God surpasses man

surprise *(nom)* lama filaan
  great surprise

surround *(act)* hareerayay
  to surround the house

swallow *(act)* liq
  swallow medicine

swallow *(nom)* barar

a cat and a swallow

swam (ydy(i(act) wuu ... dabaalashoo

Swati (nom) *Iswaati*
 Swati language

sway (act) *gilgil*
 the tree is swaying

Swazi (nom) *Iswaasi*
 the Swazis

Swaziland (nom) *Iswaasilaan*
 go to Swaziland

swear (act) *dhaarasho*
 swear that you and me will die
 (together)

swear (act) *dhaarasho*
 swear that you and me will die
 (together)

swear (act) *dhaarasho*
 swear that you and me will die
 (together)

sweep (act) *xaadhid*
 she sweeps the floor

sweet (adj) *macaan ah*
 the tea is sweet

sweet potato (nom) *baradho macaan*
 I like sweet potato

sweetheart (nom) *gacaliso*
 he is my sweetheart

swell (act) *bararid*
 swollen leg

swim (act) *dabaalasho*
 to swim well

swing (nom) *lulid*

play on a swing

switch off (act) *xidhid*
 switch off the light

switch on (act) *shid*
 switch on the radio

switch on (act) *shid*
 switch on the radio

symbol (nom) *calaamad*
 symbol of power

symbol (nom) *calaamad*
 symbol of power

Syria (nom) *Siiriya*
 go to Syria

Syrian (nom) *Siiriyaan*
 the Syrians

syringe (nom) *Silinge*
 a nurse's syringe

T

table (nom) *miis*
 chair and table *kursi iyo miis*

tail (nom) *dabo*
 a cat has a tail

tail (act) *dabo*
 to tail someone

Taiwan (nom) *Taywaan*
 go to Taiwan

Taiwanese (nom) *Taywaaniis*
 the Taiwanese

Tajik (nom) *Taajiik*
 the Tajiks

Tajikstan *(nom)* *Taajikistaan*
 go to Tajikstan
take *(act)* *qaado*
 to take medicine
take hold of *(act)* *heysasho*
 take hold of me
Takoradi *(nom)* *Taakaroodi*
 Sekondi and Takoradi
talk *(act)* *hadal*
 to talk too much
talking drum *(nom)* *Durbaano*
 dhawaaqyo kala duwan leh
 four talking drums
tall *(adj)* *dheer*
 a tall tree
Tano *(nom)* *Taano*
 Tano River
tantalum *(sci)* *taantalum*
 tantalum (Ta) has 73 protons
Tanzania *(nom)* *Tansaaniya*
 go to Tanzania
Tanzanian *(nom)* *Tansaaniyaan*
 the Tanzanians
tap *(nom)* *tuubada*
 open the tap
tarantula *(nom)* *caaro*
 a large tarantula
taste *(act)* *dhadhan*
 taste the food
tax *(nom)* *cashuur*
 to pay tax
taxi *(nom)* *tagsi*
 call me a taxi

tea *(nom)* *shaah*
 the tea is sweet
teach *(act)* *barid*
 to teach mathematics
teacher *(nom)* *macalin*
 I am a teacher
team *(nom)* *koox*
 my team
tear *(act)* *jeexid*
 tear some of the paper
tear *(nom)* *jeexid*
 my eyes filled with tears
teardrop *(nom)* *dhibicda oohinta*
 a few teardrops
tease *(act)* *foorjeyn*
 tease him
technetium *(sci)* *tejnatiyam*
 technetium (Tc) has 43 protons
technical *(adj)* *farsamo leh*
 technical work
technology *(nom)* *tiknoolaji*
 new technology
teenage pregnancy *(nom)* *uurka*
 da' yarta
 teenage pregnancy creates suffering
teenager *(nom)* *da' yar*
 she is a teenager
teeth *(plural(nom)* *ilig*

telephone *(nom)* *telefoon*
 house telephone
telescope *(nom)* *xoqad*

a black telescope

television *(nom)* telefishan
 switch on the television shid telefishanka

tell *(act)* sheegid
 he is telling the story

tellurium *(sci)* teluuriyam
 tellurium (Te) has 52 protons

ten *(adj)* toban
 ten bottles toban dhaloonyinka

tense *(nom)* kacsan
 past tense

terbium *(sci)* teerbiyam
 terbium (Tb) has 65 protons

termite *(nom)* aboor
 many termites

territory *(nom)* dhul xad leh

test *(nom)* tijaabo
 the test is difficult

test *(act)* tijaabin
 I was testing you

testament *(nom)* dardaaran
 new testament

testicle *(nom)* xiniin
 testicles of a dog

testimony *(nom)* marag
 what is your testimony?

testis *(nom)* testis - unuga soo saara manida raga
 testes of a dog

Thai *(nom)* Taay
 the Thais

Thailand *(nom)* Taylaan
 go to Thailand

thallium *(sci)* taaliyam
 thallium (Tl) has 81 protons

than *(cjn)* ka badan
 he is taller than me

thank *(act)* mahad celin
 to thank your Father

thank you *(exc)* waad mahadsan tahay
 thank you very much

thanks *(exc)* mahadsanid
 Thanks Mandela!

thanks *(nom)* mahadsanid
 thanks be to God

thanksgiving *(nom)* mahadnaqida - ciida gaalada
 thanksgiving service

that *(cjn)* taas/kaas
 I say that

that *(pro)* kaa
 that bird

that *(cjn)* taas/kaas
 I say that

that person *(pro)* qofkaa
 that person said it

that thing *(pro)* waxaa
 what is that thing I got

the *(det)* da, ga, ta
 the house

the other day *(adv)* maalintii kale
 I saw a lion the other day

the other time *(adv)* wakhtigii

kale
  she came the other time
the thing (pro) waxa
  the thing she does
their (pos) waxooda
  their house
theirs (pro) waxooda
  this thing is theirs
them (pro) iyaga
  show them
themselves (pro) naftooda
  they look after themselves well
then (cjn) ka dib

then (adv) ka dibna
  then he slept
there (nom) halkaas
  here and there
these (det) kuwan
  these books
these (pro) kuwaa
  these people came
they (pro) iyaga
  they eat
thief (nom) tuug
  he is not a thief
thigh (nom) bowdada
  chicken thigh
thin (adj) dhuuban
  thin stick
thin (adj) dhuuban
  thin stick
thing (nom) wax

  the thing; the things
things (nom) waxyaalaha
  your things
think (act) fikir
  I think that ...
thinking (nom) fekirid

thirst (nom) haraad
  I feel thirst (I am thirsty)
thirst (nom) haraad
  I feel thirst (I am thirsty)
thirsty (adj) oomman

thirteen (adj) saddex iyo toban
  thirteen bottles saddex iyo toban
  dhaloonyinka
thirty (adj) soddon
  thirty bottles
this (pro) kan
  is this your book?
this (det) kan
  lend me this book
thorium (sci) tooriyam
  thorium (Th) has 90 protons
thorn (nom) qodax
  remove the thorn
thou (pro) inkastoo

though (cjn) in kastoo
  I see though it is dark
thought (nom) u maleyn
  your thoughts
thought (ydy(i(act) wuu ... fiki-

ray

thousand (adj) *kun*
 thousand bottles
thousands (adj) *kumanaan*
 thousands of ants
threat (nom) *hanjabaad*
 stop the threats
three (adj) *saddex*
 three bottles *saddex dhaloonyinka*

three persons (nom) *saddex qo-food*
 three persons are coming
thrive (act) *kobcid*
 the ants are thriving
thrive (act) *kobcid*
 the ants are thriving
throat (nom) *Cunaha*
 clear your throat
throne (nom) *carshi*
 to sit on a throne
throw (act) *tuurid*
 the food is spoilt so I have thrown it away
throw away (act) *iska tuur*
 throw away the water
thulium (sci) *tuuliyam*
 thulium (Tm) has 69 protons
thumb (nom) *suul*
 use your thumb to vote
thumbnail (nom) *cidida suulka*
 click on the thumbnail

thunder (nom) *onkod*
 storm with thunder
thunderbolt (nom) *hilaac*
 a loud thunderbolt
Thursday (nom) *Khamiis*
 Thursday children
thyme (nom, c3) *reexaan*
 mint and water
tick (nom) *sax*
 three ticks
ticket (nom) *tigidh*
 look at my ticket
tidy (act) *nidaamin*
 tidy up the room
tie (act) *kulan*
 tie it
tie (nom) *tay*
 the tie hangs on his neck
tie-and-dye (nom) *tie-and-dye - waa midabaynta garamada*
 she is wearing a tie-and-dye dress

tiger (nom) *shabeel*
 a large tiger
tightly (adv) *xidh*
 hold it tightly
Tigrinya (nom) *Tigriinya*
 Tigrinya language
tile (nom) *leben*
 bathroom tiles
till (pre) *ilaa*

time (nom) *wakhti*

the time is up
times (nom) *mararka*
  ten times
tin (sci) *tin*
  tin (Sn) has 50 protons
tin (nom) *qasaacad*
  five tins
tiny (adj) *aad u dhuuban*
  tiny thing
tire (act) *daalid*
  enemies will tire
tiredness (nom) *daal*
  tiredness and fatigue
titanium (sci) *tiitaaniyam*
  titanium (Ti) has 22 protons
tithe (nom) *meel-tobnaadka*
  pay your tithe
title (nom) *darajo*
  "Mighty One" is a title
Titus (nom) *tituus*
  Titus 1:1
to (pre) *ku socota*
  from here to there *xagan ka timi
  ku socota halkaa*
to-and-fro (adv) *si adag*
  the swing goes to-and-fro
tobacco (nom) *tubaako*
  smoke tobacco
today (adv) *maantay*
  she arrives today
toddler (nom) *socod barad*
  toddler, where are you going?
toe (nom) *faraha lugaha*

toe and heel
toenail (nom) *cidiyaha faraha lugaha*

toffee (nom) *sacfaraan*
  lick a toffee *muudso sacfaraan*
together (adv) *wadajir*
  they went together
Togo (nom) *Toogo*
  go to Togo
Togolese (nom) *Toogaaliis*
  the Togolese
toilet (nom) *musqul*
  go to the toilet
toilet roll (nom) *waraaqda musqusha*
  to buy toilet roll
told (ydy(i(act) *wuu ... sheegiday*

tomato (nom) *xabuub*
  two tomatoes *laba xabuub*
tomorrow (adv) *berri*
  she will arrive tomorrow
tongue (nom) *carab*
  dog's tongue
too (adv) *sidoo kale*
  you are walking too slowly
too much (adv) *aad u badan*
  he insults too much
tool (nom) *qalab*

tooth (nom) *ilig*
  white tooth
toothache (nom) *ilko xanuun*

I have toothache
toothbrush (nom) *caday*
  toothbrush and toothpaste *caday*
  iyo dawo caday
toothpaste (nom) *dawo caday*
  toothbrush and toothpaste *caday*
  iyo dawo caday
torment (act) *caddibaad*

tortoise (nom) *diin/amuur*
  a tortoise walks slowly
torture (nom) *jirdil*
  torture is evil
total (adj) *wadar ah*
  the total amount
totally (adv) *gabigaba*
  it is totally burnt
touch (act) *taabasho*
  to touch her hair
touch down (act) *ka degid*

tough (adj) *adag*
  tough meat
tour (nom) *tamashle/booqasho*
  zoo tour
towel (nom) *shukumaan*
  wet towel *shukumaan qoyan*
tower (nom) *munaarad/taallo*
  Tower of London
town (nom) *magaalo*
  go into town
trade (nom) *ganacsi*
  a good trade

trade (act) *ganacsasho*
  to trade quickly
trader (nom) *ganacsade*
  I am a trader
trading (nom) *ganacsanaya*
  trading profit
tradition (nom) *dhaqan*

traffic (nom) *socod baabuur*
  traffic light
trailblazer (nom) *qof wado baabuur*
  oo cusub sameeya
  Gandhi is a trailblazer
train (act) *tobabarasho*
  he will train me
train (nom) *tareen*
  new train *tareen cusub*
traitor (nom) *khaa'in*
  two traitors
translate (act) *turjumid*

trash (nom) *xashiish*
  throw away the trash
travel (act) *socdaal marin*
  we are travelling to Africa
traveller (nom) *socdaale*
  four travellers
tray (nom) *saxan ballaaran*
  put the food on the tray
treason (nom) *khaa'in wadan*
  treason is evil
treasure (nom) *khasnad maaliyadeed*
  great treasure

tree (nom) geed
  plant a tree beer geed
tremble (act) gariirid
  his lips are trembling
trembling (nom) gariirid
  fear and trembling
trend (nom) dhankay wax isu badaleen
  a good trend
triangle (nom) saddex gees
  a triangle has three angles
trick (nom) khiyaamo
  stop the tricks
trick (act) khiyaameyn

trinity (nom) midnimo
  holy trinity
trinket (nom) dahab xaddi yar oon
  qiimo badan lahayn
  she has many trinkets
trip (nom) socdaal
  trip to India
trip (nom) socdaal
  trip to India
triplets (nom) saddex ilmood oo
  mar wada dhasha
  they are triplets
triumph (act) guulaysasho
  you triumphed
trouble (nom) dhib
  trouble and pain
trouser (nom) surwaal
  she wears trousers
truck (nom) gaari xamuul ah

  a red truck
true (adj) run ah
  it is true
truly (adv) dhab ah
  truly God is good
trumpet (nom) buun
  seven trumpets
trust (act) aaminid

trust (nom) aaminid

truth (nom) run
  she spoke the truth
try (act) tijaabin
  try again
tuberculosis (nom) tiibey
  tuberculosis is a disease
Tuesday (nom) Salaasa
  Tuesday children
tumbler (nom) koob aan dhag la
  qabto lahayn
  one tumbler of water
tungsten (sci) tangestin
  tungsten (W) has 74 protons
Tunisia (nom) Tunuusiya
  go to Tunisia
Tunisian (nom) Tunuusiyaan
  the Tunisians
turbulent (adj) qasan
  a turbulent world
Turk (nom) Turkish
  the Turks
Turkey (nom) Turki

go to Turkey

turkey (nom) *turki*

 turkey meat

Turkmen (nom) *Turkimen*

 the Turkmen

Turkmenistan (nom) *Turkimeenistaan*

 go to Turkmenistan

turn off (act) *damin*

 to turn off the light

turpentine (nom) *gaasta rinjiga lagu daro*

 turpentine and kerosene

turtle (nom) *qubo*

 a turtle swims

twelve (adj) *laba iyo toban*

 twelve bottles *laba iyo toban dhaloonyinka*

twenty (adj) *labaatan*

 twenty bottles *labaatan dhaloonyinka*

Twi (nom) *Tiwiyaan*

 Twi is an Akan language

twig (nom) *jabad*

 how many twigs?

twin (nom) *mataan*

 she is a twin

twins (nom) *mataano*

 we are twins

twist (act) *maroojin*

 twist it a little

two (adj) *laba*

 There are two bottles on the wall *laba dhaloonyinka*

two persons (nom) *laba qofood*

 two persons are coming

type (act) *nooc*

 I type fast

type (nom) *nooc*

tyre (nom) *shaag*

 roll a tyre

U

Ugandan (nom) *Yugaandhaan*

 the Ugandans

ugly (adj) *fool xun*

 it is ugly

ukelele (nom) *giitaar yar*

 play the ukelele

Ukraine (nom) *Yukray*

 go to Ukraine

Ukrainean (nom) *Yukrayniyaan*

 the Ukraineans

umbilicus (nom) *xudun*

unappreciativeness (nom) *mahadnaq la'aan*

 how do you do not sr unappreciativeness

unburden (act) *nafisiin*

 unburden me

uncle (nom) *adeer/abti*

 uncle Kofi

under (pre)

 she will sweep under the table

understand (act) *fahamsan*
  to understand something very well

underwear (nom) *nigis*
  he is not wearing underwear

undesirable (adj) *aan lo baahnayn*
  it is undesirable

unfamiliar (adj) *aan hoaray loo aqoon*
  unfamiliar animal

ungrateful (adj) *aan mahad celin*
  an ungrateful person

union (nom) *isbahaysi*
  African Union

unique (adj) *kaligiis nocaas ah*
  an unique thing

unit (nom) *cutub*
  five units

unite (act) *midoobay*
  Africa will unite

United States of America (nom) *Mareykanka*
  he was born in the United States of America

unity (nom) *midnimo*
  unity and peace

university (nom) *jaamacad*
  Legon University

unkempt (adj) *arbushnaan*
  an unkempt room

unless (cjn) *haddi aanay/aanuu*
  she will come unless it rains

unnecessary (adj) *aan daruuri ahayn*
  unnecessary insults

until (pre) *ilaa iyo*
  until we meet again

ununpentium (sci) *unuunbetiyam*
  ununpentium (Uup) has 115 protons

ununseptium (sci) *unuunsebtiyam*
  ununseptium (Uus) has 117 protons

ununtrium (sci) *unuuntiriyam*
  ununtrium (Uut) has 113 protons

up (adv) *kor*
  look up

upon (pre) *korkiisa/korkeeda*

upright (adj) *quman*
  upright person

upstairs (adv) *dabaqa sare*
  he is upstairs

uranium (sci) *yuuraaniyam*
  uranium (U) has 92 protons

urinate (act) *kaadin*
  to urinate there

urine (nom) *kaadi*
  the urine smells

us (pro) *annaga*
  show us

USA (nom) *USA*

use (act) *isticmaal*
  you will use it like that

useless (adj) *aan waxtar lahayn*
　useless work
user (nom) *isticmaale*
　how many users?
usual (adj) *caadi ah*

utterly (adv) *gabi ahaanba*
　utterly finished
Uzbek (nom) *Usbeek*
　the Uzbeks
Uzbekistan (nom) *Usbaakistaan*
　go to Uzbekistan

V

vaccinate (act) *tallaalid*
　to vaccinate the child
vacuum (sci) *fakuu*
　space is a vacuum
vagina (nom) *siil*
　you don't say 'vagina' in public
valiant (adj) *geesi ah*
　valiant woman
valley (nom) *dooxo/tog*
　hills and valleys
value (nom) *qiimey*
　great value
van (nom) *bas yar*
　board a van
vanadium (sci) *fanaadiyam*
　vanadium (V) has 23 protons
various (adj) *kala duwan*

vase (nom) *fees- weel ubaxa lagu
rido*
　clay vase
vegetable oil (nom) *saliida khudaarta*
　use vegetable oil to fry fish
vehicle (nom) *baabuur*
　a new vehicle
vein (nom) *xidid*
　blood passes through veins
Venezuela (nom) *Fenesiweela*
　go to Venezuela
Venezuelan (nom) *Fenesiweeliyaan*
　the Venezuelans
venom (nom) *sunta xayawaanka
- sida maska*
　venom of a snake
verandah (nom) *barandaha*
　let's go to the verandah
verb (nom) *ficil*
　nine verbs
verse (nom) *aayad/beyd*
　three verses
version (nom) *nooc*
　which version?
very (adv) *aad*
　you have done very well
very desirable (adj) *aad loo jecelyay*
　it is very desirable
very much (adv) *aad u badan*
　thank you very much
vibrate (act) *gariirid*

the tree is vibrating
vice (nom) *ku xigeen*
 vice and virtue
vice-president (nom) *madaxweyne*
 ku xigeen
 the vice-president has arrived
victor (nom, c1) *guuleyste*

victory (nom) *guuleyste*
 victory and defeat
Vietnam (nom) *Fiitnaam*
 go to Vietnam
Vietnamese (nom) *Fiitnaamiis*
 the Vietnamese
vine (nom) *canab*
 vine leaf
violet (adj) *buluug*
 violet flowers
virgin (nom) *bikro*
 ten virgins
virtue (nom) *dhaqan wanaagsan*
 vice and virtue
vision (nom) *aragti*
 a new vision for Africa
visit (act) *booqasho*
 do come and visit me!
vitality (nom) *koboca*
 water gives vitality
vodka (nom) *fodka- nooc alkoolada*
 kamid ah
 rum or vodka?
voice (nom) *cod*
 soften your voice

volume (nom) *mug*
 turn up the volume
vomit (nom) *hunqaacid*
 dog's vomit
vomit (act) *matag*
 you have vomitted
vote (act) *codayn*
 vote for me
voting (nom) *codeyn*
 the voting is going well
vow (nom) *nidar ku gelid*

vulnerable (adj) *baylah ah*

vulture (nom) *gorgor*
 a vulture is a bird

W

wailing (nom) *boroorasho*
 crying and wailing
waist (nom) *dhexda*
 your waist
wait (act) *sugid*
 to wait a bit
waiter (nom) *mudalab*
 he is a waiter
wake up (act) *toosid*

walk about (act) *lugeyn*
 she walks about
wall (nom) *gidaar*
 sit on the wall

walnut *(nom)* *nooc lawska ka mid ah*
 ten walnuts
want *(act)* *rabitaan*
 I want four books
war *(nom)* *dagaal*
 we are going to war
warhorn *(nom)* *hoonka ka digista dagaal*
 blow the warhorn
warn *(act)* *digniin siin*
 warn someone
warning *(nom)* *digniin*
 listen to the warning
warrior *(nom)* *dagaalyahan*
 warrior of antiquity
warriors *(nom)* *dagaalyahano*
 the warriors are coming
was *(ydy(f(act)* *way ... ahowtay*

wash *(act)* *meydhid*
 to wash the bottles
wash *(act)* *meydhid*
 to wash the bottles
wasp *(nom)* *laxle*
 many wasps
waste *(nom)* *qashin*
 the work has been a waste
waste *(nom)* *qashin*
 the work has been a waste
wasted *(adj)* *khasaariyay*
 wasted food
watch *(act)* *daawasho*

to watch football
watch *(nom)* *daawasho*
 a small watch
water *(nom)* *biyo*
 you drink water *waxaad cabtaa biyo*

water yam *(nom)* *baradho macaanta biyaha*
 cook the water yam
watermelon *(nom)* *qare/xab-xab*
 eat the watermelon
wave *(nom)* *gacan haadin*
 the waves are breaking
way *(nom)* *wado*
 the way
we *(pro)* *annaga*
 we eat
weak *(adj)* *diciifsan*
 I am weak
weakness *(nom)* *daciifnimo*
 in her weakness
wealth *(nom)* *hanti*
 we have great wealth
weapon *(nom)* *hub*
 we sell weapons
wear *(act)* *xidhasho*
 wear clothes
weather *(nom)* *cimilo*
 we have good weather
weave *(act)* *ka dhaafid*
 weave a basket
weaverbird *(nom)* *shimbirta wi-ifar*

eight weaverbirds

web (nom) *xuub caaro*
the web of a spider

website (nom) *mareeg/barta in-terneetka*
make a website for me

wed (act) *guursasho*
I will wed you

wedding (nom) *aroos*
we are going to a wedding

Wednesday (nom) *Arbaca*
Wednesday children

wee hours (nom) *saacado yar*
1am

weed (act) *harame*
wed grass

week (nom) *todobaad*
this week

weigh (act) *miisaamid*
weigh your child

weight (nom) *miisaan*
a heavy weight

welcome (exc) *so dhawaw*
welcome welcome!

well (adv) *fican*
do it well

well (adj) *fiican*

well (nom) *fiican*
well water

went (ydy(i(act) *wuu ... tagay*

west (nom) *Galbeed*

go west

Western Sahara (nom) *Galbeedka Saxaaraha*
go to Western Sahara

Western Saharan (nom) *Dadka Galbeedka Saxaaraha*
the Western Saharans

wet (adj) *qoyan*
wet blanket

wet season (nom) *xilli roobaad*
the wet season has arrived

whale (nom) *nibiri*
a large whale

what (pro) *maxay*
what is that?

wheat (nom) *qamadi*
to eat wheat

wheel (nom) *shaag*
my car has four wheels

when (cjn) *goorma*
he came when you went

where (adv) *halkee*
where do you live?

whether (cjn) *haddii*

which (det) *kee*
which child?

while (cjn) *goortii*
he danced while the old man was singing

whine (act) *cabasho*
stop whining

whip (nom) *jeedalayn*

horse whip
white (adj) *cad*
 white house
who (pro) *kee/ayo/tee*
 who is he?
whoa (exc) *wuhu*
 whoa, this man!
whole (adj) *dhan*

whole year (nom) *sannadka oo dhan*
 two whole years
whose (pro) *qofma*
 whose house is this?
why (adv) *waayo*
 why so?
wicked (adj) *shar leh*
 you are very wicked
wickedness (nom) *xumaansho*
 your stinginess and your wickedness
wide (adj) *ballaran*
 wide road
widow (nom) *carmal (gabar)*
 she is a widow
widowed (adj) *carmaloobay*
 widowed man
widower (nom) *carmal (nin)*
 he is a widower
widowhood (nom) *carmalnimo*
 a short widowhood
width (nom) *balac*
 height and width

wield (act) *isticmaal hub/qalab*
 she is wielding the pan
wife (nom) *xaas*
 my wife and my children
wifi (nom) *wifi-da interneetka*
 my phone sees the wifi
wild (adj) *duur joog*
 wild animal
will (nom) *rabitaan*
 God's will
will (nom) *rabitaan*
 God's will
win (act) *guuleyso*
 to win a competition
wind (nom) *dabayl*
 the wind is blowing
window (nom) *daaqad*
 open the windows *fur daaqadaha*

windy (adj) *dabaly leh*
 a windy day
winner (nom) *guuleyste*

winter (nom) *jiilaal*
 I spend winter in Germany
wipe (act) *masax*
 to wipe the seat
wisdom (nom) *murti*
 strength and wisdom
wise (adj) *caqli leh*
 a wise girl
wish (act) *rajee*

witch (nom) saaxirad
  she is a witch
witchcraft (nom) sixroolanimo
  practise witchcraft
with (cjn) la
  Kofi with Ama
withdraw (act) kala bixid
  she will withdraw money
witness (nom) markhaati
  three witnesses
wizard (nom) saaxir
  he is a wizard
wobble (nom) dhinac aayar u dhaqaaq

wolf (nom) Yeey
  two wolves
Wolof (nom) Wolof
  Wolof language
woman (nom) gabadh
  a pretty woman gabadh qurux badan

womb (nom) ilmo galeen
  female's womb
women (plural(nom) gabadh

won (ydy(i(act) wuu ... guuleysoay

wonder (nom) la yaabid
  wonder and love
wonderful (adj) yaab leh
  amazing story
woodpigeon (nom) xamaam
  a tiny woodpigeon

word (nom) erey
  I know 100 words
work (act) saqee
  to work hard
working (nom) shaqeynaya
  working is not trivial
world (nom) dunida
  children of the world
worldliness (nom) adduun noqosho
  she possesses worldliness
worm (nom) dirxi
  worm, where are you going?
worry (nom) warwar
  many worries
worship (act) caabud
  they worship gods
worth (nom) qiimo leh

wow (exc) waw
  wow! thank you!
wrench (nom) kiyaawo

wriggle (act) dhaqdhaqaad degdeg
 ah
  stop wriggling
wring (act) maroojin
  wring the cloth
wrist (nom) suxul
  hold her wrist
write (act) qorid
  to write a letter
writer (nom) qoraa
  I am a writer

X

xylophone (nom) qalab muusik
  play a xylophone

Y

yard (nom) deyr
  big yard
Yaw (nom) kala jeedsasho diyaaradeed
  Yaw is my son
yawn (act) hamaansasho
  stop yawning
yaws (nom) cudurka yaawis
  yaws is a disease
ye (pro) haa
  me and ye
year (nom) sannad
  a new year has come
yearly (adj) sannad kasta
  a yearly festival
yell (act) qeylin
  we will yell
yellow (adj) jaalle/huruud
  yellow flag
Yemen (nom) Yaman
  go to Yemen
Yemeni (nom) Yamani
  the Yemenis
yes (exc) haye
  I say yes

yesterday (adv) shalay
  she arrived yesterday
yet (cjn) weli
  the book is big yet I read all of it

Yoruba (nom) Yuruba
  Yoruba language
you (pro) ku
  I love you
you (pro) adiga
  you eat
you (pro) adiga
  you eat
you (pro) idinka
  you eat
youes (pro) wixiina
  the two of youes
young (adj) dhalin yaro ah
  young person
young boy (nom) wiil yar
  young boy, come here!
young man (nom) nin yar
  a young man like you
your (pos) adigu
  your house
your (pos) idingu
  your house
yours (pro) waxaaga
  Kofi, this thing is yours
yours (pro) waxaaga
  Kofi, this thing is yours
yourself (pro) naftaada
  look after yourself well

yourselves (pro) nafihina
  look after yourselves well
youth (nom) dhalinyaro
  in my youth, I was strong
ytterbium (sci) teerbiyam
  ytterbium (Yb) has 70 protons
yttrium (sci) Yitriyam
  yttrium (Y) has 39 protons
yuca (nom) kasaafada
  plantain and yuca

zoo (nom) Beer xayawaan
  zoo tour
Zulu (nom) Sulu
  Zulu language

Z

Zambian (nom) Saambiyaan
  Tendayi is a Zambian
Zambian (nom) Saambiyaan
  Tendayi is a Zambian
zebra (nom) dameer farow
  seven zebras
zero (adj) eber
  From zero to nine eber dhaloonyinka

Zimbabwe (nom) Simbaabwi
  People from Zimbabwe are called
  Zimbabweans
Zimbabwean (nom) Simbaabwiyaan
  the Zimbabweans
zinc (sci) Sinik
  zinc (Zn) has 30 protons
zip (nom) siib
  to fasten a zip
zirconium (sci) Sirkooniyam
  zirconium (Zr) has 40 protons

Somali kasahorow Library

https://so.kasahorow.org/app/l

help+so@kasahorow.org

Made in the USA
San Bernardino, CA
27 March 2020